The Hockey Stick Principles

The Hockey Stick Principles

The 4 Key Stages to Entrepreneurial Success

Bobby Martin

FLATIRON
BOOKS
NEW YORK

THE HOCKEY STICK PRINCIPLES. Copyright © 2016 by Bobby Martin. All rights reserved. Printed in the United States of America. For information, address Flatiron Books, 175 Fifth Avenue, New York, N.Y. 10010.

www.flatironbooks.com

Designed by Patrice Sheridan

The Library of Congress Cataloging-in-Publication Data is available upon request.

ISBN 978-1-250-06637-4 (hardcover)
ISBN 978-1-250-06638-1 (e-book)

Our books may be purchased in bulk for promotional, educational, or business use. Please contact your local bookseller or the Macmillan Corporate and Premium Sales Department at 1-800-221-7945, extension 5442, or by e-mail at MacmillanSpecialMarkets@macmillan.com.

First Edition: May 2016

10 9 8 7 6 5 4 3 2 1

Dedicated to my high school American history teacher,
Don Goodwin, who ingrained in me a love for learning.

Contents

The Hockey Stick Principles

The Proven Principles for Achieving Hockey Stick Growth

L aunching your own innovative business—one whose product, service, or business model you have invented—and seeing it through to success is a deeply satisfying process. I've done it twice, and there's nothing I'd rather have spent the last fifteen years doing.

As is true for so many start-up founders, I had no idea how to build a business when I started. I just had an idea and a commitment to making it work. It was a huge challenge, but it was also a highly rewarding adventure. As with so many innovative start-ups, my first company, First Research, which provides industry research reports for sales and marketing professionals, achieved classic hockey stick growth takeoff in which revenue shot dramatically up in a curve shaped like a hockey stick. Hockey stick growth is often characterized as possible only for truly game-changing start-ups, as with Amazon, Netflix, and Facebook, for example.

But I've seen the same pattern time and time again as an angel investor and advisor to many start-ups, and my cofounder and I have also seen hockey stick growth with my second start-up, Vertical IQ, which provides industry profiles to banks. In fact, a study I conducted of start-up growth patterns showed dramatically that the hockey stick curve is quite common for successful innovative start-ups, and that's true for businesses of all kinds and all sizes, not just high-tech dot-coms.

When I plotted the revenue growth of 172 successful start-ups for the first seven years from launch, covering a wide range of sectors from Web leaders like Google and LinkedIn to non-Web businesses like Chobani yogurt, TOMS shoes, and video camera maker GoPro, all but eleven saw

Inflation-Adjusted Revenue

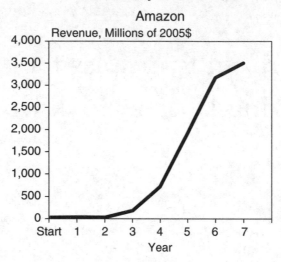

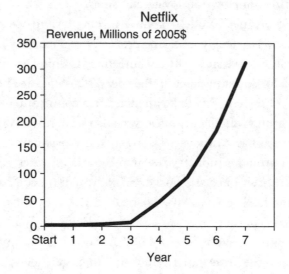

hockey stick growth. (If you want to see a selection of the graphs of the businesses I studied, they are available at the book's Web site: www .hockeystickprinciples.com.)

This shows conclusively that hockey stick growth is exactly what to be aiming for as you launch your own start-up. But if such breakthrough success is so possible to achieve, why is start-up failure reportedly so common? To answer this, I decided to delve more deeply into researching start-up success and failure to determine whether there was perhaps a proven set of best practices for dealing with the many challenges. Are there certain

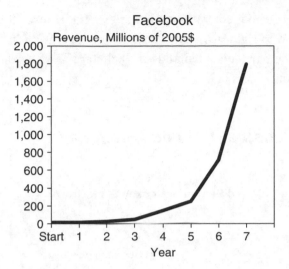

key things that successful founders consistently do that make the difference in their businesses taking off? My research revealed that there are.

I interviewed successful founders of all kinds of start-ups in depth, getting the details on exactly how they built their businesses, from how they
came up with their ideas through to developing them into viable business
models, how they designed and developed their products and services, how
they launched, and how they built their customer base and sales thereafter.
The more I delved into the founders' stories and examined the growth
curves for their businesses, the clearer it became that all successful start-
ups go through four major stages of growth, which track along the hockey
stick curve, and each of these growth stages—which I call *tinkering, the blade
years, the growth-inflection point,* and *surging growth*—presents founders
with its own distinctive challenges. As I compared the stories of more and
more founders and how they faced these challenges, the commonalities
between the businesses that succeeded, including mine and my cofounders',
were striking, as were the similarities of the mistakes that were made by
founders who failed. The result is that I have identified a set of core principles to follow in each stage of growth, which I call the Hockey Stick Principles. Following them will empower you to move successfully through
each stage and to ultimately reach takeoff growth.

The great business analyst Peter Drucker once said about running a successful business, "Management is doing things right . . . leadership is doing
the right things."[1] The founders of start-ups have to do both well; they must
constantly determine the right things to do at the right time and also work

out the best methods for getting them done. The Hockey Stick Principles show you how to rigorously tailor how you are operating in each stage according to the particular demands of that stage so that you can succeed where so many others fail.

A Closer Look at the Four Stages

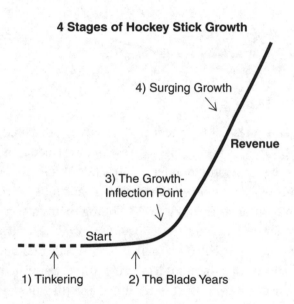

4 Stages of Hockey Stick Growth

4) Surging Growth

Revenue

3) The Growth-
Inflection Point

Start

1) Tinkering   2) The Blade Years

The building of every start-up is, of course, its own game with its own specific set of problems to solve. While some founders must grapple with complicated programming, others might have to work out details of manufacturing and supply chain management. Some might wrestle mightily with inventory control and retailing challenges, and some others might struggle particularly with finding the right recipe for online-only sales or with threats to their intellectual property. For instance, the process of creating and marketing a new type of high-tech smartwatch, as the founders of the Pebble Watch did, is quite different in the details from developing a breakthrough new mobile app like Instagram. This is what makes the underlying similarities of the challenges of each stage of the process so hard to discern; every start-up's story can seem to be unique, and in the fine details, that's true. But the fundamentals to be grappled with are universals, and having the framework of the four hockey stick stages to guide you will help you to keep these crucial fundamentals at the forefront in the heat of action.

In order to show how broadly applicable the hockey stick stages and the principles to follow for each are—and to help you apply them to your product or service—throughout the book, the stories of real flesh-and-blood founders who started successful companies in a wide range of sectors will be told and will be contrasted to those of failure. This not only makes the book an engaging read, allowing you to think through how you would have dealt with their challenges, but it also helps to showcase that as unique as the product or service your company is offering may be, you will still be grappling with the same fundamental issues as other businesses.

So let's now take a broad-brush look at the four stages of hockey stick growth.

Tinkering

This is the time during which founders are beginning to explore the viability of their idea. It begins when they start to take action to examine the idea more seriously, and it ends when they fully commit to developing the business.

While this is the least pressured of the stages, because most often the founder hasn't yet quit his or her day job or committed to a launch schedule, it still presents many tricky challenges, and too many aspiring founders never get beyond this stage. One of the most common mistakes made is that founders waste a great deal of time developing elaborate business plans, which seems so obvious as a must-do but is in fact, as we'll explore more fully, a terribly misguided action. Believing that you should develop a good business plan on the sole basis of an idea lends support to one of the biggest fallacies about the start-up process: that you've got to begin with a good idea and everything will flow from there.

Hockey Stick Principle #1, to be discussed more fully in the next chapter, is: You don't need a good idea. Viable ideas for start-ups don't just emerge whole from founders' brains; they are developed over time. This stage should be a period of actively experimenting with developing the product or service, getting out into the field and soliciting the feedback of potential customers, as well as canvassing suppliers and retailers, testing—and truly challenging—your ideas for the product and all aspects of your business model, and listening carefully to responses. It's often from this experimentation and critical listening that crucial changes to initial ideas come, which make all the difference in eventual success.

Too many founders are reluctant to discuss their ideas at this early stage and to show actual sample products for fear of competitors copying from them, and too many of those who do solicit feedback do so within an echo chamber of supportive friends and family who tell them what they want to hear. As a result, many founders fail to develop a deep understanding in this period of the market they're aiming to serve and what the true needs and desires of those they're targeting are, and they forge ahead with building a product that has no real market. Others accept the inevitable negative feedback they get too readily rather than analyzing it and discovering a deeper truth about how they could improve on their idea. Even if the idea strikes many as brilliant, and funders offer bundles of investment cash on that basis, if the needs and desires of the market haven't been understood, the product launch will fail.

A great example of a founder who did a masterful job of negotiating the challenges of the tinkering process is Bob Young, who started the $1.5 billion software services provider Red Hat. Young and his cofounder achieved phenomenal success by creating an innovative business model that gave Red Hat's core product away for free to some customers while charging others for it. Young and his partner went ahead and created their basic product, and Young then went out and tried to sell it, talking with potential customers. This led him to the company's innovative model. Young listened carefully and critically to all the feedback, and he tweaked the product, pricing, and services the company provided in creative ways that allowed Red Hat to address all the various criticisms raised. He also gave himself time for this discovery process by bringing in cash for the first couple of years with a retail business, so he had no need to take on debt or waste any time chasing funding.

Now consider the story of another software firm, GoCrossCampus, which failed despite raising $1.6 million right from the get-go and garnering major support in the press. Cofounders Brad Hargreaves and Matthew Brimer had created a computer game about which *The New York Times* wrote, "The game, a riff on classic territorial-conquest board games like Risk, may be the next Internet phenomenon to emerge from the computers of college students."[2] From what I read the founders seemed to believe that raising lots of cash up front was the key to success, so they focused a great deal on this, and very successfully, raising another $300,000 every four months as they kept developing the game. But having taken so much investment capital, they felt intense pressure to launch the product for the start of the 2007 college year, and after they did so, they ran into glitches and had to shut down the site for six weeks. As Hargreaves said in a *Business Insider* article reflecting on the debacle, "We should have spent the fall working on the project and then launched in the spring."

Another big mistake was that they tested the game primarily on friends and family, and rather than taking their negative feedback as helpful criticism, they were upset by it, which Hargreaves said interfered with their productivity. They also launched before they had figured out how the company could actually make money from selling the game. The college students they were targeting were, as Hargreaves recalled, "hard to monetize." They didn't want to pay for the game, and the founders never figured out an alternative model for earnings. Before long, the company ran out of money and had to liquidate their assets in a fire sale.[3]

The principles for tinkering that will be introduced in the coming chapters will allow you to avoid all these mistakes and other common ones made in this stage.

The Blade Years

This is the period of time when founders have fully committed to making the business work and are preparing to launch until they hit the growth-inflection point.

This is a bumpy time of highs and lows, during which many founders lose heart or become overwhelmed. They've quit their day jobs in order to devote themselves full-time to developing the business, and they're often not earning enough of a salary to pay their personal bills. My study shows that this stage usually lasts three to four years, during which revenue is often quite low, if any is coming in at all, showing up as the blade part of the hockey stick curve. The lack of adequate earnings leads many founders to focus a great deal of their energy on the quest for investment capital at this early stage, which too many founders think is the only way to fund the development process. They waste valuable time making elaborate pitches to potential funders, which most often fail to impress because they have no tangible results to point to. And if they do raise significant investment capital, as with GoCrossCampus, it often puts undue pressure on getting to market, which leads to its own common trip-ups. Hence Hockey Stick Principle #15: Raise the minimum amount you need to get to launch; financing is scarce and expensive.

A better method for success is to bootstrap during this period and to develop an alternate stream of income. This frees you to throw yourself into what should be the twin focuses of your energy in this stage: developing the market you've targeted, or searching for a different one, and simultaneously improving the product or service so that, by getting the combination of market and product right, you break through to fast growth.

Key mistakes made during this stage include spending too much on marketing and sales efforts to try to bring in customers faster, whether by pouring funds into an elaborately planned publicity push and advertising campaign or setting up an expensive sales operation. Often, after a big launch, into which founders have thrown everything they have, sales fail to gain traction, and many founders get stuck, continuing to focus too exclusively on a targeted market and pouring more and more money into the same old efforts, when they should be experimenting with alternatives, no matter how unexpected they may be. To avoid this trap, founders must keep in mind Hockey Stick Principle #33: You have no idea what your market is until you find it.

Many founders also fail to seriously consider further changes to the product during this period. Finding a market may require making a major pivot not only in the targeted market but also in the nature of the product. But here, too, many founders misstep, concluding too quickly that they should pivot when instead more measured tweaking—or developing a better sales and marketing approach for the same targeted market—are the right options. As I will show later, sometimes even just very minor tweaks can make a huge difference in results. Rather than always pivoting when the going gets tough, as we'll explore more fully, the right approach to making changes in this stage is to systematically interrogate every aspect of your business model and then decide whether to make a major pivot.

A great example of a business negotiating the challenges of the blade years and reaching growth inflection is that of The Climate Corporation, which sells weather insurance to farmers. The firm was founded by two former Google employees, and their initial concept was to sell derivatives—a highly sophisticated form of financial product—that would allow the owners of businesses of all sorts that are regularly hurt by bad weather to protect themselves against those losses. The founders were brilliant mathematical minds, and they created such an impressive basic program that they raised many millions of dollars in funding from their network of friends. But when they launched a fancy Web site and did lots of advertising, they had very few takers.

As we'll see when the story is told more fully, rather than burning through their cash by increasing their ad spending, they drilled into discovering a viable market, and they pivoted by turning the company into one that offered traditional insurance to serve a good market they identified. After that, their growth took off, and they sold the company to Monsanto for approximately $1.1 billion.[4]

By contrast, the founders of EventVue never developed a depth of understanding of their target market or branched out to experiment with other markets, and even though they recount that they did make a pivot in the nature of their product, they waited too long to do so and didn't really commit to the hard work of making that pivot succeed. Also, even though they raised a good amount of funding early, they never created a revenue stream to support further development.

As the founders recounted in a postmortem memo, they originally offered a service that would create a customized social network for specific events, such as a music concert or a business conference. They made such a persuasive case for their idea that EventVue was selected by leading start-up incubator Techstars as one of their ten companies for 2007, and they also raised seed capital of reportedly about $250,000.[5] However, after this promising start, they failed to drill into their target market. As they wrote in their memo, "At the time, we did not think about or understand the challenges of getting a lot of conference organizers to use EventVue."[6] And they continued to fail to probe deeply into the market for months and months even though they weren't getting the sales they'd hoped for, recounting that "we were basically calling on friends of friends who ran events to be our customers, we didn't learn what event organizers in general wanted or how to acquire them as a customer."[7] They finally pivoted by offering a different service, the idea they hoped would drive more attendees to events. But as they admit, they didn't do the hard work of verifying that the new product they developed would actually help increase attendance, so they again ran into a wall with the market of conference organizers. They had never really experimented with different markets for the social network product, and they never deeply researched whether or not the new product they created for their original market actually worked. Then they simply ran out of cash.

The Growth-Inflection Point

This is the wild ride of a time when revenue turns sharply upward. It's an exhilarating stage. At this point, you've honed your model, and sales are coming so much more easily. Venture firms and other investors may come calling, offering tantalizing deals that will allow you to leverage this growth momentum and scale your business way up. But this stage also poses many dangers; primary among them is scaling up too fast, so that rather than sustaining strong growth many start-ups crash and burn. Scaling too quickly has been identified as the number-one reason for start-up failure. So much has been said about the need to "go big fast," but too often this leads instead to going bust fast. In this stage, founders must always keep in mind Hockey Stick Principle #51: Don't spend lots of money to fuel fast growth until you're pouring it into a high-performance engine.

The primary job of this inflection stage is to carefully calibrate the growth of your operations so that they are in sync with your growth in revenue. Otherwise, scaling up isn't really growing; it's inflating. Too many founders invest too heavily in ramping up staff, purchasing or renting larger office space or manufacturing equipment, and expanding retail space and facilities. Before they know it, their costs have escalated way beyond their continued increase in revenue, and even though they've found a good market and are off and running, they're running out of gas.

Another trap founders fall into during this stage is making changes in a model that's working well because they think it's required in order to capitalize on the huge growth opportunity that's become clear. For example, some businesses may have been relying on Web advertising only, and then they order up a high-ticket TV ad campaign; or if they had sold exclusively online, they decide to open brick-and-mortar stores. Oftentimes, founders think they're building on their model when in fact they're perverting it. The push for these changes often comes from investors who have offered tantalizing sums to fuel growth, and founders regularly underestimate the pressure investors will exert and the amount of control over strategic direction they've given up for that cash.

One start-up that managed this stage brilliantly is e-mail marketing software services provider iContact. The founders, Ryan Allis and Aaron Houghton, started the company while they were still in college, and they had little business management experience. But after the company's sales took off in its third year, spiking up from $296,000 in 2004 to $1.3 million in 2005, they kept cool heads and focused tightly on putting the additional cash they made into stoking up sales with their existing model. We'll later read more about the smart scaling-up methods iContact employed. So well honed was their model as they scaled that they were able to raise more than $20 million in outside capital between 2006 and 2009, and with a great deal more market still to tap, in 2010, they raised $40 million in equity funding. They sold the company in 2012 to public relations software company Vocus, which became Cision, for $169 million.

In contrast, one-time "next big thing" online retailer Fab.com managed this stage very differently. Cofounders Bradford Shellhammer and Jason Goldberg launched the site in 2011, selling carefully selected specialty craft items for the home. Their model was brilliant; they offered the items through flash sales, making deals with the creators of the products, who would determine how many items would be available for sale and would take care of order fulfillment. Fab.com had no responsibility for inventory management, warehousing, or delivery. The founders had great taste in items, and their sales quickly took off. But after they raised over $40 million in outside funding, achieving a market valuation of an astonishing $900 million, they began to make a series of changes in their model that we will discuss in Chapter 5 that led them off the rails. Even having raised so much funding, by October of 2013, just two years after launch, they were forced to sell the company for the bargain price of approximately $15 to $50 million.

Surging Growth

If innovative start-ups manage the growth-inflection stage well, they will proceed into a stage of continuing acceleration of growth. During this period, entrepreneurs come to many crossroads. Their market is exploding, but so is the complexity of managing and leading a larger organization. Meanwhile, alluring offers to buy the company are often made. One way or another, a founder must grapple with the difficult transition from scrappy entrepreneur to corporate manager. He or she has three main choices: *remaining CEO* by learning how to further professionalize the business; *hiring a CEO* to manage the business, most often either then taking on another role, such as heading up research and development or becoming chairman of the board; or *selling the company*. Many founders stumble when making the transition to corporate chief and fail to recognize that they must master the requirements . . .

The qualities that were so important in taking the risks to launch the business and in bootstrapping and experimenting with new things are less called on during this time, and those of a corporate leader become primary. Too many founders fail to appreciate this and neglect to appoint top-quality managers with first-class experience to take charge of the major functions, instead often hiring from within their personal networks and promoting unqualified people from within.

A founder who managed the transition from scrappy, decidedly uncorporate, and even iconoclastic start-up creator to corporate leader is Mark Zuckerberg. He had no management experience at all before founding Facebook, having dropped out of Harvard to create the company in his sophomore year, and by popular accounts was not a natural public communicator or developer of a strong corporate culture. When first starting out, his business card read "I'm CEO, bitch." But he has been widely praised for dedicating himself to learning how to become a top-quality CEO. He's brought in many highly respected upper managers, such as Sheryl Sandberg as COO and former Genentech chief financial officer David Ebersman as CFO. He has instituted appealing and creative compensation schemes to recognize and motivate employees. And while his performance when selling the vision and message of the company was once so much in doubt that Sheryl Sandberg often accompanied him in media appearances, he has now become a polished communicator.[8]

By stark contrast, the poster child for not making this transition successfully is the founder of Groupon, Andrew Mason. He brilliantly innovated the company's online coupon business model, leading it to become the fastest-growing start-up in history at that time. But he failed to rigorously institute top-quality standards for financial reporting, even though a skilled CFO could have been brought in to do so. Just before the company's IPO, in the summer of 2011, the company roiled Wall Street analysts by introducing a new metric it called adjusted consolidated segment operating income, which was all too obviously intended to artificially spruce up the company's financial performance. The new metric was criticized as "financial voodoo" by *The Wall Street Journal*. Before long, the company was under investigation by the SEC and facing a shareholder lawsuit. As the public face of the company, in several appearances in the media, Mason was highly controversial, such as one notorious case in which he told a reporter, "Sorry, too much beer." The company was facing serious challenges to its market share and complaints from many of the businesses with whom it contracted for coupon deals, and at this critical juncture, he failed to step up as a mature leader. He was forced out by the company's board not long after the IPO.[9]

Mason's story speaks powerfully to the necessity of applying the right principles at the right time. His flamboyant and irreverent style was well suited to launching the company and getting to explosive growth but horribly suited for taking it public and managing sustained growth. Successfully navigating the changes in responsibilities and the right approaches for tackling them from stage to stage is difficult for most founders. We'll examine the cases of a number of founders who managed the transition brilliantly and the crucial requirements for doing so.

The Game Plan

In the following chapters, we'll dive more deeply into what to expect during each stage of growth, and I'll introduce the complete set of Hockey Stick Principles that will allow you to master these many challenges and become a start-up champion.

The book is divided into four sections, each dedicated to one of the growth stages, and each chapter of a section is devoted to a core challenge of that stage. Packed with stories of how successful founders managed the four stages, as well as a host of cautionary tales about why other founders failed to do so, the chapters vividly illustrate how to apply the principles no matter what type of start-up you're launching. I've chosen the stories to represent a broad range of product type, sector, business model, and scale—and also because they're just great stories. They show that the principles apply across the board for all types of business, all levels of market potential, and also all types of founders.

The stories of successful founders and their start-ups differ from one another in many ways. Some of these founders took a shotgun approach, building their businesses extremely quickly, such as Lisa Falzone, who started Revel Systems—the first point-of-sale system delivered on Apple's iPad—in 2010 with just $30,000 of savings, bringing it to a $400 million–plus valuation as of 2014. Others grew their companies over a long period of time, such as James Goodnight, founder of analytics software behemoth SAS Institute, which regularly makes lists of both the largest privately held companies in the United States and the best places to work. Some businesses have created software products, while others have created manufactured goods, such as Boogie Wipes—which makes a saline-infused tissue for children—cofounded by Julie Pickens in 2007 and sold in a deal to Nehemiah Manufacturing in 2012. Some founders had MBA degrees and lots of experience in the corporate world, such as Doug Lebda, who founded leading mortgage lender LendingTree, while others spurned the corporate life and had no business training, such as Wes Aiken, who founded Schedulefly, which offers scheduling and related services to restaurants. Some were at the very start of their careers when they founded their companies, like Ryan Allis and Aaron Houghton of iContact; others were well established in a professional career, like emergency room physician Graham Snyder, who invented the SEAL SwimSafe device out of a passion for preventing children from drowning. They all started their businesses for different reasons and with different ambitions, but what they all have in common is that they followed the Hockey Stick Principles.

I hope the advice in this book will help you achieve the great success that these and so many other founders profiled in the book have enjoyed.

Let the games begin!

Stage I

Tinkering

Chapter 1

Hitting the Ice: Beginning to Develop Your Idea

When you have an idea for a new product or service, even if you believe it's a really good one, you can worry that you might be pulling a Kramer, Jerry Seinfeld's lovable but wacky neighbor, who was always cooking up product and business ideas for his company, Kramerica Industries. Who can forget the mansiere (a bra for men), the coffee-table book about coffee tables, the roll-out tie dispenser, and the periscope for cars that would allow drivers to see better in urban traffic? Unfortunately, he had little success with any of his ideas, but that's not because they were all just wacky. One of them was to introduce rickshaws to the streets of Manhattan, which became a booming business not in New York but in dozens of other cities across the United States. Kramer's problem was that he never buckled down and wrestled with the realities of actually building a company. That is the only way to find out whether your idea will work, no matter how good the idea seems to be.

I believe that one of the most pernicious misconceptions about entrepreneurship is that the best way to go about it is to come up with a truly great idea and then right away build a slam-dunk business model and write a detailed business plan for executing it. This seems to make great sense, but there are many problems with this notion. Probably the biggest is that while some successful entrepreneurs do hit on their ideas in a eureka moment, most often ideas emerge over time, and most of them need a good deal of tinkering with.

Many hugely successful entrepreneurs started with ideas that were deeply flawed in their original iteration. If you are convinced that your idea has to strike everyone you discuss it with as brilliant and has to readily generate a good model that answers all the tough questions about market size, cost, pricing, profit potential, and competition, you are likely to give up on an idea that may well eventually be made to work.

Good Ideas Don't Grow on Trees

Hockey Stick Principle #1: You don't need a good idea.

I loved an article in *Business Insider* titled "This Man Turned Three Bad Ideas into Fortune 500 Companies," in which the CEO of Gallup, Jim Clifton, is quoted saying that his favorite entrepreneur is billionaire and former Miami Dolphins owner Wayne Huizenga. He points out that Huizenga's three highly profitable start-ups: Waste Management (the trash business), Blockbuster Video (video rental business), and Auto Nation, Inc. (a chain of used car dealerships) were arguably bad ideas. Clifton did much of the research for Huizenga on Blockbuster, and after his research, he didn't think it was a good idea.[10]

So why did Huizenga succeed in each case? (Blockbuster was a huge success until Netflix came along and ate its lunch, a danger we'll discuss later in the book.) Clifton credits his success to "extreme optimism, his unstoppable determination, and his incredible energy." The most basic reason, though, is that Huizenga figured out how to tweak, build upon, and develop his initial kernels of an idea into good ones over time.

Clifton also researched Ted Turner's Cable News Network's twenty-four-hours news idea and concluded it wasn't a good idea, either. He wrote, "No one wanted more news, and the news Ted was going to show was just a reel of reports played over and over again." He concluded, "Twenty-four-hour news is a mediocre idea." Of course, Turner went on to turn it into a fortune.

Tesla's electric car is a more recent example of an idea that plenty of analysts predicted would be bad but has turned out to be a big success. In 2003, entrepreneur Elon Musk invested $6.35 million in the business despite the fact that the big automakers were backing away from electric cars then because they were proving to be unprofitable. For years, Tesla looked like a bad idea. In 2009, it lost $55.9 million with only $111.9 million revenue, proving the big automakers were correct. So what does Elon Musk do?

He invests $75 million more to keep it afloat. By 2014, Tesla had revenues just north of $3.2 billion.

Start-up success is predicated not so much on the *idea* as on the *development* of the idea, as well as the tenacity and will to succeed. This is why the common approach of starting by writing a detailed business plan, unless it's written for the benefit of investors to better understand your basic plans, is so flawed. Even the best-researched plan is only hypothetical; it's really just the addition of more ideas to your main idea. I've seen so many founders think of the plans they've written to get started as arguments for their concept, almost as if they are a proof of concept. In no way is that true.

> **Hockey Stick Principle #2: Starting with a business plan is an exercise in self-deception.**

A real danger in writing a detailed business plan from the get-go is that having made such a good case for your idea, you may narrow your thinking too early in the process when instead you should be in an exploratory mind-set.

At First, Just Tinker

For years, most experts have encouraged aspiring entrepreneurs to "research, research, research" and "plan, plan, plan" before starting. When I did a book search for "before you start," 2,185 book titles came up. The Small Business Administration says: "The importance of a comprehensive, thoughtful business plan cannot be overemphasized."[11] But while a good business plan can be important further down the road and is essential in seeking outside funding, spending lots of time researching and writing one up front is not the way to go—and you may not even need one at all.

A fascinating study conducted by William D. Bygrave, a former director of the Center for Entrepreneurial Studies at Babson College, one of the most highly regarded entrepreneurship programs, found that there was little difference in the success of the ventures of founders who graduated from the program who wrote formal business plans versus those who didn't. "We can't find any difference," he reported.[12] Another well-respected scholar of entrepreneurship, Stanford professor Steve Blank, who is also a serial entrepreneur, has applied experiential wisdom to his study of the process. He writes, "There's only one reason for a business plan: some investor who went to business school doesn't know any better and wants to see one. . . . Entrepreneurs often mistake their business plan as a cookbook for execution, failing to recognize that it is only a collection of unproven assumptions."[13] And regarding that investor you're hoping to sway, 90 percent of the time, your plan is not going to be what gets you funding. As we'll further explore later, demonstrating proof of concept and actual revenue growth are what attract outside funding.

I've met so many aspiring entrepreneurs who spent two to three *years* researching and planning their concept and crafting their plans, imagining how the business could best work, pondering whether or not they could afford to devote their time to it, contemplating whether or not to bring in a partner, writing an elaborate business plan, analyzing their personal budget to see if they could afford to quit their jobs, and stalling because they were afraid to take the first step. Such people consider the "right" things for their business plan: market size, pricing, break-even quantities, scalability, required financial investments. And there's no question that eventually you've got to figure those things out. But don't fall into the trap of believing your plan can tell you how to actually build the business. As the founder and CEO of sports undergarment firm Under Armour, Kevin Plank, says, "I think sometimes entrepreneurs can get caught up with theorizing, hypothesizing, business planning—at some point, put the freaking pen down and go do something. Go find out if you can make your product."[14]

My study and the in-depth interviews I conducted with successful founders revealed that most successful entrepreneurs do not start in a particularly strategic manner—defining the required tasks, setting tight deadlines, keeping checklists, writing formal business plans, and developing break-even cost analyses. In fact, most of the successful founders I've interviewed and most of those whose stories are told in this book didn't start by crafting a detailed plan, and many had no plan at all.

Ryan Allis, the founder of e-mail marketing firm iContact—whose story we'll explore more in chapter 2—makes the important point that too much planning may sway you from digging into an idea you might be able to make work. "When we first started, I'm really glad I didn't know what I know now," he reflects. "Otherwise, I might not have done it, you know? Sometimes a little bit of naïveté or even ignorance helps." He says if he had more thoroughly investigated the competition, he would have found out that several other entrepreneurs were entering the same market and he thinks that might have stopped him there. That's a common mistake.

> **Hockey Stick Principle #3: No idea is yours alone; you can never escape competition—you have to outcompete it.**

The fact that others are doing what you're setting out to do—or have failed at doing it—doesn't necessarily mean you shouldn't start trying your idea out. The initial research Graham Snyder, the inventor of the SEAL SwimSafe device, conducted showed that other companies had tried using technology to prevent drownings. In the late 1990s, Poseidon Technologies had invested $30 million developing video technology to detect if swimmers are at risk of drowning, but the system was only installed by two hundred swimming pools worldwide.[15] Video detection is prone to errors, and the Poseidon system was expensive. He believed a more reliable, affordable device could be made.

I think sometimes founders focus on lots of market research and on writing business plans because it seems like the professional thing to do. They're often concerned about appearances, worrying that people, including their families and friends, to whom they may be going to ask for funding, will think they're being irresponsible if they don't draft some sort of plan. Brian Hamilton, the founder of financial-analysis software firm Sageworks, made a great point about this conundrum when I interviewed him: "Spending so much time planning is just silly. You can't explain that to someone who hasn't started a business because they will think you didn't know what you were doing. Well, the fact is it's true. You don't know—you're just trying stuff. That's what [a start-up] is."

Don't Start with a Road Map, Either

> **Hockey Stick Principle #4: Following a road map is a road to the predictable; innovating is an uncharted journey of discovery.**

You may be thinking, *But isn't there some time line I should be on or some game plan I should create with benchmarks for progress so I don't just waste my time?* After all, that's the way the leading innovators in the corporate world innovate. They've developed tools like product road maps, three-, five-, ten-, and twenty-year business plans, and a number of disciplined methodologies, such as Customer-Centered Innovation Maps, the discovery-driven planning method,[16] or the R-W-W ("real," "win," "worth it") process, developed by innovation strategist Lance Bettencourt, which industry giant 3M has used to manage 1,500 innovation projects.[17] New product projects are given strict time lines and budgets, and while trial and error is often accepted for some specified period of time, progress must be measured and reported on often. Many experts on innovation advocate for this kind of highly disciplined process, such as the authors of the book *Ten Types of Innovation: The Discipline of Building Breakthroughs,* who write, "Innovation almost never fails due to lack of creativity. It's almost always because of a lack of discipline."[18] They assert that innovation requires a "simple, organizing system—an underlying structure and order governing what works and what fails."[19]

In the corporate world, this approach can work well, but that's often because the innovation is incremental, a comparative tweak to an existing product rather than a disruptive new product with a new market. A great case to illustrate this point is Procter & Gamble's launch of the Tide Pod laundry detergent capsule. It offers the modest incremental convenience of not needing to measure and pour your detergent, which was enough to make it a big success.

But that's just one successful example. In reality, even with these elaborate and closely monitored processes, the fact is that best estimates are that 65 percent of new products created by established corporations fail,[20] which is why many corporations have been pursing alternative methods of innovation, including P&G, which has developed an open innovation program called Connect + Develop for generating new products through crowdsourcing and cocreation with outside partners.

You are not a corporation, and individuals are free to innovate in a much looser, more experimental fashion, which is vital for unleashing your creativity. Don't let any rigid process dictate terms to you. Always keep in mind that *to survive each step, founders eat the apple one bite at a time.*

Do Begin Tinkering with Your Model

What I do advocate you do at the start, as a means of beginning to think through the practicalities of how to build your product and business, is to craft a provisional business model. But you should do this *as you begin taking actions to explore your idea.* You should develop this model in tandem with making your first explorations into how feasible your idea is. Think of this early stage model not as your set of answers to how the business will work but as your set of *hypotheses* to test.

The best approach to formulating your model is to begin by considering this essential set of questions:

- Who will your customers be?
- What benefits will your product or service offer them?
- What competitors will you have, and what extra value are you offering customers?
- What processes will you be creating and then continuing to run the business?
- What financial, physical, and human resources will you need to run the business?
- How will you sell and deliver your product at a price—or prices—that generate a good profit?
- How much will it cost to produce the product, and how much can you sell it for?
- How much pricing power will you have?
- How will you market your product and build customer relationships and loyalty?

I don't suggest writing detailed answers for each of these at this early stage. It's best to come up with conjectures and then to explore the ins and outs of the practicalities for each as you proceed to take action. One device that many entrepreneurs have found helpful for organizing their thoughts about their model and coming up with action plans is the Business Model Canvas put forward by Alexander Osterwalder and Yves Pigneur in their book *Business Model Generation.* The canvas is a visual map of nine essential elements—or, as they call them, *building blocks*—of making every business, putting all of them next to one another on one page in order to help you keep them all in mind as you search for your solutions. The building blocks are:

- Customer Segments—the various groups of customers you're targeting, such as teenagers or married couples.

- Value Proposition—the commonly used business term for how your product will solve your customers' problems and satisfy their needs.
- Channels—the means by which you will sell your product, such as online retailers, your own Web site, brick-and-mortar stores, or through distributors.
- Customer Relationships—which refers to the various means you'll use to manage and build relationships with all your customer segments, for example, social media or a customer relationship management (CRM) online system.
- Revenue Streams—or where your sales will come from, such as product sales, subscriptions, or renting of office or warehouse space you may own.
- Key Resources—all of the inputs you'll need to make and deliver your product, such as raw material if you sell a tangible product or programmers if you sell an online product.
- Key Activities—everything involved in making, marketing, and selling the product.
- Key Partnerships—the people or companies that you'll outsource work to, like suppliers or anyone you might go into a co-venture with or make licensing deals with.
- Cost Structure—delineates the total set of costs you'll incur.

One thing I like about the canvas is that it doesn't suggest a linear, step-by-step process but, by putting the blocks side by side, suggests one on which you will be working toward solutions for multiple components at once. One of the first things entrepreneurs learn is that the building process is simply not a straight, sequential one. As we'll see more in chapter 3 on getting to market, once you're engaged in earnest in your lead-up to launch, you will have no real choice but to work on parallel tracks in developing your product, your sales, and your marketing, and those tracks will be looping ones, often with byways you find yourself going down. Sometimes you'll have to take three steps back on one track just as you're taking two forward on another. The sooner you begin getting used to this, the better, and it's more helpful to not even have a conception in your mind—or on paper—of a linear, orderly series of next clear steps.

You may want to use the canvas, or you may want to create your own schematic for writing up and updating your hypotheses about each of the core elements. Maybe you prefer to list ideas under a heading for each, or maybe you prefer to create a PowerPoint deck or a spreadsheet. Whatever format you choose to use, what's important is that you treat your initial ideas about your solutions as hypotheses and then continually update and refine them—or, as the case may be, overhaul your model as you test those hypotheses.

You certainly don't have to have proposed solutions for each of the key questions right at the start, and for some, you might be better off starting with a set of possibilities. For example, regarding who your customers will be, you may want to specify a target market with a good deal of demographic precision—maybe that's males ages eighteen to thirty-five—or if it's a business-to-business (B2B) model, meaning a company that sells to businesses instead of consumers, a high degree of specificity about the type of business being targeted, such as pet store chains and independents. Or you may want to start with a broader definition, such as small business owners, and refine your targeting over time. For sales channels, you may want to start with just one or two as propositions, such as a company Web site and e-commerce sites for sales, Internet advertising for marketing, and order fulfillment from a warehouse by mail delivery for distribution. Or you might want to list a set of all the available possibilities that you'll need to research and test out as you go. Do not spend days and days working on this plan; rough it out and get going with the first actions to get your business actually up and running.

Learning by Doing

You should begin the way the feeling moves you to. That might be working on the product itself first, discussing the idea with potential customers or retailers, going out and checking competing products, or reaching out to specialists you'll have to contract with for design or manufacturing and getting costs. More likely, the process involves doing some of all of these things at once.

It's vital to keep an open mind, which is true all through the building process but especially so in this stage. You may discover a whole different way to make or deliver the product than you've expected; you may come to the conclusion that you need a partner; or you may even come up with a whole different idea that you think is better to pursue.

Hockey Stick Principle #5: A foolish consistency is the road to failure.

Ralph Waldo Emerson wrote, "A foolish consistency is the hobgoblin of little minds" in his essay "Self-Reliance," suggesting that it's important to change your mind about things. In building a start-up, it's often important to change both your mind and your methods. When Lisa Falzone started having conversations with restaurant owners that led her to pursue creating the first point-of-sale system for an iPad, which became the very successful Revel Systems service, she was exploring the idea of a restaurant ordering and delivery mobile app, along the lines of the Seamless app. But when the demand for a better POS system was expressed repeatedly, she listened and totally changed course. Red Hat founder Bob Young was trying to build a newsletter business about Linux software and a catalog business reselling Linux and UNIX products when he kept hearing from customers about the man who would become his partner, Marc Ewing, who was selling a version of Linux he had programmed. Bob didn't abandon his newsletter and catalog businesses right away, but he kept them running to sell Red Hat as a complement, and that was the business that eventually took off.

Of course, your early tinkering may also provide you with just the confirmation you need to be confident in going forward as you've wanted to and in taking the risks that may be required. One of my favorite stories of such a case is that of Graham Snyder and the tinkering he did to explore his idea for the SEAL SwimSafe device. He began tinkering in his basement, often staying up as late as two or three in the morning while his family slept. The first device he assembled was too complicated and too large and heavy to be practical for a child to wear. It also only worked some of the time. But it did provide good reason to believe that a much sleeker and more foolproof device might be possible to create, and by building it, he got the proof of concept he needed to decide to invest considerable personal funds to get a highly functioning prototype made by experts. Probably no mechanical engineer or corporate product manager would have advised him to do this tinkering, because he knew very little about the work required, but it has led him to a remarkable feat of innovation.

You Don't Need to Be an Expert

One of the most common pieces of advice offered to aspiring entrepreneurs is to build a business in an area in which they have expertise. That can work well, but it's by no means required, and many entrepreneurs who start businesses they're experts in fail.

> **Hockey Stick Principle #6: It's not what you know that matters; it's what you learn.**

Graham Snyder had no expertise whatsoever in building any kind of mechanical device and very little business experience at all. He was an emergency room physician. The only background he had in any sort of machining was hanging around the garage of Ed Patterson, a neighbor of his when he was growing up, who invented things for the sheer enjoyment of it. Ed showed him how to use lathes and specialty saws, but that wasn't the kind of work he'd have to do to create his antidrowning alarm. As an undergraduate, Snyder had studied chemical engineering, which also had no direct bearing on making the device. As he told me, there was one way in which he felt his medical experience was relevant: "When people are broken, I can help get them fixed."

Many successful founders had no expertise in the business they developed when they started. Fred Smith, the founder of FedEx, conceived of the idea for a competitor to the US Postal Service in a term paper he wrote at Yale, and he had no knowledge of the postal service business. In 1976, Howard Head invented the Prince oversize tennis racket because he had so much trouble hitting the ball in the sweet spot of a traditional racquet. Talk about not being an expert![21] Bing Howenstein worked in film and TV production when he created BackJoy, a medical device that improves your posture and helps prevent back pain. I could go on and on.

This doesn't mean that you should proceed without any expertise. Graham Snyder managed to create a workable, if clunky, prototype because he threw himself into learning everything that he needed to know, no matter how arcane. One of the first things he did was take apart a flood sensor to figure out how it worked. As he explained to me, "I didn't know whether a device could sense water intake and then use that to deploy alarms," and he figured a flood sensor was a good place to start finding that out. For more than eighteen months, as he learned more about what would be required to make the device, he taught himself about circuit board layouts, capacitor timers, CAD software, programming, and other electronics. Engineers told him he should pay someone with the expertise to figure it out, but he refused. He told me, "I needed to understand this at the base level. And so I did. I learned what's called assembly language. It's not quite programming using 0s and 1s, but it's almost that complicated."

You could absolutely say this was quixotic of him, but the fact is that by learning a great deal about the engineering involved, he developed the knowledge that allowed him to work closely with trained engineers on the further development of his product.

The big takeaway here is that while expertise is not required for first pursuing an idea, developing expertise as you do so is crucial.

Irish playwright and cofounder of the London School of Economics and Political Science George Bernard Shaw wrote, "Geniuses are masters of reality."[22] It's the realities you want to be mastering, not the planning process. As is so often the case, Graham discovered that, as the saying goes, "the devil is in the details." And it's by beginning to confront these details during the tinkering process that you discover not only what's really going to be required but whether or not you have a passion for tackling the job.

Don't Be Afraid to Socialize Your Idea

An aspiring entrepreneur recently told me about his idea, which involves creating online contests for personal home videos. (Nothing inappropriate—just good, clean fun.) He was walking me through the complexities involved with getting it going, telling me, "To even start this business, I'll need at least $50,000. It'll require secure hosting. Advertising is critical to getting enough customers to break even. I'll need a business plan. I figure I'll need X content entrants to break even at Y revenue per entrant." He'd clearly put a good deal of thought into the concept, and he was already thinking seriously about its scalability.

This entrepreneur would be better off simply starting by creating a version of a video contest on an inexpensive hosting platform, such as YouTube, and inviting his friends and family to participate. That would give him all sorts of feedback for taking the concept from there. But when I suggested this, he responded that he didn't want to give the idea away.

Contrast that anecdote to the approach Darren Pierce took in investigating his idea for his successful business etailinsights. His premise was
that with e-commerce booming and so many sites springing up, companies
needed help in targeting those sites, getting the contact information for
their buyers, and crafting their pitches to them by getting a richness of data
about the firms. He went out and started discussing the idea with potential
customers with just a very preliminary "vaporware" demonstration product consisting of just a screenshot prototype drawing, having done no
actual programming. From that, he got the message loud and clear that, as
he says, "They had a pain, and we had a remedy."

> **Hockey Stick Principle #7: Ideas are made to be shared, not
> stockpiled.**

There's no substitute for discussing your idea with potential customers,
as well as suppliers and retailers. The quality of the information you will
gather is richer and more nuanced than any survey or purely online method
of testing can provide. Potential suppliers offer great advice, can save you
lots of mistakes, and help you understand how much the product will really
cost to build. For instance, retailers can give you good feedback in particular about packaging and pricing.

Many founders I've recommended Hockey Stick Principle #7 to have
worried about protecting their idea, concerned others will steal it. To my
mind, in most cases, you shouldn't worry about that. The truth is most
people have their own lives and passions, and very few are in a position or
have the desire to knock off someone else's idea. And the process of creating a product and developing a market requires so much input from others
that keeping it truly under wraps is normally impossible, anyway. Furthermore, big ideas that involve selling to mass markets generally end up with
hundreds of new entrants, anyway.

Protecting trade secrets and confidential information is a whole other
thing. I wouldn't teach my potential partners—who could just as easily become my competitors—exactly how I produce industry profiles and how
much they cost, at least not without noncompetes or nondisclosure agreements. And when you contact suppliers, having them sign a nondisclosure
agreement might be a good idea. For proprietary information about design,
costs, and specifications and for your logo and name—and also protection
of your confidential customer information—you should absolutely have

people sign such agreements, and you should register for trademarks, copyrights, and patents, and it's best to do that as soon as possible. The good news about that is that getting this paperwork done is generally easier than you might expect.

You should also involve an experienced corporate attorney *early* in the process to guide you about how to protect your idea and company. I wouldn't advise trying to save a few bucks by managing all this yourself because the process is too complex, and a good lawyer will already know all the pitfalls. There's no need to be intimidated by the process because normally it doesn't have to be a big deal or very expensive, but it's critical to get a lawyer involved because before launch you're often negotiating with potential partners, customers, manufacturers, suppliers, and consultants, and you'll need to protect your interests. Most experienced corporate attorneys won't charge you for an initial meeting, so you can at least gain a broad understanding of what's needed before starting out. My attorney, Byron Kirkland, says, "I recommend entrepreneurs go talk to two or three attorneys. I do that all the time. I meet with them and don't charge them for the first few meetings to just help them get along. But maybe they'll come and hire me one day."

With the protections you need in place, generally, you should begin sharing your idea with those who can help you to craft it, those who can help you sell it, and those you'd like to buy it from very early on. This means at the very least having a series of conversations with potential customers, suppliers, and retailers.

An Idea Is Only a Figment of Imagination

When doing this outreach, whether in person or online, it's best if you can provide those you're consulting with some type of prototype or demo, so you should work on getting that made early on in the process. For potential customers or retailers, you should try to actually sell your product to them on the basis of your prototype for future delivery. Although early sales might help you raise some funds, the main reason you do this is to *learn from their rejection.* You'll probably get a lot of "maybes" from them, and you should follow up by asking them why they won't commit now. That will help you flesh out your understanding of shortcomings in the benefits you're offering and in how you're describing them.

Going to trade shows is another great approach to product and market research that many of the successful founders I interviewed found very valuable. The founders of Boogie Wipes, Julie Pickens and Mindee Doney, attended a number of trade shows during their first few months of development to get hands-on feedback and product awareness. This may strike you as going right to the competition to give your idea away, but remember, it's not the idea, it's the development of the idea that's key. Julie and Mindee had a fundamentally simple idea—to add saline to tissue wipes—and they might have worried that Kleenex or another major brand would hear about it and swoop in and steal it. But instead, they took samples as they were developing the product in order to get feedback from retailers, which proved important to the creation of a final product that got a good reaction once they went to market.

You may even want to canvass reactions more widely by tapping the power of the Web. Julie and Mindee did this by targeting the network of "mommy blogs." "We put it out there to a lot of mom bloggers at the time," Julie recalls. "There were some really large ones that drove interest to some of the big retailers. We got them to review [the concept], and we based some of our criteria for success off the reviews. We got them to react to both the idea and the name of it."

Another founder who tapped the power of Web feedback is Lending-Tree's Doug Lebda. He had written a great business plan, but when he took it to funder after funder, they turned him down. He was also running into a chicken-and-egg problem in trying to get buy-in from banks. He thought he needed them to agree to offer loans on the site in order to build it, but as he recalls, "The big question with the banks was, are consumers really going to do this? They asked, 'Why would a consumer put their confidential information on the Internet to fill out a loan application? Nobody's going to do that.'" Finally, when a potential angel investor he pitched to requested that he get some proof that consumers would respond positively to an online mortgage application process, he got a great idea for a market test. He asked a Web developer acquaintance to build him a very basic site, which he did at no charge. Then, to see if he could attract consumers to the site, Doug invested $1,500 of his own money to buy search-engine keyword advertising from Yahoo!. The campaign attracted more than three hundred borrowers, which was a stellar result. That simple test became the hardy sprout that grew into LendingTree, providing the basic proof of concept that got him his first funding.

If you are going to put your idea out in the world, the only caution I would pass along for blogging or putting your idea on the Web is not to include confidential information, such as business processes, details about costs, business plans, and projections.

Minimal Viable Products Can Be a Virtue, but They're Not the Only Way to Succeed

Most entrepreneurs should expect their tinkering process to take at least several months, and it often extends to well over a year. My Hockey Stick study showed that the average founder tinkered with his or her idea for 10.6 months before actually officially starting his or her business.

A popular method for shortening the time it takes to get a product on the market was introduced by successful entrepreneur Eric Ries in his book, *The Lean Startup*. It's a rapid prototyping and market-testing process. The core of the method is to create a minimal viable product (MVP), an inexpensive version of your product with only enough features to satisfy a first set of early adopter customers, as quickly as possible. You then sell it to those targeted first customers and get customer feedback from them, conducting analysis of which features are most popular and which aren't being used as much. Then you use that information to make improvements to the product. Ries summarizes the method with the phrase *Build, Measure, Learn*. He developed this method after his painful experience of putting everything he had into a long product development process as an employee for a 3-D virtual world program called There.com, which had to close its doors. He had taken a class in entrepreneurship with Professor Steven Blank at Stanford, and he combined Blank's insights about being customer-centric in your development with the lessons of the lean manufacturing process created at Toyota, as well as the discipline of agile software programming, to craft this new way of working. For his next start-up, the 3-D social network IMVU, he and his cofounders used the method to great success.

This method can certainly work well, and you should consider whether or not it's a good way for you to go. Lisa Falzone and her partner took this basic approach in launching the Revel Systems to great effect. For them, speed to market was very important. When restaurateur Michael Lappert mentioned that he wanted a better POS system to replace the complicated ones available at the time in 2009, he outlined the basic features he was looking for, and Lisa told him on the spot, "We'll build it for you!" The annoyance of the available POS systems had come up in a number of conversations Lisa had had before with restaurant owners. Meanwhile, the iPad had recently come out, and a system using that, connected to the cloud, seemed feasible. It was a great idea, and they knew someone else might have it soon.

They immediately followed up with a written contract to deliver Michael the product, scheduling a follow-up meeting for a week later to get more precise information about what he'd need. During that meeting, Lisa says they "just storyboarded [the product layout] and said, 'What do you think about this? Is this right?' And he said, 'Yeah, we want you to build it.'" They told him they'd deliver the system in two months, a very challenging time frame because Chris not only had to write the software but they had to find hardware to handle credit card swipes, and a stand to hold the iPad had to be designed and manufactured. They hired an outside programmer to help Chris with that part of the project, and Lisa worked on getting the hardware developed and crafting their marketing. The first stands she ordered weren't right, but on the next try, they hit the mark, and she ordered one hundred stands to start.

They didn't even try to raise any outside funding; they invested $30,000 of their own savings. Rather than a full-blown business plan, they wrote an executive summary and created a PowerPoint pack to tell the story of the product.

The product they delivered was bare bones, offering only the simplest POS functions, but it was much easier to use than other systems, and they got lots of great feedback for improving it from Michael and the other early customers they sold it to.

This method works best for software products and has more limited relevance for manufactured products, with which an MVP might spell disaster. If Graham Snyder's SEAL SwimSafe device failed in use by early adopters, even once, he'd almost surely have had no second chance. And the device had to go through rigorous safety testing and receive regulatory approval in order to go on the market.

The official Lean Startup description of the development cycle shows how tailored to software products the method is, including how the Build-Measure-Learn cycle is translated to "code, data, ideas," meaning that after you've written the code, you gather and analyze data from users to get ideas about improvements and then do more coding. But even for software, the market you should be selling to may be unclear, and you may start with a misguided target, so the feedback you get could be counterproductive. For example, Sageworks's cofounder Brian Hamilton first tried to sell his financial analysis software to small business owners for their own purposes of learning more about their business. Only after running into a wall with them did he stumble on certified public accounts as his core market.

Even software products sometimes simply require that they function at a very high level before they should be sold. With LendingTree, given the extensive network of mortgage brokers, Doug Lebda had to be sure his system was offering a very strong set of loan offers to choose from before he launched.

So the Lean Startup method shouldn't be considered *the* way to go but rather a very useful process that might work well in your overall development approach. The tinkering process I recommend is a more informal, hands-on, trial-and-error exploration of product possibilities that allows you to identify clues for moving the idea forward. And you should expect it to take some time. If getting answers and coming up with solutions is taking longer than expected, don't panic; just keep trying more new things. Learn what you need to learn. That's a big part of the satisfaction.

Some Feedback Won't Be Pleasant At All

There are a few key things to keep in mind about this process. One is that some people are inevitably going to tell you your idea is horrible, and many won't mince their words. Be aware it can be very hard to take. What can help with keeping your bearings and not letting harsh responses derail you is to always keep in mind that the fact that you're asking for feedback doesn't mean you should believe all of it, even if—and sometimes especially if—it's from experts.

> **Hockey Stick Principle #8: Feedback is meant to be challenged, not bowed down to.**

Before starting First Research, I asked my target market, bankers, about my idea, pitching it to Bank of America and Wachovia. The people who managed industry research for them rejected it flat out. When I persisted and pitched it to a woman who worked for one of the men I met with, she said, "There's no money in industry research." A few of my good friends were feet-on-the-street business bankers, and so I decided to also ask them what they thought about my idea for the reports. They didn't even take the concept seriously and saw no real opportunity to make money from it. I was still getting poor feedback even after I had quit my job and was selling a finished product, but I was stubborn because I was confident in the value of the reports. I'm sure glad I persisted.

Almost every successful entrepreneur I've ever talked to or read about has been told their idea was flawed, even ridiculous. Marc Benioff, co-founder of cloud computing behemoth Salesforce.com, recounts in his book *Behind the Cloud* that he was told by programmer Dave Moellenhoff, who would later become one of the company's cofounders, that his idea "was 'a crackpot idea' and would never work."[23] Recall that both Wayne Huizenga and Ted Turner were told by an expert researcher to forget about the ideas that they're best known for today.

Expertise Is a Tricky Thing

Negative feedback from experts can be disorienting and especially hard to take. So consider this. Ravi Mehta, a professor at the University of Illinois, has conducted studies of how experts evaluate new products. He says, about the research he and colleagues have performed, "There is a blanket assumption that knowledge and expertise are always good. What we show is that it's not always true. Expertise is a double-edge sword."[24] It can cloud people's judgment with biases, and Mehta found that when experts evaluate new products, they often make inaccurate comparisons with prior products.[25]

This is why, as said earlier, industry insiders aren't often the ones who make the biggest innovations in their own industries. The experts you consult may simply be wrong. I'd say that the lawyers you go to for advice about contracts, trademarks, and patents are an exception *when it comes to those legal issues.* I'm not saying that you shouldn't consult any experts; you probably should, because they can be a font of important information. But keep in mind that Steve Jobs said, "We built [the Mac] for ourselves. We were the group of people who were going to judge whether it was great or not. We weren't going to go out and do market research. We just wanted to build the best thing we could build."[26]

Listening to advice—and this goes for all the advice you get, whether from potential customers, suppliers, or retailers too—requires a challenging balancing act between being receptive on the one hand and persistent on the other. People are going to tell you all kinds of things, and they'll often be conflicting. You've got to be digging into the feedback, thinking through why people are reacting the way they are and whether there's some message within their message that you should be discovering. You can't use any formula for this, such as if eight out of ten people like it, then you're good, or vice versa. Eight out of ten people can be wrong, and so can ten out of ten.

A founder I interviewed who did an especially deft job of managing this balancing act and figuring out how to challenge and dig deeper into the feedback he was getting is Bob Young, cofounder of Red Hat. The breakthrough business model that led to the successful launch of the company came out of a combination of rejecting the chorus of nay-saying he got from industry insiders and potential funders he approached on the one hand and brilliantly recognizing how he could reconcile conflicting feedback he got from potential customers on the other. Challenging the feedback he got and thinking deeply about it provided the insight he needed to create a counterintuitive business model that made sense out of selling software that was available for free, a model related to the now-popular freemium model of giving away a version of your software or service but also offering a paid premium version, like the model that's used by Dropbox, Skype, and so many others.

Bob was a standout exemplar of taking the right approach to market research. He was like an anthropologist, going out in the field to get firsthand insight and studying responses thoughtfully. That led him to a radical sales model that has earned billions. So adept was his approach in the tinkering process that it's valuable to take a closer look.

What Microsoft, IBM, and Apple All Missed

In fiscal year-end February 2015, Red Hat earned $1.8 billion in revenue by offering support service for clients who run their servers and applications with a particular kind of high-demand open-source software called Linux.

When Bob started the process of creating the company, he didn't have any experience in building a software firm, which helped him spot an opportunity to build a unique business model around Linux. He and the partner he built the business with, Marc Ewing, were willing to move into a market dominated by such behemoth firms as Microsoft, because they believed that they could offer a proprietary version of the free Linux at a low enough price that it would appeal to the programming crowd that was adopting Linux and because the big firms weren't showing any interest in offering a version of Linux themselves. The success of Red Hat is a true David-and-Goliath story, and it illustrates one of the great paradoxes of innovation, dubbed the "innovator's dilemma" by Harvard Business School professor Clayton Christensen. Quite often, large market-dominating firms do not pursue emerging opportunities within their business domain because they consider them too small. This is another way in which industry experts can be biased.

The business idea that led Bob to Marc and then to their breakthrough Red Hat model was much more modest than the game-changing concept that emerged from their tinkering—it was a newsletter for users of the UNIX computing program, called *New York Unix*. Bob started the newsletter even though he had no knowledge of programming. At the time, he was in the business of leasing the big computers that UNIX ran on, and he had discovered that programmers regularly had meetings to talk about the latest trends with the program. He began crashing those meetings, even though initially he couldn't speak their language, and that's how he got the idea for the newsletter. His business model called for making all his revenue by selling advertising, but it turned out that advertisers were only somewhat interested in his specialized offering. While he was trying to make a go of it, though, he developed a close relationship with the UNIX programming community, and he was always asking them, "What do you want me to write about that you can't get from other publications?" Again and again, they said they were curious about the free software known as Linux, an open-source, Unix-based language originally created by programmer Linus Torvalds to improve on UNIX (Linux being short for Linus's UNIX).

Bob's first pivot was to start *The Linux Journal,* but that still wasn't making him enough money. He recalls that his family was "living on the knife edge," using credit cards to pay all their bills. So his next pivot was to branch out into catalog sales, selling applications for UNIX and Linux, books, and other computer-related products. He finally started to make some money, but not all that much. In the process of working on lead generation, though, a customer told him about a programmer, Marc Ewing, who had written a proprietary version of Linux, called Red Hat, that was easy to use. Bob asked some other programmers about it and learned that Red Hat was being well received by the wider community. Bob's first proposal to Marc was that he become Red Hat's sole distributor, and they made a deal.

After a couple of months, he and Marc realized that the distribution deal wasn't optimal. It led to complications about who would set the price, and it was stopping Marc from pursuing other sales channels. So they discussed combining their businesses into one company. But before he made that commitment to quit his Linux catalog company and take a huge risk, Bob made the very smart move of going out in the field to meet with leading-edge customers for Linux. He wanted to understand the market potential better.

On an early trip to the NASA Goddard Space Flight Center, he interviewed programmers and learned that "they were not using Linux because it was better, faster, or cheaper technology; they were using it because it gave them control." The engineers at NASA—and, as he was to discover, at many other organizations and companies—wanted to be able to customize the operating system running their programs, but they had no alternative system—not from IBM, not from Microsoft, not from Sun, not from Apple. The engineers were saying to him, "I really want to see you guys succeed. But if you layer proprietary software on it, I can't use your stuff. I'll build my own. If you just share your code with me as quickly as you can, though, I'll use Red Hat rather than making my own."

The engineers were saying that if Red Hat would share its Linux upgrades, such as improved methods for printing or managing Web pages, then they'd use Red Hat's version. However, if Red Hat charged money for those improvements or refused to share the source code, they would just keep working with Linux. That left Red Hat with no way of making more money, which might have been extremely discouraging.

But Bob didn't stop there; he also decided to talk to people at companies that *weren't adopting* Linux. He discovered that they were rejecting it because Linux was too complex for them—more than six hundred separate programs make up Linux—and they didn't have the staff to maintain the programs and keep track of updates and changes. Another issue was that Linux nonadopters tended to think of the "freeware" programming community as long-haired radicals—not exactly the kind of team they wanted to rely on for mission-critical company functions. They wanted to have support, security, confidence, and backup plans from their software providers. They also wanted "official" documentation to show their bosses and auditors that they had a legal right to use the programs. Linux didn't offer any of that. So Bob and Marc decided Red Hat would.

But these insights left them with a tricky market complication to manage: How could they sell a product to the Linux nonadopters without alienating the avid Linux community? They made the bold decision to distribute the same product in two different ways:

- a free, downloadable version that included the software and source code, and
- a CD-ROM "official" version that customers could purchase.

The two versions were exactly the same software program, but the official version included a product serial number, installation guides, a how-to manual, and customer service and support. To its buyers, the Red Hat Linux paid version stood solidly between hackers and the establishment.[27] These buyers regarded serial numbers and support as insurance against loss. Meanwhile, Red Hat got top-quality R&D from the programmers who downloaded the software for free, as they made many improvements that were helpful for all users. And because Red Hat didn't have to invest the man-hours to build Linux, it could compete aggressively on price. Red Hat Linux, therefore, retailed for $49.95, compared to Microsoft's Windows NT's retail price of $150 and up. You could describe the model as a two-way freemium, as the free service provision worked both ways, allowing the company to gain insight and input from the extremely talented programmers that were using Red Hat at no cost.

When Bob and Marc were pitching their model, not one of the industry experts thought it had the potential to achieve major growth. But through all their tinkering, they had learned one of the great truths of new-product success. As Bob puts it, "I'm a sales guy. I don't sell features. I sell benefits." Bob came to realize that listening to customers would be the key to Red Hat's success. "I saw an opportunity. I saw the benefit of open source articulated by guys like [the engineers] at Goddard Space Flight Center, which all the business guys working for Oracle and Sun Microsystems and Microsoft and all the rest didn't have the opportunity to see because they weren't asking the questions."

The features of the software were the least valuable part of what they had to offer; their customers had articulated two clear benefits—control over the code and professional documentation and support—and Red Hat figured out a way to offer both.

You Don't Need to Quit Your Day Job

One great lesson from the Red Hat story is that as you are tinkering with your idea, you do not need to go "all in" and sacrifice your source of income. Bob and Marc kept their catalog sales going until they saw that Red Hat was catching on. Many of the successful founders I interviewed either stayed at their jobs while they tinkered or did consulting or other work on the side as they tinkered.

> **Hockey Stick Principle #9: Successful entrepreneurs take as little risk as possible.**

A common notion promoted about entrepreneurs is that they have a propensity for risk taking, sometimes characterized as a need for risk if not an outright obsession with it. Taking risks is certainly at the core of starting an innovative business, and some successful entrepreneurs do seem to relish the danger, but as long ago as 1961, Harvard professor of psychology and leading entrepreneurship expert David McClelland conducted a study in which he found that entrepreneurs are generally rather moderate risk takers. Much subsequent research has backed this up, and some has even shown that entrepreneurs tend to be risk averse. Malcolm Gladwell wrote in a *New Yorker* article about entrepreneurs that "their entrepreneurial spirit could not have less in common with that of the daring risk-taker of popular imagination. Would we so revere risk-taking if we realized that the people who are supposedly taking bold risks in the cause of entrepreneurship are doing no such thing?"[28]

Work on Your Whole Model

Another lesson from Red Hat is that as you tinker, you should be exploring not only how much interest there might be in the product or service and the costs and other practicalities of making it but also tinkering with your hypotheses about delivering it to the market. Many start-ups fail because they didn't create a good sales and distribution model and also because their product wasn't competitive. One of the most glaring cases in point is how JVC's VHS (Video Home System) pummeled Sony's Betamax in the once-lucrative market for home video recording devices and cassettes. Sony was out the gate first with Betamax, and it had better picture quality, a slicker design, and smaller, more storage-friendly tapes. However, JVC won the war by tweaking its business model and engaging other manufacturing firms to build their own recording devices that could play VHS technology. They would earn money by selling their own recording devices and gaining market credibility but would also learn important insights for product improvement from their competitors. JVC eventually won a nearly 90 percent market share.

Doug Lebda was also able to strike gold with LendingTree by making a new model for selling mortgage loans work. Michael Dell did the same with a new model that allowed customers to customize their computers and order them by mail. Jack Dorsey hit it big with his Square point-of-sale system by removing hidden fees and charging all retail customers the same rate to process credit card orders. Daniel Ek and Martin Lorentzon broke Spotify out with a new model of offering access to millions of songs on their computers and mobile devices for a monthly subscription.

> **Hockey Stick Principle #10: A great product is not a business model.**

The point here is that many great business successes weren't the result of an invention or physical product; they were the result of a clever business model. You may not even need to invent a new product in order to achieve phenomenal success. Amazon didn't get into product development until many years after launch, but it's an innovation pioneer based on its pricing, sales, and delivery model. Another example I love is the endearing start-up Dollar Shave Club, cofounded by former digital marketer Michael Dubin, who, I should point out, wasn't an expert in the business of manufacturing or distributing razors when he started. The genesis of the idea came in 2010 when Dubin met cofounder Mark Levine at a holiday party, and they started chatting. "I don't know how we got on the subject of shaving, but we started talking about what a rip-off it is," Dubin recalls.[29]

A common scenario for men when purchasing razor blades is that they go to a grocery store or drugstore, stare at the display offering a wide array of blades, hope they don't accidentally purchase the wrong ones, and out of frustration from the decision-making process, curse all the way to check-out before paying thirty-five or forty dollars for a purchase they're unsure about. They use the blades for too long because they're so expensive, and that results in dull blades and some painful shaving. (Okay, so this is my personal experience, but I bet many men would agree.)

Dubin came up with the idea to sell razors with a subscription plan that ships replacements automatically. Basically, he applied a well-established model to a well-established product. As of 2014, Dollar Shave Club had more than 650,000 customers and was growing fast.[30]

Finding a Cofounder

Don't let the mythology of the lone genius stop you from collaborating. Another important consideration during this early tinkering process is whether or not to get hooked up with a partner. Sometimes cofounders cook up an idea together, of course, but often, deciding to find a partner is motivated by the realization that you need someone with complementary skills. It can also be a great help to have someone to share responsibilities and to make the thousands of decisions you've begun to realize are in store. The Hockey Stick Research Study showed that 85 percent of the successful start-up firms had more than one founder. Sixteen percent had more than two.

Many times, cofounders are friends, but if you don't have a friend who's interested or has the skills you need for a cofounder, it can be difficult to find one. The process took me eighteen months from when I had the idea to start First Research. When I decided to give my idea for First Research a try, I started by crafting some very rough research reports and that quickly allowed me to realize that I really needed to find a partner to do the report writing. It just wasn't my greatest strength, and I realized that I wanted to focus on marketing and sales. I had no idea how to find someone to write the reports, and I just figured I would need to partner with a big firm, so I sent my business plan to Dun & Bradstreet, Frost & Sullivan, and other large research firms. I made the mistake of thinking that I'd have to partner with a large, established company and that doing so would also give the business credibility.

During those eighteen months, all the established firms I approached rejected me, and I realized that it's actually uncommon for big companies to partner with individuals. Fortunately, those efforts pointed me in the right direction. One of the people I met with to discuss my idea was Rafi Musher, CEO of Stax Research headquartered in Boston, and though Rafi wasn't interested in partnering, during our lunch, he shared with me three names of people he knew who did do business research. One name was Ingo Winzer. He was a self-employed real-estate-analysis guru whose second-bedroom company was called Local Market Monitor. He'd been quoted in *Barron's, The Wall Street Journal,* on CNN, and other media. He had credibility, so I called him. This was the gist of our first conversation:

Ingo: "I can create a research product, but I can't sell."
Bobby: "I can sell, but I can't create a research product."

After that call, I decided to go meet him. Ingo picked me up at a street corner in Boston, arriving twenty minutes late in an unwashed, gray Toyota Camry. I figured he'd be big-city serious and formal, but he wasn't like that at all. With hair falling slightly below his shirt collar, in black jeans, a gray T-shirt, and cowboy boots, he was a superintelligent, laid-back Yankee cowboy. Meanwhile, I was in my pressed khakis and a blue sports coat, an intimidated, small-town Southern banker. We might not have seemed a likely fit, but I soon discovered that Ingo had humility and sincerity to go along with his brilliant mind. He took just a day to design a nifty, efficient process for creating industry reports, and he turned out to be a great partner in building all aspects of the business.

> **Hockey Stick Principle #11: Going it alone may mean going nowhere.**

Many of the cofounders I interviewed brought complementary skills to their businesses. Bob Young had experience in customer development and management while Marc Ewing was the specialist in programming. Lisa Falzone took the lead in marketing, sales, and manufacturing while Chris Ciabarra took the lead in programming. Wes Aiken was stalled for two years in launching Schedulefly because he didn't want to do the marketing and sales and did not have any real sense of how to go about it, and bringing in Tyler Rullman as his partner to take charge of that aspect of the business was a vital decision.

A number of organizations have sprung up to help founders with the process of finding a cofounder. One example is cofounderslab.com, an on-line matchmaking service that counts its membership community as hav-ing forty thousand founders, advisors, and interns. Another is Startup Weekend, where aspiring entrepreneurs come together for fifty-four hours in one weekend to share ideas and form teams. One benefit of attending this event is "cofounder dating." If you do a Google search, you'll turn up other such organizations.

It's also fine to just go it alone and find independent contractors or hire staff as you need specialty skills and extra hands to manage the flow of work. As we'll dig into more in the next chapter, partnering involves shar-ing control and splitting equity, which can be quite tricky to manage. One thing is for sure about whether or not you seek out a partner: The decision has to be made carefully. A few things to consider when choosing a partner are you have to be sure that you have a shared vision, that you have similar goals in terms of how far you'd like to take the business, how many hours you feel are acceptable to work each week, and how you treat employees.

No Hard Line between Tinkering and Committing

The simplified explanation as to how a business starts—that a founder first gets an idea, creates a plan, and then executes on it—has led to a false notion of there being a clear planning phase and then a development phase. The truth is that tinkering often morphs seamlessly into serious development. You may find yourself well into product development from very early on in your tinkering process, maybe because there's no other way to even begin figuring out whether the product is viable—as with Graham Snyder's SEAL SwimSafe device—or because you quickly discover that you are very seri-ous about going ahead and that you should do so as quickly as possible, as was true for the Revel founders who launched in two months. But even the Revel founders kept tinkering after their launch. And, as we'll discuss in the blade years chapters (chapters 3, 4, and 5), most founders have to and should. You should really never stop tinkering.

But you may also find out during this stage that you have to do lots of other legwork before you can begin your actual product development and that the development is going to cost a substantial amount, as was true for both Doug Lebda in founding LendingTree and Graham Snyder in creating the SEAL SwimSafe device. They learned they would have to come up with lots of money to hire expert developers.

You know that you've passed from tinkering into prelaunch development once you have gained a deep conviction about pursuing your idea and you truly commit to it. This often involves quitting your day job, and even if it doesn't, committing to actually making the product work will inevitably involve many more hours and a greater intensity of development, as well as more money. So I strongly advise that when you arrive at this juncture, the one key thing you should take the time to reflect on deeply is how you're going to have enough money to launch your business and make it through the blade years. Does that mean you should now start drafting a detailed business plan so you can pursue angel investment seed money? Should you ask your family and friends for money? If you're still working at a day job, should you quit so you can focus entirely on the business? Should you figure out ways to bootstrap during this development process so you don't need outside funding?

As you move out of the tinkering process and into the blade years, these questions about funding are pressing, and we'll dive deeply into them in the next chapter.

Chapter 2

Skating on Thin Ice: Leveraging Seed Capital to Get Started

Many founders launch their start-ups with the expectation that they'll begin to earn income from the business not long after going to market. This is a big mistake. One of the most common misconceptions about building a start-up is that soon after you launch, you'll be able to pay yourself a good—or at least an adequate—salary either out of your revenue or out of capital raised. The truth is that very often, revenue is not enough to cover expenses well into the blade years—often three years—and that getting the business solidly into growth mode usually requires that the lion's share of earnings and of any capital raised be invested back in the business. This money should go toward paying for increasing operating expenses, such as salaries for employees and office space; to make product improvements; to do more marketing and advertising; to maintain the product; and to expand operations. You should plan to reinvest in the business rather than pay yourself a desirable salary even when revenues are quite healthy.

Don't Plan on Paying Yourself

> **Hockey Stick Principle #12: Earning a living from your start-up will take at least twice as long as you think.**

Take the case of my brother-in-law Brad McCorkle, which is a pretty typical experience for entrepreneurs. He started his company when he was thirty-six years old and was married with two young children, so he had several mouths to feed, and he hadn't been saving up for launching a business. He wasn't expecting to become an entrepreneur, but he seized a good opportunity when he saw it.

Brad was working as a salesman of ophthalmic drugs, which treat ailments of the eyes, and when his employer, Alcon Labs, wanted him to relocate to become the manager of a sales territory, he decided that he didn't want to move his family. Instead, he left Alcon and started Local Eye Site (LES), a Web-based service that connects eye care practices with job applicants, which was the first of its kind. He had determined that Monster.com and the other job boards weren't doing their job in the eye care business because his clients often asked him to help them find new employees.

To get started, Brad raised $60,000 from two angel investors to build the LES site and a sophisticated recruiting tool. One angel was a well-connected leader in the eye care industry, and I was the other. Brad made a full-time commitment to the business and owned 51 percent of the firm. He used none of this seed money to pay his living expenses, instead drawing from his savings for those, and as his revenue slowly grew over the next several years, he started to pay himself a very small salary. Even when revenue grew to $429,000 in the third year, he continued to dig into his savings to pay his family's living expenses and poured most of that revenue right back into the business.

This may seem foolish, but one of the important truths of achieving start-up success is that being willing to continue to put a vast majority of earnings and capital raised into fueling growth is often the differentiator in getting your business to take off. So founders must plan on this. It's true that some start-ups do manage to generate enough cash from sales early on to provide a good flow of founder income while also investing adequate funds into growth, and in a bit, we'll discuss great models for generating cash up front and a predictable future cash flow, but even in these cases, pulling in an adequate pool of first customers may take quite some time. Meanwhile, raising outside capital is much more difficult than most founders predict. The result is that far too many end up raiding their personal finances and drowning their prospects for success in overwhelming debt.

So often, founders anticipate they'll have to work for no or low pay for six or maybe as long as twelve months, but that stretches out to twenty-four months or longer. Keep in mind that the Hockey Stick study found that the average time from starting a company to growth takeoff was three to four years. Not anticipating the financing challenges of this period means that far too many founders are forced to abandon a business that might have great potential because they're broke and have maxed out all of their credit cards.

It's vital not to plan to pay yourself a sizeable salary from either earnings or financing for the duration of the blade years, and to not delude yourself about how long these lean times will last.

> **Hockey Stick Principle #13: Accurate predictions of costs and revenue are not possible; plan to spend more than you think you'll need and to earn little to nothing.**

Financial projections to help you navigate through this stage are important, and you should definitely calculate detailed ones. But they're likely to change. Product delays and redesigns are the rule, no matter how well you've planned, and they always cost something, whether in more outlays or loss of sales. When we started Vertical IQ, our first interface was confusing and had to be completely redone, delaying launch by three months. That mistake cost us roughly $20,000 that we'd originally projected from advance sales I'd made, and another $15,000 to redo the interface, so suddenly our operating budget was much tighter.

Even businesses that end up becoming huge successes take off slower than planned. For example, the music-streaming service Spotify, which in late 2014 was worth $8 billion and seems to have exploded virtually overnight, took much longer to make into a viable business than its founders, Daniel Ek and Martin Lorentzon, expected. As early investor Sean Parker recounted, "The thing that made Spotify very different when I first met Daniel and Martin was that they had this incredible stubbornness. . . . Daniel said, 'I think it's going to take six weeks to get our licenses complete.' It ended up taking two years."[31]

This is why the only prediction you should truly rely on is the rule of thumb that you should expect achieving sizeable earnings to take at least twice as long as your gut tells you you'll need, and therefore, your financing will be spread much thinner than you've hoped.

Fast Growth Is Way Overrated

The problem of financing in the blade years is often made much worse by founders throwing far too much cash into trying to speed up the process of growth. One of the most dangerous misconceptions about the early growth phase is that you can speed it up by pouring cash into attaining scale. The Startup Genome Report, conducted by entrepreneurs Bjoern Herrmann and Max Marmer in collaboration with Stanford lecturers Steve Blank and Chuck Eesley, researched thousands of Internet start-ups. One of its findings, from an analysis of more than 3,200 firms, is that "one reason for failure has shown up again and again: premature scaling."[32]

As we'll consider more fully in chapter 6 about the right way to scale up, premature scaling occurs when a start-up builds up large fixed expenses by hiring employees, overbuilding the product without enough customer feedback, and investing in expensive marketing and customer acquisition strategies. In short, it occurs when start-ups throw a bunch of money at an idea before they truly understand how the idea will actually work. Practically speaking, a start-up gets ahead of itself and skips the tweaking needed to make its model work.

The scaling mistakes of high-profile Internet and software firms account for a great deal of the press coverage about the problem, but they aren't the only types of start-ups that scale prematurely. The founders of any type of business can be tempted to do the same. Start-ups that sell physical goods are especially vulnerable. After achieving some early success, they often purchase too much inventory, which they then have trouble selling. Many of these founders also don't fully understand the challenges of customer returns and slow payers, so they miscalculate their cash flow. What happens next? They end up with more bills than they can possibly pay, and a good idea goes bust.

Rather than planning to quickly ramp up spending—such as with a big marketing campaign—and achieve fast growth, founders should plan for the blade years to be a patient time of deep market investigation and product and marketing trial and error, while continuing to learn what's working well for their business and what isn't.

So many founders miscalculate how much funding they'll be able to raise in this stage. With so much press coverage of high-profile start-ups receiving big funding, investment money can seem to be plentiful. During the blade years, though, the hard truth is that it's not.

So rather than focusing on how to raise funds from the professional investing community, we'll start by taking a good look at the best tricks of the trade for getting through the blade years with only minimal—or even no—seed capital, largely using out-of-pocket funds or money from friends and family. Then we'll consider how to approach professional funders.

Models for Customer-Funded Growth

Some start-ups lend themselves to making at least some money early on, and sometimes, though rarely, these earnings can take off fast. The ideal method for raising capital is to earn it from paying customers, and as pointed out by London School of Economics professor John Mullins in *The Wall Street Journal,* this is in fact the most common way that founders raise cash. In his book *The Customer-Funded Business,* Mullins highlights that there are five main business models to consider: 1) matchmaker models (e.g., Airbnb) wherein you don't have to hold inventory or maintain an expensive product, you just connect two parties; 2) pay-in-advance models (e.g., Threadless) wherein customers pay you the full amount or a deposit for a product before you build or ship; 3) subscription models (e.g., Netflix) wherein the product or service is delivered to a customer on an ongoing basis but the customer pays up front; 4) scarcity models (e.g., online retailer Zara) wherein the customers make purchases before you pay your vendors; and 5) service-to-product models (e.g., iContact) wherein businesses start out providing a service to a customer, and that service transforms into a product.[33] For example, iContact originally provided the service of writing more efficient applications for sending e-mails to customers, and the founders then got the idea of packaging their e-mail marketing solutions into a marketing software product.

Founders can either copy such successful models or can experiment with their own versions. For example, if you have a Software as a Service (SaaS) business model, instead of billing customers monthly, as is typical, you could offer them a discount if they pay up front for a full year. Getting paid up front for annual subscriptions made a world of difference in funding First Research's first year or two. In fact, we couldn't have hired our first salesperson as early as we did without these customer commitments.

These models may not work for your business, and if one or another does, the cash you raise this way may well not cover costs. At this early stage, you most likely will not be making a substantial amount of money, so you're also going to have to become a great bootstrapper.

Everybody Should Bootstrap, Funding or Not

Hockey Stick Principle #14: "Bootstrapping" should be the start-up founder's word for "standard operating procedure."

"Bootstrapping" is the hands-on, low-budget, hand-to-mouth method of starting a business that minimizes the amount of financial capital required. A great deal of advice in recent years has encouraged founders to bootstrap as opposed to raising outside capital early from professional investors. I agree that this is generally the best way to go, but what I think has gotten somewhat lost in the discussion is that it's also generally the only real choice.

There's no widely accepted definition of what qualifies as bootstrapping. Must the founder begin with *no* financial capital? Or just a little capital? Is $20,000 or less the cutoff? How about $50,000? Is that too much to constitute bootstrapping? Any attempt to draw the line would reinforce a false distinction. I've found that most successful founders of innovative firms bootstrap in the earliest years, regardless of whether or not they've raised substantial funding.

The most important question regarding funding that founders should be asking themselves from their earliest days is not, "Should I bootstrap or should I try to get outside financing?" but instead "What is the appropriate mix of human, social, and financial capital that I can leverage to get my start-up going and sustain it long enough to discover the improvements that will lead to takeoff?" The discussion of capital can often be too focused on financing, but it's really the human and social capital that make any financing effective, and all the money in the world won't make your business take off without them.

Leveraging the Three Types of Start-Up Capital

Harvard Business School professor Noam Wasserman, author of the excellent book *The Founder's Dilemmas,* highlights the need for all founders to maximize the use of the three sources of start-up capital: human, social, and financial. He defines *human capital* as the founder's "skills, knowledge, and expertise,"[34] including his or her work, school, and managerial experience; industry knowledge; and experiences from outside his or her schooling or work life, such as hobbies.

He defines *social capital* as the "durable network of social and professional relationships through which founders can identify and access resources."[35] In referring to resources, he means advice and connections that help founders discover partners, suppliers, marketers, and customers as well as financing.

The definition of *financial capital* seems obvious, but it's important to appreciate that it can take many forms, which have different implications for your freedom in building the company. As said earlier, the ideal source of financing is revenue generated by the business, but many founders need to raise cash up front in order to get the business launched and to fund operations until earnings cover costs. The main ways of doing so are:

- Out-of-pocket money from savings and credit card debt
- Loans from friends and family or a bank, with repayment terms
- Investments from friends and family, which may or may not involve a transfer of some shares in the business to them, often referred to as an equity stake
- Investments from angel investors, which do involve the transfer of some portion of equity in shares
- Investments from professional venture firms, which also involve equity transfer, usually at a higher, and quite a substantial, stake.

The term "seed capital" is generally used to refer to the money drawn on before revenue is coming in. However, the lines have become fuzzy because new venture creation has become much more fluid, with launches coming earlier and more models for raising cash before product delivery emerging, most prominently crowdfunding.

The real line to be aware of is between money to fund your initial growth, your seed capital, and venture capital (VC). VC is not usually offered until substantial earnings have been achieved and indications are strong of substantial additional growth. In 2014, only 1 percent of VC investments were made at the seed stage.[36] The rest were early-stage, expansion, or later-stage investments.

Despite the popular mythology that businesses raise a significant chunk of change up front and then develop the product, many new ventures actually begin with the founders tinkering and injecting only, say, $1,000;

working on development part-time for a month; borrowing another $3,000 off their credit cards; working another three months and then raising $100,000 as a "seed round" from friends and family or a professional angel investor.

> **Hockey Stick Principle #15: Raise the minimum amount you need to get to launch; financing is scarce and expensive.**

There is no formula to use for figuring out your seed funding plan. When it comes to making this assessment, each founder must discover the right recipe for him or herself. While some businesses can be grown with virtually no up-front money and minimal operating expenses, relying almost entirely on the founder's own talents and contacts—and less so on revenues coming in—others require a great deal of cash investment up front in order to even get going at all. But as a best practice, when first starting out, you should raise only as much as you absolutely need to begin testing your idea and then, once you've determined to go ahead with building the business, only as much as you need to get to launch.

As we'll explore further later in the chapter, outside capital is very hard to raise at this stage, and you have to pay a significant cost for it, usually either in interest on a loan or in equity shares in the business. Even if you do raise a large amount, that money can give you a false sense of security about not needing to watch your expenses. Before you know it, you've spent a huge amount of your cash on a fancy Web site design or on getting samples of your product made, and then when you discover you've got to make fixes in the site or the product—which is inevitable—you don't have the cash to pay for them. As chapter 3 will explore fully, this is the stage when you're experimenting with your idea, and you will *always* have to make some changes to your plan or fixes in your product. It's best to waste as little money on those experiments as you possibly can and to raise funding in increments as you make progress.

The Hockey Stick study shows that the median amount of money raised during the tinkering stage (before committing to it full-time) was $3,500. The median seed money the founders required was $150,000 but that ranged widely, from $600 to $4 million.

No matter how much money you need to get to launch and how much you're able to raise, you must be intensely careful when spending and consider all other means for getting work done.

Bootstrapping Best Practices

The best way to think about bootstrapping is that you are always looking for ways to leverage your creativity, ingenuity, time, living space, sweat, and connections so that you don't need to spend cash. Bootstrapping entrepreneurs wear many hats, doing most tasks themselves that established companies usually hire professionals to do or finding a partner or partners with the complementary skills for doing them. They design their own marketing brochures, draft their own customer agreements, devise their own bookkeeping systems, and, if required, sell door-to-door despite having no sales experience. They often barter for services or supplies. They generally either keep their day jobs through much of the blade years or find alternative means of making income, often a hodgepodge of odd jobs, allowing them to take very little or no earnings out of the start-up. They often work out of their homes, in the garage, or in a spare bedroom, and they zealously look for all sorts of cost-cutting opportunities.

I'll use the story of how the founders of iContact, the $50 million–plus revenue provider of e-mail marketing software, achieved growth takeoff without raising any seed capital as a guide for considering the best tactics for making bootstrapping work. Their tactics are relevant for all founders, but of course if you're building a tangible goods business, then it's generally not feasible to make do entirely without seed capital. If a product must be manufactured, warehoused, and distributed, seed capital of some kind is required. So later on page 64, we'll consider the many sources of seed funding.

How Two Bootstrappers Struck Gold with Negative Income

Ryan Allis and Aaron Houghton brilliantly leveraged their human and social capital, allowing them to launch iContact with no seed funding. They started the firm in 2003 and grew it to be used by more than 70,000 organizations in 2012, the year it was acquired by Vocus for $169 million. Though e-mail marketing software is now a crowded business with a number of large rivals, such as Constant Contact, MailChimp, ExactTarget, and VerticalResponse, the business was in its infancy in 2003. Only a few companies provided the service, and hardly any businesses purchased it. Small- to medium-sized businesses with little technical ability could easily install iContact's software and use it. Given how big the business has grown, one might expect that iContact took off rapidly. The founders had certainly hoped it would, but, as Ryan recalls, the first year was a brutal surprise. They earned $11,964 and had $17,000 in expenses. As Ryan put it, "We had worked a year of our lives to lose $5,000. I just thought it would go faster. It took three years to get to a million dollars in revenue, and I thought it'd take a year and a half."

Ryan and Aaron made it through this lean period and were able to put all their scant earnings back into the business because they managed their expenses well, divided up responsibilities to maximize their human capital—which they had a good deal of—and leveraged their social capital in order to get valuable advice for free.

Ryan was an eighteen-year-old UNC–Chapel Hill freshman, and Aaron was a senior when they started the company. When the two met at UNC's Entrepreneurship and Venture Capital Club, both had started Web-based companies previously. Ryan was running a Web consulting and design business, Viranté, while Aaron was running a Web design company called Preation, Inc. Aaron was a talented programmer, and he had developed several Web products, such as an online calendar and an affiliate marketing tool. Ryan's eye was struck by another service Aaron had created for one client, a small business called Mountain Brook Cottages, which was an efficient system for sending bulk e-mails to customers or registrants. Ryan had experienced trouble in sending bulk e-mail newsletters to his customers, and he thought lots of small businesses would be interested in the service.

The two decided to work together to market the product through a joint venture between their firms, with Viranté handling the marketing and Preation the product development.

In making the arrangements for setting the company up, they smartly tapped the social capital of relationships with their business professors for advice about how to establish the company. One recommended that they create one company instead, which would streamline administration duties and simplify finances. Others advised them about the legal agreements to sign, the best practices for corporate governance, and equitably dividing shares of stock, with Aaron receiving a larger stake because he had written the software. Ryan became CEO, and Aaron was chairman of the board and CTO. They smartly divided their responsibilities according to their strengths, with Ryan, who knew more about marketing, taking charge of sales and advertising, and Aaron, who was a more experienced programmer, taking charge of making product improvements.

If you aren't in college and don't have these connections, you can get this type of advice from one of the nine hundred Small Business Development Centers supported by the Small Business Administration (SBA), SCORE, a mentor program supported by the SBA, and local entrepreneurial organizations found in most communities around the country, such as the Center for Entrepreneurial Development in the Research Triangle area of North Carolina, where I live. And as I pointed out in chapter 1 but is worth repeating, I strongly encourage you to reach out to many lawyers who are willing to offer entrepreneurs some basic advice at no charge.

Find Alternative Sources of Income

Both Ryan and Aaron kept their separate businesses going while they got iContact off the ground, which brought in moderate income. Many entrepreneurs find odd jobs to help them through the early years that are synergistic with the work of their start-ups, such as consulting in the same field. Jim Goodnight, John Sall, Jane Helwig, and Tony Barr, the cofounders of giant software services provider SAS, used consulting income to help pay monthly expenses during the company's first year. Bill Gates and Paul Allen wrote specialized software for a number of PC companies while developing their Microsoft products. When starting First Research, I was pitching an economic developer in a rural North Carolina county when the man said, "Bobby, I don't believe I need your research portal, but if you'll research these five companies and their CEOs, I'll pay you $1,000 for your time." I gladly accepted the deal. He was pleased with what I produced and referred me to other economic developers in surrounding counties. I had myself a little minibusiness and earned about $10,000 doing this until First Research was up and running. This income wasn't only helpful in paying my bills; even more importantly, it boosted my confidence during these especially tough years.

> **Hockey Stick Principle #16: Making money by other means allows you to leverage your time to support the building process.**

I cannot recommend more emphatically that you have a plan worked out about how you'll pay your living expenses by other means during the blade years. My main backup plan was that I would get a job as a waiter at nights. Graham Snyder, founder of SEAL Innovation, continued working as an emergency room physician on weekends. Nick Woodman, founder of GoPro, maker of handy wearable video cameras, which today is worth more than $3 billion, helped pay the bills by selling Indonesian shell necklaces from the back of his Volkswagen bus.

One option for finding work is today's "sharing economy," with services such as Uber, Lyft, and Airbnb, to sign up as a driver or host, as well as services that hook freelancers up with jobs, such as TaskRabbit and Upwork.

Be a Maniac about Keeping Costs Down

Ryan and Aaron were extremely rigorous about keeping the company on a shoestring budget, watching every nickel, and they took out no loans to fund operations or marketing, not even to pay for a backup server after their server broke and the service was offline for a week and a half, during which time they lost 35 percent of their customers. That was a painful lesson, but it is typical of the setbacks that founders should expect in the early going. It simply isn't realistic to think that you can anticipate every problem.

Creative scrimping can get you a very long way. Ryan told me, "I remember going down to UNC Surplus for a twenty-dollar desk and a forty-dollar computer. I ate at the same sushi restaurant day after day where you can get six pieces of sushi for a dollar. I sat in the hallway of our dorm working because we ran out of space. I jumped into dumpsters to get proof-of-purchase tags off our chair boxes to get the fifty-dollar rebates at Staples."

Darren Pierce, founder of etailinsights was a clever money-saver. "We just didn't have much cash, and the little cash we did have we invested into our product. I shopped for everything in our office on Craigslist. We bought these huge desks from an insurance agency going out of business. I persuaded my sweet wife to help me move them in late at night using her employer's work truck. When we got there, the desks didn't fit, so we had to take them apart in the dark, move them inside, and reassemble them. Also, phone systems were ridiculously expensive, like $5,000, so I just set up Vonage phone lines and a free Google voice number that I could point at any of our other phones, which at that time worked great."

I watched every dime during First Research's first two years, and that philosophy naturally carried over to my personal expenses, as well. While I lived in Wilmington, North Carolina, my ten-year-old, beat-down Nissan Maxima and I would drive four hours to Charlotte, North Carolina, to make a few sales calls. If I spent $20 on gas and sold $500 worth of product, I'd make a $480 profit. This was my early-formulation growth. But in August 2000, a little more than a year into my venture, my intern and I made this trip when my passenger-side window was stuck permanently down. It was rainy the entire trip, and my intern had to just deal with it because I simply couldn't afford to get it fixed. These sacrifices are common for founders. I consider them badges of honor.

Even Amazon founder Jeff Bezos watched costs zealously. For example, instead of paying for an expensive automated system for updating information about book titles on the Web site, he had his small staff manually input the information. Those first employees also had to kneel on the concrete floor of the warehouse while packing books to ship out until one of them, Nicholas Lovejoy, suggested to Bezos that he buy packing tables. Bezos recalls, "I thought that was the most brilliant idea I had ever heard in my life!"[37]

Use Creativity in Lieu of Cash for Marketing

iContact had no budget for advertising, so Ryan put in thousands of hours of sweat equity, leveraging creative Internet marketing strategies, such as SEO, permission-based e-mail marketing, and pay-per-click advertising, to find customers. One creative and effective tactic Ryan tried was lining up affiliates, or sales partners, to promote iContact to find their own paying customers in exchange for a 25–30 percent lifetime referral commission on iContact's earnings from them. iContact used technology to track the referrals and offered affiliate partners with support, such as statistics, banner art images, and instructions. As Ryan says, "The great thing about affiliate programs is that you pay out only after a sale is made. You already have the money in your bank account before you write the check for the commissions, completely eliminating risk." To persuade companies to join the program, they made sure it was easy to sign up for, using win-win partnership agreements rather than cash to incentivize affiliates and build the network.

Ryan also used ingenuity when contacting Web sites and convincing them to link to iContact, which improved the company's presence on Google. "The entire summer of 2003 was all about getting links from other Web sites to link to us," he recalls, "so we could get #1 in Google for e-mail marketing software. Because once you have that, it's free traffic. We set up five or six hundred links that summer."

They were also willing to use one of the most effective customer acquisition tactics; they gave the service away for free to a select number of local restaurants. Many founders are reluctant to offer giveaways because it's a direct hit to earnings. But Ryan and Aaron understood that this was a way to do high-quality user research with which to make more improvements. Free giveaways are harder for companies selling tangible goods, because of the variable costs involved in both making and distributing the product. One way to lower those costs is to offer a deep discount instead, so that at least you cover your costs and are only forgoing profit.

Offer Equity to Partners or Employees

Another smart move Ryan and Aaron made was to hire a top-quality Web designer their second year to help them improve the product even more. They couldn't afford to pay him market rate, so they leveraged their future equity by offering him shares, paying him a below-market-rate salary. They did the same to bring in their second employee, a customer service representative to man a phone line.

> **Hockey Stick Principle #17: Equity is worth incalculably more than its current value.**

If you're going to offer equity, you want to carefully consider the implications for the future. This may sound obvious, but it's important to keep in mind that your early ownership allocations are just the first ones and that if you're successful, you'll have to dish out more ownership later. Let's say you start a company with a cofounder who agrees to work with you for no pay for two years, and you also agree to work with no pay. You negotiate that he or she will get 40 percent, so you get 60 percent. Some people disagree that a founder should get a premium for coming up with the idea, because it's really the execution of the idea that matters. But in most cases, when founders bring in a partner, they have spent some serious time formulating the idea, investigating it, and have probably invested at least $5,000 or so to get it started. So I think such a division is generally fair.

Now say that six months later you can value the business at $500,000 and you're able to raise $100,000 but have to give away another 20 percent for that cash. Now your partner owns 32 percent and you own 48 percent and you haven't yet set up a stock option plan for new employees or raised additional capital for future growth. In essence, you've already given away *control* of your business. Of course between you and your partner, you still own 80 percent, but if you disagree about future strategic decisions, you no longer have the majority stake with which to definitively win the day. Some entrepreneurs are fine with owning less than 50 percent, and with the risk they take, due to the rewards gained. The risk is that you lose voting control of your company, which can lead to founders being fired from the companies they started. The rewards are that you have more partners to share responsibilities with and to help in decision making, and you have more cash to fund growth.

The calculation for how much ownership to maintain depends upon what your goals are. But many founders I interviewed strongly advise retaining majority ownership. As Brian Hamilton of Sageworks put it, "It's a simple formula. Keep 51 percent." Some people argue that it's better to have 10 percent or 15 percent of a billion-dollar company than a majority share of a ten or twenty million–dollar company. But if you truly believe your company can grow that big, also consider that it might be well worth taking longer to get there. After all, a majority stake in a billion-dollar company is even better. And stories of founders being forced out of their own companies, which were then run into the ground, are plentiful.

The Founder's Dilemmas offers helpful insight about making your calculations in splitting up early equity. Wasserman identifies four contributions as the main criteria to be factored in: past contributions (capital, the idea), opportunity cost (sacrifices founders have to make), future contributions (level of commitment, titles), and founder motivations and preferences (wealth motivations, risk aversion).[38] He also advises against splitting equity between founders and divvying it out to employees in the very early days. He cautions that "seventy-three percent of teams split the equity within a month of founding, a striking number given the big uncertainties early in the life of any start-up."[39]

Ryan Allis voiced these equity ownership concerns about the early share offers he and Aaron made: "I wish I had known how valuable equity is and not given it away so easily. We gave our first employee 7 percent of the company. Fortunately, we vested him over four years, so when he left eight months later, he only got 1.5 percent. Theoretically, it was worth little then, but it ended up being worth a lot. Our second employee got 15 percent, and he vested the whole thing.

"I wish I'd had a better ability to translate equity into what the potential value might be down the road so we hadn't unnecessarily diluted ourselves as much early on. I should have explained, 'What do you think the proper compensation would be for four or five years of work? Maybe a million bucks a year, risk-adjusted? But not three million bucks a year!' "

By contrast, other founders I interviewed followed the principle Wasserman suggests and split shares more in keeping with contributions. For example, Jim Goodnight, cofounder of SAS, told me that when it came time to divide up shares between him and his cofounders John, Tony, and Jane, "There was a lot of negotiation. . . . I tended to want to be egalitarian, but the attorney said no because [Tony and I] deserved a lot more than the other two since they had been working for us only a short time."

Microsoft cofounder Paul Allen recalls in his memoir, *Idea Man,* what a shrewd negotiator Bill Gates was about splitting early shares. He writes, "I'd assumed that our partnership would be a fifty-fifty proposition. But Bill had another idea." Gates made the case that "You had your salary at MITS [a computer company where Allen worked at the time] while I did almost everything on BASIC [the computer language Gates used to write software] without one back in Boston. I should get more. I think it should be sixty-forty." But the split didn't end up there. Allen further recounts:

> Bill's intensity was nonstop, and when he asked me for a walk-and-talk one day, I knew something was up. We'd gone a block when he cut to the chase: "I've done most of the work on BASIC, and I gave up a lot to leave Harvard," he said. "I deserve more than 60 percent."
>
> "How much more?"
>
> "I was thinking 64–36."

Allen agreed.

This is a great example to keep in mind for negotiating your fair share, because as a start-up evolves, the proportion of work each founder puts in usually evolves, as well. There's nothing wrong with asking cofounders for more equity, but you should be sure to do so thoughtfully and with a light touch, because this issue can be highly sensitive.

The timing of offering shares must also be considered carefully. If you split shares too early, you risk miscalculating how much each shareholder will actually contribute. Say one founder says he or she will contribute twenty work hours a week, but then circumstances change and he or she can only contribute ten work hours a week. What happens then? Negotiating a change of terms might be complex and combustible. On the other hand, if you wait too long and nothing has been put in writing between founders as they're building the business, negotiations to split up shares after you've launched and are growing can be brutal. My advice is that you agree on terms very early in the process.

To split up the shares for Vertical IQ, my four cofounders and I agreed within the first month that ownership would be primarily based upon cash and nonpaid work contributions. We basically all came up with the idea for the company, so there was no premium for that. The only special consideration was that one shareholder received a relatively small amount of bonus shares for his contribution of intellectual property. We created a spreadsheet that tracked everyone's nonpaid work contributions at eighty dollars per hour and cash invested. But to close the deal, we had to estimate future nonpaid work contributions, which required a vesting schedule—an agreement making the award of shares contingent on work being completed. We waited a year before signing the shareholder and other legal agreements in order to avoid managing the complex issues and expenses associated with that until we confirmed there was interest in our product and that the equity split was a good formula. In the end, this solution worked very well for me and my partners.

Leaving Bootstrapping Behind in the Haze of Your Gold Dust

All the tactics Ryan and Aaron deployed began driving revenue, and by the middle of year two, August 2004, revenue had improved to $20,000 a month, and total revenue that year was $296,000.[40] But they still didn't draw salaries. Instead, they hired more employees and invested heavily in Google AdWords advertising. That ramped sales up nicely, and Ryan recalls that "by the end of that second year, in May of 2005, we were at $60,000–$70,000 a month in sales with about twelve employees." That's when he decided to commit full-time to the business. Aaron had graduated from college the year before, and Ryan decided that he should quit college, which worked out well, as it was in that year that the company hit its growth-inflection point.

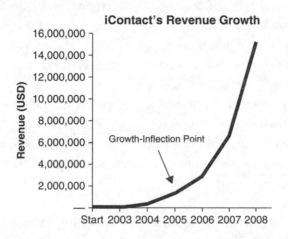

We'll pick up the balance of the iContact story in chapter 7 when Ryan and Aaron learn to raise capital and discover explosive growth. For now, the takeaway is that for more than two years, they invested very little cash into building the business, and they invested just about every dime of revenue back into building it.

Of course, sometimes there's no way around getting some up-front funding—sometimes quite a bit of funding. The good news is that there's a wide range of options founders can pursue. However, this doesn't mean the quest will be easy. It means you've got to be open to a wide range of possibilities, and most founders who raise cash tap several of these sources.

Chasing Cash

Knowing where to start when it comes to funding can be overwhelming, so here is a good basic list of the possibilities to consider.

- "Love money" from family and friends
- Individual angel investors
- Professionally managed angel funds
- Investments or loans from customers, suppliers, or industry insiders
- Incubators
- Seed or early stage venture capitalists
- Pitch-offs and demo days for investors
- Bank debt financing
- Nonbank debt financing from lenders, such as OnDeck, Lending Club, and IOU Financial that lend money at higher interest rates than traditional banks
- Crowdsourcing
- Grants from federal government entities, such as Small Business Innovation Research (SBIR)
- Grants from local and state governments, such as economic growth initiatives
- Grants from nongovernment entities, such as foundations and organizations that support entrepreneurship
- Advocacy groups

Not to harp, but the single most important thing to keep in mind when pursuing outside funding during the blade years is that it won't be easy. Sramana Mitra, founder of incubator One Million by One Million (1M/1M), points out in *Harvard Business Review* that the most difficult time to raise money is the seed round before you have a proven business model and execution capacity: "To be precise, the capital gap is in the sub-million dollar revenue level," she explains.[41]

This is probably the key reason that self-funding out of savings and personal borrowings is by far the most common scenario. Of the founders in my Hockey Stick study, nearly 80 percent invested their personal funds. Just less than half of those also received other funding mostly through angel investors. That finding is in keeping with the results of a study by Noam Wasserman that showed that 77 percent of the firms he had studied had at least one founder who contributed money early in the life of the start-up.[42]

One of the great advantages of self-funding is that you typically retain control. Of course the downside is that you expose yourself to financial loss, and there are too many stories of founders who get themselves into dire financial straits this way.

> **Hockey Stick Principle #18: Don't invest any money that you aren't willing to lose.**

How much of your own money you should be willing to devote to getting the business into growth mode is again, of course, a matter of personal choice, but doing so with the expectation that you will not see that money again really helps to motivate creative approaches to finding other means. Because so many founders fall into the trap of cashing out their 401(k)s and mortgaging the equity they have in their homes—resources that are extremely difficult to make up for if the business fails—I advise great rigor in following this set of guidelines when deciding to use personal money to back your business:

Calculate Your Amount of Affordable Loss

Many successful founders have made the choice to invest every dime they have in order to keep their building efforts going. Doing so is certainly a valid decision, but you must first conduct a serious analysis of what the consequences of losing that money will be.

I advise operating on the principle of affordable loss, proposed by Professor Saras Sarasvathy of the Darden School of Business, who has studied how successful entrepreneurs make what she and her coresearchers call the "plunge" decision about whether to go all-in and how much money to commit. The principle is that founders should calculate an upper limit to what they're willing to lose, calculate a worst-case scenario of losses, and then weigh that against how important it is to them to give the idea their best try.

One of the worst and most common mistakes entrepreneurs make is determining how much money they're willing to commit based instead on a prediction of costs and returns, such as: "If I put in $250,000 and in two years I'm making $1 million, and I can keep my costs at that time under $750,000, then I'll be at breakeven or better." The hard truth is that it is simply impossible to accurately estimate these costs. Recall Hockey Stick Principle #13 on page 48. Accurate predictions of costs and revenue are not possible.

Factor in the Opportunity Costs of the Time You Devote to the Business

Opportunity costs are the amount of money—or other kinds of payoff—that you might have earned by doing something else with your time. Founders should make a hard-nosed assessment of the costs of the time they're taking away from their former income-generating work when figuring out what their losses may be. If you're making $150 an hour at your job and you walk away from it to work full-time on your start-up, then you're not only spending the money you may be putting into the business out of your savings, but there's also a considerable amount that you're not earning by not working. You may be able to compensate for some of this loss of income by beginning to pay yourself out of first earnings, but remember that, as said earlier, for many start-ups, earnings won't allow for this for a couple of years.

Ensure You Receive Adequate Compensation for Your Input and Loss of Income

Because founders so often don't factor in their loss of income from the job they would have been doing had they not quit it to start the company, they sometimes settle for too small an ownership portion. They also fail to take advantage of other means of compensating themselves appropriately for that lost income. This becomes especially problematic the longer the business takes to earn revenue sufficient to provide them with a good salary. One way to ensure adequate compensation is a clause in the shareholder agreement that allows a founder to receive more shares if it turns out over time that he or she is committing more than expected. You can also set up a deferred compensation plan, which stipulates wages that will be owed to the founder in the future by the company. Those wages will be paid once the company can afford to do so or if the firm is sold. An attorney can easily draw up the paperwork for this.

Doling Out Equity

In preparing to approach potential funders, another key issue to consider is how dilutive the funding source will be, meaning how much equity you'll have to give up. Professional investors tend to require substantial equity stakes of 10–45 percent. Rarely do they take more than 50 percent, because they want the founders to be motivated and empowered to succeed. However, professional investors require stringent corporate governance and often board control so that if the company isn't performing well they have options to replace management (a.k.a. you). This is a key reason to think hard about how much control you're willing to relinquish and make no mistake: Trading equity for cash is always giving up some degree of control.

This is one reason that as an alternative to investors, you might want to try securing a loan from a bank, because bank loans are rarely dilutive at all, and they are also a relatively inexpensive source of capital.

Let's say you need $100,000 to get your business going. If you borrow the $100,000 from a bank at 5 percent interest and repay it in five years, you'll pay roughly $13,200 in interest. However, if you receive $100,000 for a 25 percent stake in your new venture (assuming a $400,000 valuation of your business) and in five years your business has become worth $4 million, you've given up $1 million for that $100,000—overwhelmingly more expensive than the 5 percent bank loan.

But obtaining a traditional bank loan for a new venture is difficult because you generally have no proven source of repayment. Banks generally want to make only very safe bets because they're lending their depositors' money. So for the most part, the only way to get a bank loan is by having a very strong secondary source of repayment, such as putting up high-quality stocks, bonds, or equity in your home as collateral, or you might get someone else who can easily repay the loan to cosign, which is often a parent.

Occasionally, you can qualify for an SBA loan guarantee program or another special loan program to get a strong secondary source of capital. Most traditional banks can underwrite SBA loans, and you may qualify if you're willing to guarantee it with your personal assets. This is why it's smart to speak with a small business banker to figure out if you are eligible. Try to meet with two or three different bankers from different banks, because they often have different levels of experience and banks have varying degrees of appetite for offering these types of loans.

Knocking on the Doors of Angels

The definition of an angel investor isn't simply a wealthy individual who likes to invest in companies at early stages of the growth process. Angels are accredited investors. This means that, according to the requirements of the SEC, which regulates the terms according to which you can officially offer shares in your company, they must have a net worth of at least $1 million and make a minimum of $200,000 a year (or $300,000 a year jointly with a spouse). According to a study by Harvard Business School professors William R. Kerr and Josh Lerner and Sloan School of Management professor Antoinette Schoar, firms started by founders who received angel capital were significantly more likely to survive the blade years than those that didn't. The advice and connections angels provide may be an even more important factor than the capital itself.[43] Many angels have a great deal of wisdom to offer, but keep in mind that while they're called angels, they're no pushovers. Most angel investors are or were successful entrepreneurs themselves, and they have a knack for knowing if an idea is good and if a founder is experienced enough to make it successful. They can poke all sorts of holes in your pitch, so you should make sure that you have your ducks in a row before approaching them.

When you approach a potential investor, even if at first just informally, you must have a well-organized business plan in hand, but you cannot expect the plan to make the case for you. While almost all investors want to see one, most know enough not to believe them.

> **Hockey Stick Principle #19: Business plans don't raise seed money; tangible results do.**

The experience of Doug Lebda in raising seed money for LendingTree is typical in this way. Doug benefited a great deal from the wisdom of the angel investor he got his first money from, even though the investment was for much less than Doug had asked for—it was only $10,000. There is no question that in this case, the advice was much more important than the cash. And though Doug had written a fantastic business plan, that wasn't what got him the money.

The investor was Lee H. Idleman, who had a long and illustrious career in investment research and portfolio management for Wall Street firms, and at the time Doug approached him, he was a member of the board of trustees of Bucknell University. In other words, Lee was no slouch as far as giving advice goes. He told Doug that he'd invest $10,000 if Doug could show him three things: that customers would want the service, that a bank would agree to offer loans through it, and that Doug could line up a professional banker to work for the company. This advice is what led Doug to build the proto–Web site that got such a strong response from potential customers. It also spurred him to approach banks again, and he managed to get a letter of intent from National City Bank, which Idleman deemed sufficient for his second condition. And for the professional banker, Doug convinced a former Goldman Sachs investment banker to agree to work with him to raise funds. That wasn't quite what Idleman had stipulated, because investment banking is different from mortgage banking, but he found it acceptable nonetheless.

Doug's creativity and persistence in meeting Idleman's demands made all the difference in impressing him and convincing him that the plan that looked so good on paper might actually be made to work.

Doug's first capital raise for LendingTree is a lesson in not wasting your time approaching even the early stage investment community with only a paper promise; approach them when you have some actual progress to show. And ideally you won't have to cold-call them. When it comes to pursuing angel investors, I recommend you first try to seek them out through warm introductions from other successful entrepreneurs you already know. Many angels are entrepreneurs themselves, and even if they are not, they generally like to learn about new ventures from other successful entrepreneurs. Most of the time, the process of raising funds from them is very different from approaching banks or VCs. They don't generally invite you to a conference room meeting to pitch your idea with a PowerPoint presentation. Instead, many angel investors try to spend lots of time with founders before they make a commitment. The process is iterative and ongoing: you might meet several times trying to solve business challenges together.

Also, most angel investors have particular types of businesses they like to invest in, so don't get discouraged if the first few you speak with aren't interested; that's normal. Ask instead if they know of angels who might have an interest in your type of firm. This is especially wise to do because identifying potential angel investors can be difficult and can take quite a bit of time. Doug Lebda advises that founders should leverage the law of averages to find seed money—meaning the more people you talk to, the better your chances are of getting funding. "Raising money is just really a conversion funnel, so a quick no is okay. You just need to know where your conversion funnel is. If you need one investor, you need to get three offers to consider, which means you need to get fifty meetings, which means you need to mail three hundred business plans and make three thousand phone calls. Whatever the numbers are, it's just a numbers game. So work the numbers."

To speed the process, you might want to also contact angel groups, which pool investors' resources and develop portfolios of companies they've invested in. You can find a listing of them online from Angel Capital Association (ACA), a trade association of angel groups.

Another option is to seek funds from one of a number of platforms for crowdfunding of angel investments, such as Crowdfunder.com or Angel-List. These sites were made legal by the JOBS (Jumpstart Our Business Startups) Act passed in 2012. Before that, crowdfunding platforms were not allowed to facilitate the selling of equity shares. The act, however, opened the door to making equity deals on these sites—but only for accredited investors—to protect novices from being burned.

Time Is Not Only Money, It's Progress

In making the call about whether or not and how much to pursue outside funding, it's vital to think through the opportunity costs of the time the chase takes away from working on the product and on sales and marketing to customers.

> **Hockey Stick Principle #20: All funding comes with hidden costs.**

Figuring out your game plan for fund-raising is again a personal choice. Some successful founders will tell you that every minute they spent hustling for funding was worthwhile. The founder of online course company Udemy wrote a blog post titled "Udemy's $1M Fundraising: Lessons Learned about Pitching Investors from a First-Time Entrepreneur," in which he recounted how constant hustling paid off: "I went to every conference I could and literally killed myself while there. I attended tons of networking events and met as many entrepreneurs and investors as I could. While at events/conferences, I rarely ate dinner because I was too busy schmoozing and grabbing business cards. During the weekdays, I'd spend hours e-mailing potential [investors] to start using Udemy."[44] This is a typical story for plenty of founders.

But in thinking this through, you've got to factor in that you're most likely going to have to keep at it and go back to the well repeatedly. A common misconception about raising seed funding is that you can get a good lump sum up front and that will carry you through to growth takeoff. Sometimes that does happen, but what's much more common is that you won't get the amount you're looking for from one source or all at one time, and you'll have to seek multiple sources and repeated injections.

One piece of wisdom to take away from this is that founders should be flexible about what they really need for funding versus what they'd like to get. Savvy founders leverage what money they do get in order to build momentum to get more money if they need it. You might think it's more efficient and orderly to get as large a sum up front as possible and to devote a serious chunk of hustling time to that so that you can then focus exclusively on building the business. But in fact, planning for an ongoing process of fund-raising is not only more realistic, it gives you better odds, because you're asking for less. As you move into a more serious development phase, you're going to have to get used to doing all sorts of different kinds of tasks all at once, so it's better to get used to this juggling act now before you're in the heat of the run-up to launch.

The Friends and Family Plan

The difficulty of raising seed money from professional investors or from banks explains why it's so common for founders to rely on "love money." Yet many aspiring entrepreneurs are reluctant to ask family and friends to make investments because they believe it's brazen to do so.

> **Hockey Stick Principle #21: Taking love money is nothing to be ashamed of when you're open and optimistic.**

Asking for money from those who will feel a special incentive to offer it is brazen only if you do so dishonestly. If you're forthright about the status of your operation, the challenges you face, the prospects for growth and your plans for achieving it, and if you're clear about the risk of failure, emphasizing to your loved ones that they may never see the money again, then they are making a legitimate choice to support you, and it's fine to offer them this opportunity to invest in your business. Taking money from people you care so much about is also a very strong incentive to work even harder. And keep in mind that the amount friends and family will invest is usually the amount they're comfortable losing. Many of them offer the money with little or no expectation of getting it back—though, of course, sometimes they do, and sometimes they get it back many times over.

One founder I interviewed had a memorable take on this issue. Bob Young decided to seek seed money from friends and family, and eight of them offered funds, for which he compensated them with a total of approximately 10–15 percent of Red Hat's stock. He was aware they were investing without expectations, and the way he saw it was "a love-money round is precisely what it says—people are investing in your business not because they know anything about your business or because they think you're clever. They're investing because they love you." Investopedia, an online platform that provides a financial dictionary and investment advice, wisely says about this issue that the terms on which love money is offered "are usually based on qualitative factors and the relationship between the two parties, rather than on a formulaic risk analysis."[45]

Suffice it to say, those love-money Red Hat investments turned out to be good ones. Bob's aunt Joyce Young, who donated $40 million to the Hamilton Community Foundation out of her proceeds, told *The Hamilton Spectator* about her good fortune: "It was exactly like buying a lottery ticket. You don't expect to win. . . ."[46]

One piece of advice when it comes to accepting money from friends and family is to treat them like any other shareholder, both in terms of communication and documentation. As consultant and author Wayne Rivers of the Family Business Institute warns, the lines between business and family can get uncomfortably blurry. "Families operate informally, but growing successful businesses requires formal rules, roles, responsibilities, accountability, and communication in order to function. Your family rules and roles are what they are; don't make the mistake of superimposing them onto your business. You'll find they hold back your company's success and add tension during the times when you're trying to relax with the ones you love." In other words, just because a relative offers you funding, even a parent, doesn't mean that he or she is a member of your management team. You must establish clear limits to their input. Not only might you face extremely difficult disagreements otherwise, but you'll scare away other investors who don't want to be bullied or be the odd-man or woman-out in family quarrels.

Build It First and Investors Will Come

If you don't believe enough in your product or service to go ahead and put some of your own money into building it, you should not feel entitled to ask others to fund it.

One founder I interviewed who was ultimately able to raise substantial seed funding is Graham Snyder, the inventor of the SEAL antidrowning device. His story is exemplary of the belief that you should have in your product and the tenacity that will be required of you to get others to back it. It also demonstrates how different your results might turn out to be once you've raised some funds to develop early versions of your product to a point that allows you to show investors proof of concept.

After his considerable tinkering on a rough prototype, Graham realized he'd have to pay a professional engineer to create a much more effective device. But after eighteen months of pitching to potential investors—about twenty angel investors and venture capitalists—he had no takers. As he recalls, "Selling an idea with a plan when you're not well known and don't have a track record is very, very difficult." So he decided to do what most founders have to do—invest a considerable amount of his own savings. "I was at a highly feisty point where, if the investors didn't do it, fine," he told me. "I'd put my own chips in. I would just basically do everything . . . short of ending [my] marriage, to advance it."

Most engineering firms he looked into were too expensive, but he found one with good ideas and paid $20,000 for the firm to improve his prototype. He expected that the $20,000 would get him a product he could manufacture. But that was not so, not by a long shot. The firm had worked for several months on improvements that made the device much less clunky, but it was still nowhere near ready for the market. "I didn't quite have 'buyer's remorse,' afterward but I thought, *That's it?* I wanted more. What I saw showed me I wasn't even close to done."

So he got more work done, hiring two other part-time engineers who had particularly good experience in working with start-up inventions, this time paying them with a combination of cash out of his savings and stock options. This time, the result was a device and business model that Graham believed was ready to show to investors. The new engineering team had not only raised the reliability of the device above 90 percent and made it smaller, they had also made the smart suggestion that Graham offer the product two ways, one for individual purchase and the other for purchase by the owners of public swimming pools, which would monitor all the swimmers in a pool. Swimmers could be given a SEAL device when they registered at the pool, and the lifeguards would have monitors that could keep track of all the swimmers.

Graham quickly applied for a number of patents on the invention, and when he was awarded them, he decided that the best way for him to pursue further development of the product was to sell the rights to a large company that had the expertise and funds to get it to market much faster than he could on his own. But what he discovered after a great deal of traveling to pitch companies was that "what most large companies do now when it comes to consumer products is they let another company develop the device, and then they buy the rights to it or buy the whole company. A guy who owned a large national safety firm told me, 'We've got 140 products in the queue. The only way you get moved to the top is if you're already selling. Then, it makes sense for us.'"

By this time, nearly three years into the project, Graham had invested $100,000 of his own cash for engineering, marketing, materials, patents, and travel expenses. He believed the SEAL SwimSafe had been improved enough that he decided to test market interest by meeting with several national swimming organizations. Though he got their blessing that the SEAL SwimSafe concept was good, they also told him that his prototype needed more work. "It did the job," he explains, "but it looked like a medicine bottle swinging from your neck. And it wasn't durable. That was a nonstarter. It has to be virtually indestructible so pools can use them for many seasons." With more consultation with his engineering team, he determined that making the necessary improvements would require another $350,000.

In light of that large sum, he set out to raise capital, focusing exclusively on high–net worth individual investors. He had learned by this time that the product still wasn't far enough along for venture capitalists, so he took a smart approach, pitching first to investors who he didn't think would be a good fit, which was like practicing with a net. Rather than money, what he was really looking for was feedback from these investors. The presentations were fairly simple, done in his home with PowerPoint and some product videos he had made and live demonstrations of the prototypes in an aquarium and his hot tub. It wasn't ready for prime time, but it was impressive enough for these motivated investors. He made fifteen presentations to forty serious investors, and some of them wanted to hear the presentation four or five times before they made a decision. But most liked his pitch and believed the SEAL SwimSafe had a good chance of success.

During the fall of 2010, Graham successfully raised $365,000 by selling 15 percent of his company's stock to fifteen individuals, with the investments averaging about $24,000.

Graham also personally invested another $40,000 in order to maintain majority ownership and voting control of the company, assumed the chairmanship of the newly formed board, and demonstrated to the investors that the price was fair. He also decided not to pay himself any salary out of the funds, investing almost all the money directly into product development.

The SEAL SwimSafe story is a good representation of the twists and turns to expect when getting any product ready enough for pitching to professional investors. Of course Graham's product is an especially complex one, but even with much simpler requirements, getting your product to the level of proof of concept that most professional investors want to see will almost certainly cost a good deal more money and take much longer than you've originally calculated.

This is why I am so adamant that founders have a good plan for earning money by other means during their blade years.

Alternate Funding Sources

One of the biggest developments in recent years regarding entrepreneurship is what's often referred to as the "democratization of funding" through such new sources as crowdfunding and increasing numbers of accelerators and incubators. The federal government and many state and city governments have put a new focus on encouraging entrepreneurship and have created programs and awards to assist founders with funding. You should seriously investigate all such options, but it's important to keep in mind that some of them can take considerable time to pursue and some have potential pit-falls.

Crowdfunding and "Pretailing"

Kickstarter and Indiegogo are the two largest crowdfunding sites, and there are many others worth looking into, such as Crowdfunder and RocketHub. Crowdfunding keeps booming, and more than $6.5 billion was raised for "business and entrepreneurship" in 2014 according to estimates.[47] Many start-ups have received huge boosts from their campaigns, such as Pebble Watch, which raised $20.3 million on Kickstarter, and Coolest Cooler, which also raised $13.3 million through Kickstarter.

And, of course, the boost is not only in funding but in publicity; campaigns can ignite a tremendous amount of buzz. While at the start, most campaigns asked for donations and offered those who contributed relatively moderate rewards—such as posters, T-shirts, and mugs—more recently, campaigns have been increasingly using crowdfunding sites for preselling products, sometimes referred to as "pretailing" or "pre-commerce," which can be a good way not only to raise cash but to get product feedback. By racking up preorders well in advance of launch, you can also fine-tune your initial order of stock, which is one of the trickiest judgments to make for launch. The process allows you to test your pitch and the story you're telling about your product, as well.

But it's important to be aware that this process also takes quite a bit of time, and it has some potential problem areas that can get founders into trouble. The time you spend on writing your pitch and making product or pitch videos will surely be well spent, as you should be creating these regardless of whether or not you're going to pretail. But they're only a relatively small part of the job. You can't just post your content on the platform and expect the platform to drive interest; you've got to drive eyeballs to your product page, and the primary way of doing so is through an e-mail campaign. That takes creating a curated e-mail list and crafting your e-mail and sending follow-up e-mails, as well. You should also be posting on all the social media sites to promote your crowdfunding page.

Research by Indiegogo indicates that "personalized e-mail is the most effective channel of online communication for your campaign" and that at least three follow-up e-mail updates are advised. They also advise creating a dedicated Facebook page and Twitter account for the campaign, and their research shows that "on average, about 22 percent of the funds raised by a campaign come from people clicking on social media posts."

You may also want to send out a press release, and you should be prepared to respond to press inquiries whether or not you do, as some campaigns attract a good deal of press attention if they've gained good traction. You should also be prepared to respond to queries from backers or customers.

Time is another big factor in managing customer expectations. Once you've promised a product to people and have given them an expected delivery date, the clock begins ticking furiously for you to actually make your product ready for market. Many products have run into serious delays, as with the Pebble Smartwatch, which attracted almost sixty-nine thousand backers who were then eagerly awaiting their cool new watches. Shipment was delayed for many months due to a number of manufacturing glitches, and some backers still hadn't received their watches by the time they were available in some retail locations, leading many of them to voice great irritation toward the company.

You may also end up delivering quite a different product, for a different price, than you'd initially advertised in your campaign. For example, the campaign for the Bluetooth- and Wi-Fi-enabled Lockitron keyless door lock that allows you to unlock your door from a remote location through your wireless device generated fourteen thousand preorders, totaling $2.2 million—though in this case, those were only pledges, and the cash wasn't actually sent. The campaign generated a ton of press, which drove people to the company's Web site and generated another seventy thousand preorders. But only fourteen thousand of all those orders were fulfilled because they ran into manufacturing problems with the factory they had selected in China. The founders decided to switch gears and totally redesign the product, so more than two years after the expected delivery date, all those who hadn't received the first version—apart from the ten thousand who canceled their orders—were still waiting for the product to arrive. Imagine the stress of that for the founders, not to mention the ill will you risk generating in the market.

You may well be able to recover from such a setback, as the founders of Pebble did, going on to successfully launch a growing line of watches. But you also risk turning the early adopters you're hoping will become evangelists for your product into evangelists against it. As Daryl Hatton, CEO of the Vancouver-based FundRazr crowdfunding site, cautions, "You have to be careful how much you hype your product. You're putting yourself in a much more transparent position than you used to be. Your actions are monitored. An unhappy customer can create a lot of grief in your community." Another pitfall he highlights is failing to factor in all the costs and logistics of order fulfillment, including packaging, warehousing, shipping, and customer support. As he says, "What are you committing yourself to when you receive $50 from someone? Will it mean $100 in costs?"[48] It's vital that before you launch a campaign you calculate every single cost that will be involved with fulfilling the commitments you've promised to contributors.

Pitch-Offs and Demo Days for Investors

These events and conferences are good venues that offer the chance to pitch, normally in ten minutes or less, to several investors at the same time. Universities and local entrepreneurial organizations put them on often. They are highly competitive, so winning one takes serious preparation, and the amount of prize money varies greatly. Most are in the low five figures to low six figures, but some seven-figure prizes are also awarded. Spending the time to participate in some of these may well be worthwhile, not only for the award money but probably even more importantly for the networking and the potential to receive some great advice from top investors and entrepreneurs.

Grants or Awards from Government Entities

Federal, state, and local governments are active in supporting new business ventures and offer financial support. For example, the Small Business Innovation Research Program (SBIR) provides awards of up to $100,000 for "approximately 6 months support exploration of the technical merit or feasibility of an idea or technology." These programs can be great for certain types of technology, but applying also requires lots of work, and the odds of winning are minimal. One company I invested in applied for a $50,000 grant from NC Idea, a program in North Carolina that gives five or six awards per year. The founder spent a great deal of time applying and got down to the top ten finalists. He then had to do a great deal more work, and in the end, he didn't win. Meanwhile, he'd been pulled away from actually building his business.

Nonbank Lenders

If you type *nonbank business lenders* into Google, you'll get thousands of results. These are firms that offer loans but do not have a banking license. One reputable nonbank lender on the rise is OnDeck, which has loaned more than $1.7 billion in only seven years. The key things to keep in mind here are that they almost always charge higher interest rates than banks, and that while some are reputable, others simply are not. Instead of going into one cold, ask your attorney, banker, or CPA for a referral.

Incubators and Accelerators

There are dozens of incubators and accelerators that provide mentoring support, funding grants and investments, and physical locations to work. The important thing to know is that each incubator has its own vibe and criteria for selection. Techstars, for example, has twenty-two locations and provides $118,000 in seed financing in exchange for 6 percent equity, plus a wealth of support from mentors and educational programs. Other prominent accelerators are Y Combinator, Capital Factory, DreamIt Ventures, and Flashpoint.

Seed and Early Stage Venture Capitalists

While most venture capitalists fund later-stage growth, some focus on early-stage, as well. Generally speaking, they look for firms that have managers who have already been successful and transformative and big ideas that have big potential. Many of these firms are in Silicon Valley, but there are some in other areas that are hotbeds of entrepreneurship, as well. To learn more about early-stage venture capitalists, I recommend you contact the National Venture Capital Association (nvca.org) that, for a fee, provides a detailed list of VC firms organized by various categories, one being "stage of development."

How to Craft Your Best Plan

There is no way around the fact that you can never know what sources of funding will come through for you or how much you're really going to need before you're fully funding your operations with earnings. To do the best job possible of preparing to start a company, though, here is a set of questions that all founders should carefully consider:

- What capital investments and ongoing expenses are necessary to create a sellable product?
- How much salary, if any, do I have to earn for myself until the business can support me?
- How long am I willing to work on growing my business before I am earning the salary I want to make?
- Do I want to have financial partners in my business?
- Do I have the personality type that seeks advice and ideas from partners who might have more experience than I? Or is this venture about providing me with the opportunity to build something on my own?
- How much ownership am I willing to give up at this very early stage of my new venture?

By thinking carefully about these questions right when you start planning your business, you will set yourself up much better for success. And the better you are at anticipating the costs you'll have to pay and the hit to your income you'll take, the more rigorous a plan you'll be able to come up with for getting through these lean years. If you seriously consider how long it may take to grow your business to the point that you're earning the salary you aspire to—which generally requires three to four years—you will have a much better understanding of how much your current lifestyle is likely to change while you're building the business due to the need to cut back on expenses. Right at the start, if you begin to consider whether or not you're open to partnering with someone to build the business, you may be able to find someone to take some of the load of work off your plate and also complement your own skills, as well as easing some of the financial burden. But it's important to think through these ownership and control issues right from the get-go, as well, because the decisions you make at the start have such significant consequences later on. Wrestling with all these questions before you get going in earnest with the building process will help to assure that your expectations match with the reality of what the commitment will require of you and to assure that you are prepared to make that commitment.

Stage II

The Blade Years

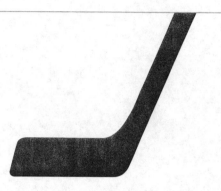

Chapter 3

Let the Game Begin: Getting to Market

So you've fully committed to making your idea work, and you're now entering the blade years. You've come up with a plan for funding your development. Now what? I love what essayist, entrepreneur, and cofounder of seed capital firm Y Combinator Paul Graham says about how businesses get off the ground:

> Startups take off because the founders make them take off. There may be a handful that just grew by themselves, but usually it takes some sort of push to get them going. A good metaphor would be the cranks that car engines had before they got electric starters. Once the engine was going, it would keep going, but there was a separate and laborious process to get it going.[49]

Hockey Stick Principle #22: You can't build it and expect a market to come; you have to build your market as you build your product.

So how do you crank the engine? So much of the emphasis in writing about entrepreneurship is on crafting the product. But getting an innovative start-up up and running is as much about developing a market as about developing a product. As marketing specialist Charles Spinosa writes:

> We tend to think that the inventor produces something for an already existing market and then establishes a more or less traditional company

with traditional departments to produce and market the new thing. But entrepreneurs time and time again tell us that this is not the case. The market is always being developed along with the product.[50]

You will also need to craft your brand at this time. You might think of a brand as the name of a product, which is one meaning of the term, but it's also used to refer to the identity and reputation a company creates in the minds of consumers. Building your brand involves not just naming your company and your products but also crafting all aspects of the look and feel of your offerings—the actual design of the product, your logo, the look of your Web site, the nature of your content marketing, the quality of your customer service operation, and the style of your advertising. In this phase of serious product development, you must be working on the product, the market, and your branding simultaneously, which makes it a very challenging time.

This is one of the biggest differences between a start-up and an established business. In established businesses, these functions are almost always divided up into separate staffs, and many even have professional product managers to monitor the progress of each group. You may be able to divide up responsibilities, especially if you have a partner, but even so, founders must keep very close tabs on product development, customer service, marketing, sales activities, and operations. Otherwise, one or another part of the process will inevitably get off track, and you'll be working out of sync. For example, if your product prototype is all set for promoting in a crowd-funding campaign but your branding is lagging, you'll have to postpone the campaign by a couple of months. Or you'll be racking up lots of great preorders from retailers, but you won't be able to fulfill in the time agreed, and retailers will start canceling them.

Juggling One Thousand Important Things at Once

How do you juggle multiple important tasks, each of which is probably equally important for success? A great product with poor packaging can flop. Great packaging or a great user experience for purchasing on your Web site can't make up for lack of quality in the product. And a poor launch strategy and ineffective branding and pitch can lead you to believe the market isn't interested in the product when in fact it would be with better promotion. Meanwhile, if you don't incorporate in the optimal way and apply effectively for patents and trademarks, you might face serious tax consequences later or lose control of your branding or other intellectual property. There is no way around working on all these things at once, so you must become adept at switching tasks and adjusting your day to the unexpected while always still driving toward your goal.

> **Hockey Stick Principle #23: Be both rigorous in your daily planning and highly flexible about going off-plan at any moment.**

As you head into your blade years, on any given day you might have to interview a new potential part-time employee, work on a product feature, provide a demo to a potential customer, discuss a future stock option plan with your attorney, write and mail checks to your suppliers, return a call from a potential angel investor who's looking for an update about your progress, and request that your Web site developer make a number of tweaks to your landing page. And the next day could be totally different. Dealing with so many aspects of the product and business all at once is one of the most difficult parts of the whole start-up process. F. Scott Fitzgerald famously wrote, "The test of a first-rate intelligence is the ability to hold two opposed ideas in mind at the same time and still retain the ability to function." Well, the test of a first-rate entrepreneur is the ability to hold multiple streams of development in mind all at once and not go crazy or freeze up.

The process is all the more challenging because most founders have very little practical experience doing some of the required jobs. A founder who has good experience building prototypes may have little experience building a marketing platform or meeting with potential customers. Some know a lot about manufacturing but little about setting up a corporation or managing day-to-day business operations. The process can feel overwhelming.

I've seen this stage of development cause many founders to get stalled, putting off decisions just when they should be going full steam ahead. Some founders focus almost exclusively on the task they feel most comfortable with and badly neglect others. Some become highly agitated and begin lashing out at partners or suppliers. Many simply give up, largely due to fear and self-doubt.

The flood of advice coming at entrepreneurs during this stage can contribute to the problem. A case in point is a *Forbes* article that warned, "Failure to properly obtain a trademark could put your fledgling business at risk—not to mention that the time and money you have invested in establishing your business name could go to waste if someone else owns the trademark."[51] That's sage counsel, and I'm not picking on it, but if you've had the paperwork on your desk for weeks to apply for a trademark for your company or product name when you read that piece, you might find yourself thinking, *Oh *#@%, I'm so behind. I just don't know what I'm doing!* The trick is to accept that you're simply not going to be able to do everything according to an optimal schedule, no matter how well you've anticipated what's required and plotted a time line, while also constantly looking for better ways to get tasks done. Regarding that trademark application, a great way to go would be to hire a lawyer and offload the burden. Plus, a lawyer can normally do the work for about $1,500 and without much involvement from you.

> **Hockey Stick Principle #24: Building a start-up is a physical challenge as well as a mental one.**

In this phase of the process, you often feel like you're trying to control chaos; just as you're finishing up with one thing, some new information comes in about a problem you thought you'd solved earlier, and you've got to switch over to attend to that. Meanwhile, your plan for the thing you had been working on goes off the rails because some negative feedback comes in, or a supplier screws up, or you find out your cost estimates were all wrong.

Even for the best multitaskers, the pace of decision making and the constant changes in your plan can be very challenging to adjust to. Anyone who's worked a job of any level of difficulty has had to make a host of decisions every day. But the intensity of problem solving in this lead-up to the launch of a start-up, and the pressure you feel about making these decisions, can be truly fierce and badly depleting.

Psychologist Roy Baumeister has conducted fascinating studies about what's called decision fatigue, showing that making a decision really does drain energy from your brain. His work revealed that glucose is the fuel for decision making and that each decision we make zaps our brains of some of their reserve of glucose, so the more decisions we have to make in a day, the more depleted our brains become, literally, and the quality of our decisions is compromised.[52] This is why many founders will tell you that they were often exhausted much of the time as they built their companies. It doesn't help that when you finally knock off for the day and try to get to sleep, your brain is often racing with thoughts about the decisions you've just made and those you've got to deal with the next day.

The key to surviving this crazy stage when juggling so many tasks at once is to enjoy the ride. While challenging, starting a new company will likely be one of the most memorable times of your life. To relieve stress, be disciplined about taking time for yourself and enjoying activities such as sports, yoga, hiking, traveling, good times with friends, hobbies, movies, and reading non-business books. You'll need balance in your life because the journey is a long one.

Using Tools to Make Your Life Easier

To combat the fatigue and frustration and to get perspective on where you are and where you are heading, it's also a good idea to make use of some of the planning, organizing, and strategizing tools developed for start-ups. The goal is to find tools you like to use that will make planning and then keeping track of the progress on all fronts more efficient. This will relieve you of some of what's called your *cognitive load,* or the amount of information that you've got to be actively retaining in your mind at any given time. Different people prefer different tools, and some are more appropriate for some start-ups than for others. For example, if you're building your business all by yourself, then software that facilitates efficient team communication won't be particularly helpful. You should take a good look at the range of possibilities and check out products on their company Web site, which generally will have great tutorials and examples for how to use the tools. The main ones to know about are:

- **Accounting tools:** These help you manage your payables, receivables, sales, and purchases, as well as processing credit card orders and doing your payroll, all of which can be a real hassle to stay on top of otherwise. Far too many founders have lost track of bills and receipts or failed to make payments on time or to chase down a payment that's due to come in. These systems also help to identify potential cash-flow problem areas in advance so that you can plan ahead to manage them. A great bookkeeping system is a godsend, and most of the programs require no training in accounting at all. This kind of financial software is often built specifically for your type of business— for example, for SaaS, retail, or manufacturing. Examples include Intuit's QuickBooks, NetSuite, Cheqbook, and Xero.

- **Project management tools:** These facilitate planning and coordination of your development process, allowing you to create a time line that includes all parts of the process to help you create to-do lists; to make information available in one, reliable location, such as marketing copy that's being developed and status reports; and to stay on top of the flow of tasks that are getting done and those that are coming up for completion.

  These are especially helpful for keeping teams well informed and on track about what each member is working on, highlighting which deliverables are due when, facilitating efficient and transparent communication among all members of the team, and alerting you to potential problems, such as what the ripple effects would be if it were to take longer than expected for you to get your samples for a promotional event. Putting the dates for getting the samples and for the event into the system might help you consider that you need to push the date for the event back to give more wiggle room, and it might also make you think of researching a plan B venue for the event in case the original one you've picked won't be available at the later date.

  By creating an overview of the whole process with a schedule to accompany it, this kind of planning tool also helps you make sure you're not overlooking tasks you'll need to do in the future or are planning on completing either earlier or later than you should. These tools allow all members of the team to interact online, which is a great help in cutting down on the number of e-mails flying around among team members. They can also save documents, so that they're immediately retrievable. Examples include Basecamp, Active Collab, Asana, LiquidPlanner, and Freedcamp.

- **HR process management tools:** Despite the fact that start-ups generally have few employees, managing the laws and complexities of payroll tax, paycheck calculations, and benefits is a confusing and time-consuming process for founders. It's best to outsource the risks and the management of these complexities to experts, but if you can't, these tools are up to speed with all the latest legal issues and tax provisions, which you really don't want to be spending time digging into. Examples include ADP, Paychex, or Intuit.

> **Hockey Stick Principle #25: Start-up process tools do not have a brain.**

Opinions are all over the map about the utility of these tools, and you should feel free to make use of the ones that appeal to you or to craft your own methods for organizing and monitoring. No matter which tools you use, you can't expect that these programs will be doing the actual thinking or evaluation of work for you. Even if you input an exhaustive list of tasks that must be done into a project management tool, you'll inevitably learn that you didn't anticipate certain tasks, and you'll have to make adjustments to the plans according to reasoning that only you can do, not a computer program. For example, you might input "critique Web site design" as a task and allocate two days in the schedule for that, but in the process of reviewing the site design, if you learn that you want to find out more about customer relationship management tools so that you make sure you're getting the best system for that built in to your site, then you might also discover that you want to read up more on content marketing and take more time to think through your plan for that. Should you push back your schedule for getting back to your developer, or should you respond as planned and then follow up with changes? How important is it that your Web site be optimized right at the start? Maybe it's best to go ahead with the plan as it is and make improvements later. Only you can decide.

These tools don't solve problems for you, and you'll still have to rigorously assess your progress in a continuous way and make all sorts of judgment calls about the issues they help to surface. But they definitely can help with lifting some of the cognitive load of managing the flow of work and communication, and they can be a huge help in thinking the logistics of the process through.

Get the Team Together

One way lots of people hope that these kinds of online planning and management tools can help is in eliminating live conversation and face-to-face meetings. Cutting down on meetings and phone calls is usually a great thing to do, but it's important to have a certain number of face-to-face meetings and voice-to-voice calls. Meetings that bring most or all of your team together regularly, whether in person or on the phone or with video calling, can be a fantastic tool for monitoring progress, and they often stimulate discussion of issues and generation of ideas that might not have come up otherwise.

When starting First Research, I hosted a weekly conference call in which Ingo and I, and additional staff as we brought them in, simply discussed who was doing what and the kind of progress made, which worked wonderfully for us. In starting Vertical IQ, my cofounder, Bill Walker, proposed sending out a weekly update listing all the tasks in the works (normally, there were dozens of them), who was responsible for each, and the status, which we then quickly discussed. This process has also worked smoothly for that business. In both cases, we solved many problems with great efficiency. I've found that regularly scheduling opportunities to have actual conversations is invaluable, and I strongly advise that you don't rely solely on electronic communication. I think we often underestimate just how efficient human conversation can be as a communication and decision-making practice. Making it work in person or over the phone just requires you to run an organized meeting by having an agenda and making sure the group sticks to it.

Working with Cofounders

The upside to having a partner or several partners is that they bring additional man power and decision-making bandwidth for coping with the controlled chaos. They usually also have complementary skills, so you can divide responsibilities in ways that make good sense, and they have the same kind of skin in the game as you. Often, they're also willing to work without pay. The downside is that, as discussed in the last chapter, you have to share ownership, which not only affects your financial position in the company but can also make working together as a team difficult.

In 1965, Johns Hopkins University sociologist Arthur Stinchcombe published his frequently cited paper "Social Structure and Organizations," which highlighted four common problems that cause new organizations to fail, and three of them involve interaction between founders: disagreement over dividing up financial rewards, the difficulty of determining and learning roles, and developing good working relationships. The fourth is a lack of relationships with outside parties vital to success, such as suppliers and customers.[53] To overcome these challenges when working with partners, new ventures require an environment of open-mindedness, sharing of opinions, and mutual respect.

> **Hockey Stick Principle #26: Avoid fifty-fifty partnerships.**

Clarity of decision-making responsibility and authority is also key. This is the main reason I advise against fifty-fifty partnerships. They can lead to awkward stalemates and messy negotiations. Generally speaking, I think cofounders work best together when there's one person clearly in charge. The way to accomplish this is to have one president and for that person to own at least 51 percent of the stock. This doesn't mean the majority owner should act like a "my way or the highway" head coach, though. If the majority owner is a bully, is selfish, and doesn't work well with people, the organization is probably doomed; it's that simple.

To mitigate disputes, I advise that if partners haven't clearly divided responsibilities right at the start, they do so when heading into the serious development phase—and that the president also "own" particular responsibilities, which should be in areas of his or her greatest strength, whether that's marketing, sales, product development, or customer service.

Note that the goal here isn't to squelch disagreement. I believe there's nothing wrong with heated debates between cofounders; in fact, I encourage it, and that's often where the best solutions to problems come from. But a predetermined agreement about who has the last call is a great aid in conflict resolution.

Follow the Eighty-Twenty Rule

Another great aide to efficient decision making is the well-established principle that 20 percent of inputs generally account for 80 percent of outputs, which is based on the work of Italian economist Vilfredo Pareto, and hence is also sometimes called the Pareto Principle. Having noted that

80 percent of the land in Italy was owned by 20 percent of the population, Pareto later noted that only 20 percent of the pea pods in his garden accounted for 80 percent of the peas. The principle has been applied to business in many ways to help focus time and effort most effectively. For example, the rule holds that 20 percent of your customers account for 80 percent of your sales, that 20 percent of your products account for 80 percent of business brought in, and 20 percent of your employees account for 80 percent of your results. You can apply it to your decision making and the allocation of your time in the start-up phase, as the rule suggests that 20 percent of your decisions and 20 percent of the tasks to be completed will account for 80 percent of your results.

The concept for how to apply the rule to your business is that you should identify the most highly productive 20 percent of work processes, customers, employees, and partners and focus more of your time and attention on them. The eighty-twenty split is by no means a hard-and-fast scientific fact; you should think of it just as a general tendency and good rule of thumb for focusing your efforts.

For example, let's say your business has one hundred customers, and you find that in fact twenty of them provide 80 percent of your revenue. I'm not suggesting that you don't worry about providing high-quality service to your bottom eighty customers. Instead, devise a good system for providing those eighty customers with high-quality service using a standard, automated process that takes care of most of their needs very well. And for your top twenty customers, provide them a more individual, customized experience, and in addition to that, give them your proactive attention.

Another way you could apply the rule would be in prioritizing tasks to focus on every day. Most days, you will have a good ten or more key things that need to get done, and a common mistake people make in their time management is to put off harder, more consequential tasks and get a bunch of smaller, less important ones out of the way. We might do this because we're dreading diving into the bigger tasks, perhaps due to anxiety about the outcome or because we think that if we can just cross all of those annoying smaller items off our lists, we'll make more time to concentrate on the more important ones. For sure, we've got to get to the smaller tasks sometime, but tackling the most consequential ones with the greatest possible efficiency is the route to the greatest productivity. Keeping the eighty-twenty rule in mind can really help with disciplining yourself to do this.

I've found keeping the rule in mind is helpful in three key ways. For one, it helps me be more vigilant about focusing my time on the right tasks on my own plate and also to help those working for me to do so, as well. It also helps me not to worry so much about the other 80 percent of things I haven't gotten to yet. And finally, it helps me make each decision faster. Indeed, some time management specialists have pointed out that the eighty-twenty rule implies that 20 percent of the time spent in making a decision accounts for 80 percent of the result. You're never going to get your decision-making time down to that pure 20 percent, but I've found that keeping this concept in mind helps with not obsessing over getting more and more information and overanalyzing.

Speed of Activity versus Speed to Market

While the Lean Startup approach of getting a minimal viable product actually out to the market and in customers' hands as fast as possible may not be right for your business, the emphasis on speed of process that's at the heart of this approach absolutely is. Regardless of whether you start to actually sell early, it's important that you keep up a fast pace of development and get feedback from potential customers, suppliers, and retailers early. You've got to stress *speed of activity*.

> **Hockey Stick Principle #27: Impatience is a virtue.**

I remember watching a TV show in which Donald Trump was asked what the most important attribute he looks for in a leader is, and he said, "Impatience." I fell out of my chair, because in entrepreneurship for sure, I've observed that the best leaders of the process are impatient; they are just about hell-bent to get as much done as fast as humanly possible. And by getting more done faster, they improve their chances of success for many reasons: They make more sales calls; they complete more marketing activities, such as case studies or content marketing pieces; they build more product features; and they meet with more investors.

One of the most impatient entrepreneurs I know is Darren Pierce of etailinsights, and I believe this has been key to his success. When his product team was adding a feature that involved an advanced algorithm, they had to hire a statistician to build it. Those involved in the project were getting stuck in the process and deeply analyzing each aspect of how the feature should work best for the customers, but the process of generating customer feedback and testing it was slow-going, and Darren could see that it was going to take months, which was just too long. So he halted the process and went live with the feature as it was. "I just pushed the feature live myself, and we started selling it, and our customers loved it," Darren recalls.

You might be reading this and thinking that Darren is too quick on the draw and doesn't often think through things well, but he does. He just understands that projects have to be completed fast enough so that the company is able to move on to the next one and allow customers to provide feedback as quickly as possible so improvements can be made.

Always keep in mind that while getting your product to market may require many months—or even years—of development, all along the way, you should be striving to accomplish each task as efficiently as possible. If you are disciplined with your time, the amount you can get done in a day may surprise you.

Delegate and Outsource

We have entered a golden era for finding part-time and contract workers. The online resources for finding talent are extraordinary, and you can reach out all the way across the country or around the world.

A very effective means of freeing up your time to focus appropriately is to identify repetitive tasks that don't require a great deal of skill but require a great deal of time and then hire an employee at comparatively low cost to do it for you, such as a college student working as an intern (which should be a paid internship) or someone with experience but who is only looking for part-time work. This doesn't require all sorts of paperwork; you just have to get a Form W-9, Form I-9, or a Form 1099 and a standard employment or consulting agreement from anyone you're going to be paying. The nice thing is that part-time interns will often come aboard for ten to fifteen dollars an hour just for the experience of working at a start-up. So for ten hours a week, you pay only about $150 and free yourself up to use those ten hours for much more productive development work. It's not often in business that you can count on getting such a great return on an investment.

Hockey Stick Principle #28: Allow others to solve your big challenges.

You should also consider all opportunities to outsource jobs. The fact that lots of programmers are available to help build software and Web sites and lots of marketing firms offer brand development, publicity, and advertising services is well known. But there are independent contractors in all other sorts of fields. The Boogie Wipes founders Julie Pickens and Mindee Doney knew very little about the chemistry required to produce their wipes. They easily found a chemist to work with to develop them, and he was right in their community. Graham Snyder found highly qualified engineers to develop his device. With First Research, neither Ingo nor I had the time to edit our research reports, so we lined up a professional outside editor to do it for us.

The rule I recommend is that you first outsource the functions that are critical to your success and that you or your cofounders have no skills in, and if you have the funds, you might also consider outsourcing work that you do have some expertise in because you have the network to find high-quality people and the skills with which to evaluate their work efficiently. For example, if you worked in branding, maybe you could decide to hire a firm to create your logo and a set of taglines to choose from so that you could focus more time on a critical function that only you can take charge of. If a function is critical to success and will require constant attention and pull too much of your time away from other equally important parts of the business, you might consider bringing in another cofounder or employee to perform the function. You might also consider offering stock options as well as pay to outside specialists you contract with for this work, as that means they're also vested in a positive outcome. But remember, make sure your stock option plan has a vesting schedule that stipulates a duration of time the person must work for the company before the shares offered actually benefit them. That way, if these employees or consultants quit working for you prematurely, they're not taking part of your company with them.

If you can afford it, I also recommend you consider outsourcing non-core business functions to create administrative efficiencies for your business. Examples could include managing the day-to-day accounting duties, such as check-writing and booking sales, payroll processing, inventory record management, and booking travel.

It's often best to seek small shops with talented, innovative people and low overhead. I mostly find partners through word of mouth—asking people whom they know with a particular skill. I recommend this approach over searching online, but plenty of founders have had success with the latter. Julie and Mindee found their chemist that way. In all cases, it's critical to have a lawyer-prepared "work for hire" contract signed, and in many cases also a noncompete letter. If you're contracting for software code, also make sure you can take the code with you in case you have to switch to working with a different programming firm, which is not uncommon. You should also make sure contract workers have their own insurance and provide you with a certificate of coverage; otherwise, make sure your own policy covers contractors. You don't want one freak accident to take down your entire new venture.

Smaller companies are often much more personal and easier to work with than large ones. Partners who work with your business consistently can become part of the family if cultures are shared and the passion is there. To reinforce this sense of team commitment, I give stock options to partners critical to our success. For example, Vertical IQ delivers our product via the Web, but neither Bill nor I have skill in database programming, so we hired a programmer and gave him stock options.

The value that the right outside talent can bring to your business can make an enormous difference in your outcome. One example of this is the striking bottle designs that the founders of Method ended up with. Cofounders Eric Ryan and Adam Lowry had determined that to differentiate their soaps, they needed truly striking packaging, and Eric was a big fan of top product designer Karim Rashid, who has many designs in museum collections. They wrote him an impassioned letter, telling him that "the design goal is to reinvent the banal dish soap that looks like a relic of the 1950s and sits on every sink across the landscape of America. We want you to approach it not as a packaging assignment but from a product perspective to create an object for the kitchen that is as iconic as a salt and pepper shaker." Rashid found that mission intriguing, and he agreed to sign on as their chief creative officer, designing a stunning series of bottles that opened the door to a big order from Target and connected powerfully with customers.[54]

Of course, this process doesn't always go so smoothly. Lots of people will tell you horror stories, like the Revel Systems founders, who invested their savings into getting their first iPad stand built only to have it fall far short of the mark. They then had to go into overdrive and spend more of their tight budget on another source for creating the stand. Doug Lebda's first attempt at outsourcing the programming for LendingTree resulted in software that didn't work at all. But don't let these stories discourage you; just expect that some such setbacks will happen for you too, and plan on working your way through them.

> **Hockey Stick Principle #29: Screwups happen; let go of them and move on quickly.**

Redos and tweaking are also almost always required for every piece of work you have done. So communicate clearly to contractors at the outset that you expect the project to be iterative, with possibly more than one round of changes being required, and ensure that they agree to that process. There's an inherent conflict between your interests and theirs in this regard. The goal of every independent contractor is to get the work for you done and to move on to the next project as efficiently as possible. Your goal is often quite the opposite. You will want to tweak and revise until you're confident the quality of the product is the best it can be. In the eyes of the contracted firm, you're disorganized, changing your mind constantly, dragging the project out, and all this "redoing" isn't worth the money. This is another reason that going to a smaller, often one-person shop is preferred; they generally take a more artisanal approach to their work and tend to better appreciate that you do, as well.

In addition to the obvious questions, such as whether or not you can afford to outsource a task, here are some others to consider when deciding whether to outsource something or do it yourself.

- How much time would this project require if I did it myself? Can I leverage this time more effectively doing something else?
- Might it be more effective to ask a consultant to train me so I can complete the task myself?
- Is this task absolutely necessary to get this business off the ground? Or, alternatively, could I table this task and get more feedback first?
- Is the amount of money I'm paying for this task a good return on investment? Or, alternatively, should I look at outsourcing a different project that could get a larger return on investment?

Don't let the anxiety about handing off some of the process to others stop you. Most founders find working with a new person or firm can be really rewarding and sometimes a great deal of fun, which can counteract some of the inevitable frustrations.

From Concept to Store Shelves in Less Than a Year

Two founders who became deeply engrossed in all the details of getting their business off the ground and very smartly developed their market along with their product are Julie Pickens and Mindee Doney of Boogie Wipes. They also managed to get the work done fast, working on all fronts at once. They're a great model of planning effectively and managing for efficiency. Even though they were developing a consumer-goods manufactured product, they got to market within a year.

The idea for their product was first conceived in February of 2007; they then incorporated that May as Little Busy Bodies, Inc., and in December, they sold their first pack of wipes. Because of good product development, strong marketing, and good retail distribution, they hit $1 million in sales their first year.

A big emphasis was on getting early versions of wipes made and then testing them with potential customers. One of the keys to the success of the product was making the wipes with the proper amount of saline, which required skills neither Julie nor Mindee had. They also had no connections to find someone with the relevant experience. So they searched online, and they found a chemist in Portland to help them.

There were several challenges with finding the right combination of saline and cloth to make for a perfect product. "You're putting a wet wipe on your nose to wipe a wet nose," Julie explains. "The wipe has to be wet enough to deliver the saline, but still have some absorbent capacity in it because you're still wiping your nose." Another product design challenge was getting the right amount of saline to work "with your body" to be effective and ensuring the saline and cloth combination didn't have abrasive qualities. "It was tricky to get all that right," Julie recalls. "We were very hands-on. We learned every aspect of the business as we went and were very involved in every piece of it. As we started to evolve the wipe's [design] with the chemist, we learned all about it and started testing and doing different things and putting different things together to see if it would work, and we were very instrumental in creating the actual product itself."

Developing samples allowed them to get market feedback from very early on. In their case, they were sure of who their market was: moms. And, as covered earlier, they first socialized the concept and tested their product name on blogs popular with mothers. Having received good feedback, they moved forward quickly with developing their branding, intent on creating desirable packaging. Maintaining a low budget, they hired a local freelance graphic designer in Portland. The outcome was a loose plastic container with creative graphics: black-and-white cute, cartoonish baby faces nestled into a fun, green-and-orange font. "Our designer, along with myself and my business partner, just sat down and came up with what we wanted the package to look and feel like," Julie told me. "The three of us collectively designed it. It took us about a month."

The Boogie Wipes team attended trade shows in these early months to get hands-on feedback about their samples, as well as to build product awareness. Julie told me, "We did a lot of trade show sampling to get feedback. But it wasn't like we were out researching, 'Should we do this?' We were researching as we did it." Once they were happy with the quality of the wipes, and before they had their packaging finished, they put sample wipes into generic white packets with a Boogie Wipes logo stuck to it and took them to the shows. In addition to handing out these samples at trade shows, they elicited feedback in two other key ways, while also building brand awareness: by leaving samples in doctors' offices and kids' clothing boutiques. And they didn't limit this sample testing to their own backyard. "We geo-targeted pediatricians' offices all over the country so that they could have them in their office and spread the word. Obviously, that's our front line: moms who have sick children. We did it for feedback. We did it for exposure."

Once they had nailed the product formula, they moved forward efficiently in applying for patents for both the formula for making the wipes and for their packaging. Since they were on a low budget, Julie worked very hard on much of the product patent application herself, even though she had no experience in the work, though she did get advice from an experienced lawyer. As I advised earlier about getting trademarks, hiring a lawyer to do this work might be a good way to go, but a number of founders I've interviewed have done much of the legwork for the lawyers themselves. Even Graham Snyder, whose device is so complex, wrote his patent applications himself—saving himself money when the attorney completed the legal work.

With their intellectual property protections in place, Julie and Mindee's next order of business was figuring out how to manufacture the wipes, which as Julie says was the "tricky part." This is generally true for novel manufactured products for two key reasons. One is that most manufacturers don't want to take on small-quantity orders, and entrepreneurs usually want to start small, as they almost always should. Also, often it's hard to find a manufacturer with the right equipment and experience to produce what you need.

For these reasons, most founders have to pay for first stock at a per-item premium above what an established firm would pay. So Julie and Mindee decided to go with a manufacturer in Israel. They ordered a twenty-foot container, which was a minimum condition, which amounted to 3,300 cases, or 39,000 units, costing roughly $20,000. That might seem like a big gamble, but they were quite confident in the market from the ongoing sampling they'd done.

Also, in discussing their decision to go ahead with this order, Julie stressed that they had carefully calculated that they could actually afford the order, and really knowing and understanding their financial situation was a key part of this decision. One thing to look out for during this step is that the process of getting your inventory often takes longer than expected, and if you have been banking on cash flow from sales earlier than you're able to get the stock out to market and moving off shelves, you'll quickly become cash-strapped.

I see so many new entrepreneurs struggle with cash flow and learn the hard way just what a big impact timing differences make on their working capital. Just consider how much cash gets eaten up to order and sell a typical physical product. You send $30,000 to a manufacturer; they take sixty days to produce your goods and ship them to you. Remember, you're still incurring overhead expenses, which may include rent, payroll, and phone bills throughout this whole waiting period. Once you finally receive your finished product, you then have to pay to have it warehoused. You ship it to several retailers, who in turn take forty-five days to finally pay you for it. Some retailers also drag out payment even longer. So that's 105 days without your $30,000 and nothing coming in. And, depending upon what agreement you reach with retailers, they may be able to return what doesn't sell or is defective in some way, so you have to plan for that, as well. If you're selling your product online, you should also plan for chargeback, which occurs when consumers don't believe the product fits their standards and demand a refund from their credit card company.

Because this process of managing cash inflows and outflows involves so many unknowns, it's important to create a detailed set of monthly cash flow projections before each quarter of the fiscal year. This, at least, allows you to do a good job of anticipating possible hits to your bottom line and to build in some cushion of cash to make up for any loss of income you might suffer. For example, if you are expecting a big reorder from a customer in March, you might want to keep enough cash in reserve for your March expenses to cover the expected income just in case the order doesn't come in until April. You can create your own spreadsheet or utilize an easy-to-use preprogrammed tool like Intuit's QuickBooks to manage this task. Each month you should begin with a cash balance, and below that, list sources of cash inflows and add them to the balance, and then list sources of cash outflows and subtract them, leaving you with your new cash balance. Update the numbers with budget versus actual each month. This will allow you to prioritize expenses well in advance and anticipate if you'll likely need funding so that you can begin the process of chasing those funds.

You should also avoid waiting until right before launch to establish what your retail channels will be, and don't put your hopes in only one basket. Julie and Mindee smartly moved on several fronts at once when pursuing retail placement. They pitched to boutiques and to grocers, exploring both the specialty and mass markets. They struck gold when they approached the buyer at the Fred Meyer chain, which is a division of Kroger in the Northwest, who put in an order for placement in about 120 stores in the baby section.

It's vital to approach a range of retailers and experiment with sales channels. Hoping to be picked up by a major retailer like Walmart, Target, or Whole Foods and pitching to their buyers is just fine and a smart thing to do, but planning on them ordering from you isn't. Most often, you need to have sales traction within independent stores or small chains before a large retail chain will take a chance with your product. You need to be able to show them how you're already selling hundreds if not more of your product every day. You should probably also be aiming for sales through e-commerce sites and may also want to approach TV sellers, such as QVC and Home Shopping Network, if your product is right for those channels. Another route to retailers is to build relationships with distributors, who can act as a bridge to the retailers they work with.

One of the keys for Julie and Mindee's success was doing a good job of deciding which critical functions should be outsourced versus which ones to do themselves, while also keeping closely engaged in the work they outsourced. They knew they had to go to a specialist in chemistry to figure out the way to combine tissue paper with saline, yet they were very hands-on with him in developing the right formula. They also knew that the design of the packaging would be critical to success, so they outsourced that as well and again worked very closely with the designer. For their marketing and publicity efforts, they had the expertise and skills for this, so they did all the blogging and outreach themselves.

In order to do a good job with this balancing act, I advise that you follow these three rules:

1. If you are good at a particular task and enjoy doing it, you should strongly consider taking charge of it yourself.
2. If a task is absolutely critical to success and you aren't certain you can do it flawlessly yourself, then you should bring in experts to do it.
3. For simple tasks that are mostly administrative in nature but that can require a great deal of time and energy, you should outsource if you can afford to do so.

Beware of Estimates of Time and Cost, Even from Experts

No matter what kind of product you're making or how detailed your plan—even if it's fairly far into your development—and no matter how well you manage the process, expect that your costs will escalate and the time it takes you to be ready to launch will stretch out. This is as true for Web-only software products as it is for manufactured ones and brick-and-mortar services.

> **Hockey Stick Principle #30: Your time and cost estimates will always be wrong—always.**

A great case demonstrating this is Doug Lebda's experience in building LendingTree. His experience also speaks to the wisdom of getting started with building prototypes and market testing them right away. Recall that he wrote a strong and successful business plan that won second place in a competition at the University of Virginia. He received the advice of a consultancy with experience in the business of building Web site services for making his projections, and his plan called for building the application and marketing it on the Internet for two years, by which time positive cash flow was predicted. Doug's original expectation was that building the Web site and writing the software to support the business would be fairly straightforward, and the plan was to pay two computer programmers fifteen to twenty dollars each per hour and to hire a Webmaster, who would be paid $40,000. But instead, Doug hired a consultancy that projected it would take only sixteen weeks, and cost much less, about $30,000. As Doug says now about the advice he got from the consultancy, "That team just didn't have a clue." What they delivered wasn't close to what Doug needed to satisfy the banks or to process customer applications.

Fortunately not long after, Doug was able to raise $1 million from a group of angel investors headed by banker Jim Tozer, and he spent $300,000 of that to hire a high-quality programmer, Rick Stiegler, and hundreds of thousands more to hire a technology staff to work under Rick's direction who spent several months building a workable application.

Graham Snyder ran into the same problem with predicting the true costs of building a functioning version of his antidrowning device. Recall, he'd already paid an engineering firm $20,000 but didn't get close to having a finished product. These are stories you hear again and again when you talk to entrepreneurs about their product development process. My advice about this stark reality is to not get down on yourself if you miss your cost and time estimates, even if by a great deal. Even when building Vertical IQ's product, which was my second go-around for a similar business, the process required twice the investment we had originally expected.

Agile versus Waterfall

You may not be developing a software product, so this section may not be relevant for you. But if you are, the following is important for thinking through the approach you want your development team to take.

Doug Lebda's experience with a faulty estimate of the amount of time it would take to program the site, and the innumerable headaches his programming team had to deal with over the course of three years, is a perfect example of the problems that have plagued software development and is what inspired the innovation of the agile development process to replace the established waterfall approach. Agile has steadily gained ground in Web product development, and Eric Ries incorporated the agile method into his Lean Startup approach. The agile and waterfall approaches are easily summarized by these schematics:

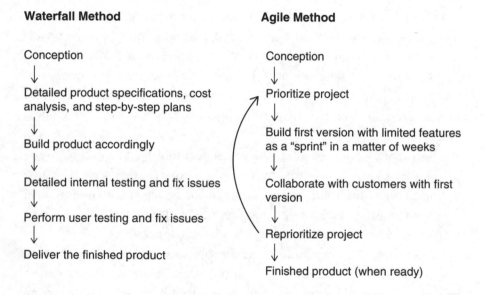

Waterfall Method

Conception
↓
Detailed product specifications, cost analysis, and step-by-step plans
↓
Build product accordingly
↓
Detailed internal testing and fix issues
↓
Perform user testing and fix issues
↓
Deliver the finished product

Agile Method

Conception
↓
Prioritize project
↓
Build first version with limited features as a "sprint" in a matter of weeks
↓
Collaborate with customers with first version
↓
Reprioritize project
↓
Finished product (when ready)

Which method is best? The right answer depends on your product type, personality, and budget. Generally speaking, the more established and predictable a product you're building, the better a fit it is for the waterfall method. More innovative projects are usually better suited for the agile method because it's so much more fluid and allows you to make plenty of mistakes along the way and correct for them as you go. Another positive of the agile method is that you bring the customer into the development process more, and they are both more engaged and better informed about what you're building.

Once again, you're not a corporation, and you are free to make your own choice in this regard. If you prefer to work in a more tightly planned and structured way, you might be best off with the waterfall method, and if you're more comfortable with a more fast-moving, exploratory, and flexible way of working, waterfall will probably drive you mad. The truth is that many developers blend the two, which is often most realistic. A good way to do that is through embracing plans, details, and processes up front, but not spending so much time and energy on trying to perfect them. Then building a good prototype and quickly getting input from customers, much earlier in the process than you would according to the classic waterfall approach.

How Do You Know When You're Ready to Launch?

The traditional approach to a product launch was to get the product all ready, get stock in stores, and then send out press materials to drum up as much coverage in as big a push as possible. Today, a big launch could mean pushing out videos introducing founders and product, social media announcements, user events, free product giveaways, and an e-mail campaign encouraging people to buy and spread the word.

Sometimes you've got to plan a "hard launch" because you've lined up an advertising campaign, scheduled a calendar of multiple events, for which you've had to book venues, or you're tying your product into a specific date, such as Valentine's Day. Also, if you've pushed a significant volume of product out to retail stores in advance, this is the kind of push you want, because you've got to get inventory to turn around as fast as possible to keep those commitments from the retailers and usually to also pay for that stock.

> **Hockey Stick Principle #31: A big launch may not be best.**

But the process for many products has become much more complex and much less clearly delineated by a line in the sand of pre- and post-launch. Beta launches have become commonplace with Web products, relying on early adopters becoming engaged with your product and helping to tweak it with their feedback. With development of e-commerce and the innovation of Point of Sale (POS) sales systems, such as Square, a more gradual, measured, "soft launch" approach is becoming popular even for tangible goods. That might involve starting out with Web promotion and sales through your Web site and on e-commerce sites only, or perhaps setting up some "pop-up" retail locations, renting space within a retail venue or an empty rental space in prime territories for reaching your target customers. Another approach is mobile boutiques, such as fashion trucks, that bring their product right to the neighborhoods where their target consumers live. This innovative approach to selling can become part of your brand and integral to your marketing.

A soft launch might also mean limiting retail to a select number of independent stores. This approach allows you to gauge market response and learn more about your market while also containing your initial inventory and cash flow needs.

Making a huge push right at launch may catch you by surprise with market demand and the intensity of follow through you'll have thrust yourself into. A great example of this was the launch of Warby Parker's lower-cost, elegantly designed eyeglass frames. They had truly identified a market gap. Stylish eyeglass frames were running in the $400 to $500 range, and Warby Parker offered appealing alternatives for just $95.

As one of the founders, Neil Blumenthal, recounted of the launch, "We knew we only had one shot. We launched on February 15, 2010, and it was mayhem." Their PR operation had been hugely successful and articles had run in both Vogue and GQ. They sold out the inventory they ordered of their top fifteen styles, which they had anticipated to last their first year, within four weeks and had to tell twenty thousand customers that it would be three months before they could fulfill their orders. They handled the crisis well with high-quality customer relationship management, and the company went on to become a huge success. Still, it's a cautionary tale regarding the intensity of an all-out, hard launch push.

> **Hockey Stick Principle #32: No matter how big your splash, sales may not come.**

Even if you do make that big push, you may have the opposite problem, the market response equivalent of one hand clapping. You've fired on all cylinders and yet have generated virtually no coverage and little to no sales. Now what? You've experienced one of the great truths of entrepreneurship: Early adopter customers can be very hard to find. Maybe you've misjudged your market, maybe you've promoted to it ineffectively, maybe your pricing is off, maybe you just need more time to find your market, or you need to find a whole different market from the one you were targeting. Whether you launch hard or soft, chances are that you're going to have to do a good deal of market development. The good news is that there are so many powerful tools and methods to keep trying, and we'll dive into those in the next chapter.

Chapter 4

Always Be Shooting to Score: Marketing and Selling During the Blade Years

E ven with the best product development and market testing, the fact is that getting adoption by the market you've targeted is often quite difficult, let alone convincing people to pay the price you'd like to charge. And this is true even when there's an obviously compelling value proposition for a well-targeted group of buyers. Sometimes you've correctly identified the market to sell to, but even so, getting your first customers is like pulling teeth. You may have to convince them of the value of your product even when it seems obvious to you. Other times, you might simply be wrong about the market and you have to find another one.

Focus, but with Flexibility

The prevailing wisdom is that founders should narrowly focus on one market. Craig Wortmann, serial entrepreneur, professor at the University of Chicago's Booth School of Business, and a leading specialist in entrepreneurship, and his coauthor Waverly Deutsch advise in their paper "Entrepreneurial Selling" that "most entrepreneurs sell opportunistically to everyone they can. [But] it is critical to narrow the target to be effective." This is sage advice, as marketing your product to highly targeted buyers is extremely helpful in allowing you to continue to tweak and customize it to specific needs and also to focus your marketing strategy and tailor your sales pitch. But there are also some caveats. Some founders narrow their focus *too early,* and then if they're not getting good responses in market testing or when they begin selling, they conclude prematurely that there is no market.

> **Hockey Stick Principle #33: You have no idea what your market is until you find it.**

You may have a wider market than you originally anticipated, with segments you never thought of showing up for the product. And those you've targeted may also purchase for reasons other than your original value proposition. A few cases in point are: the large additional market for Kleenex, which was originally marketed only as a wipe for women to use to remove their makeup; Avon's body lotion Skin So Soft being purchased as a bug repellent; and the popularity of Arm & Hammer's baking soda as a refrigerator deodorizer. Our First Research industry profiles have become very popular with CPAs who must calculate business valuations, but I didn't discover that market until two years after starting.

On the flip side, your market may be narrower than you've planned for, but that might also be fine if those customers are willing to pay a price that yields a good profit. Michael Bloomberg's model for the Bloomberg Terminal, a.k.a. the "Bloomberg box," which is a desktop monitor system that provides a constant stream of real-time financial market data and allows finance professionals to make trades, was to charge a very high annual fee—at the time of writing $24,000—to the high end of the investment firm market, and that's served him quite well. Niche markets can be rich veins to tap.

If you're not getting the market response you expected, you've got to be open to exploring a wider range of possibilities. And even when you do get a good response, you must carefully evaluate whether your strategy is as wide or as effective as it should be.

> **Hockey Stick Principle #34: You cannot find your market through research; only through selling.**

A common problem is that founders lean too heavily on one key strategy, as an open sesame kind of solution. They believe they've determined the best way to reach the market they've identified and often will stay the course for too long instead of switching to other options.

Knowing how long to keep plugging away at your current approach is not a simple matter of hitting a target conversion rate of pitches to sales or some magical click-through rate on your ads. According to a study by Monetate, a company that works with businesses to improve their e-commerce results, the average percentage of clicks on online advertisements that led to a sale was 2.65 percent for Q3 2014.[55] But what if your rate after one year of trying is only 0.2 percent? Experts also say that the success rates for cold-calling and telemarketing should be about 5 percent. What if after six months you're only converting one out of five hundred potential customers you call? You can't just give up. You've got to be prepared to hit some walls and try new ideas. You should be prepared for a longer struggle than many founders plan for.

Getting Your First Customers

The famed late professor Everett M. Rogers, who held a Ph.D. in sociology and statistics, wrote in his classic book *Diffusion of Innovations* that new ideas or technology are adopted by society according to a consistent pattern whereby they are first embraced by a relatively small group of people, whom he called innovators, who are relatively open to trying new things. These innovators are then instrumental in spreading the word to a next group he called early adopters, who need more convincing but are also quite receptive, and they then help spread the word to a group of early majority buyers, who like to wait to hear about innovation from the earlier adopters. Once that group has come on board, the two last groups—the late majority and the laggards—finally embrace the innovation. This pattern has been found to hold for all sorts of innovative products (versus well-established ones with preexisting markets that firms can seek to take share from).

Though the innovators and early adopters are described as relatively receptive in practice, they can be hard to identify, and then getting them to purchase can require a good deal of persuasion about the merits of the product. Just finding a first customer can take months. In the Hockey Stick study, for example, I found that the average time from product launch to closing the first customers was four months.

Also, sometimes the customers you've identified simply turn out not to be interested in actually buying your product at the quantity you've predicted, even if you have tested the market. Extensive market research and the most elaborate product development procedures can sometimes mislead you or simply fail to identify markets you should aim for. PepsiCo had a huge flop with Crystal Pepsi, a clear cola drink it launched in the early 1990s, even though the company had done market tests in a number of cities carefully selected to represent varying regions of the country—Denver, Sacramento, Dallas, and Providence—and the response was positive in all of them.

Also, as said earlier, sometimes you've got to develop the product fully—or very close to fully—and then go to the market for its response. The Segway scooter is regularly used as a case of failing to do a rigorous job of market assessment, and one can argue that there were good reasons to have anticipated it wouldn't take off for broad consumer purchase. But its inventor, Dean Kamen, arguably had no practical choice in pursuing his dream for the product but to build a highly engineered version because the essential selling feature of the Segway is its extremely refined motion control. Doing extensive testing of anything less than the real deal would have left open the question of whether people might not respond much better to the perfected product.

Kamen wasn't wrong that the Segway would be an amazing new kind of vehicle and have a market; but the market turned out to be much smaller and more specialized than he'd anticipated, largely comprised of public services like police and fire departments and security guard firms. I'm not saying mistakes weren't made. The company way overhyped the nature of the Segway in the lead-up to launch, claiming that it was going to revolutionize transportation, which was absurd and badly miscalculated. This is a textbook case of why no matter how much publicity you generate in advance of your launch or how good the product is—the Segway really was a brilliant accomplishment—you cannot depend on your intended market flocking to your product.

The Market You Never Thought Of

If you're not capturing the market you've aimed for, you might find an entirely different one out there if you keep trying out possibilities. A case in point of a start-up I invested in is My LifeSite. The company sells analysis of the quality and financial health of high-end retirement communities.

The founder, Brad Breeding, reasoned that financial advisors in particular would be a strong market, because helping clients make a choice of retirement home is a common requirement for them. The plan was to target that market at the start and then to expand to other potential markets, such as the retirees themselves. Financial advisors seemed like a slam-dunk market to buy the product to me, so I made the investment.

But three years later, our largest market by far is retirement homes themselves, not financial advisors, and yet we hadn't even considered them as a market. A regional sales director for a retirement home learned about My LifeSite in a retirement publication article about analyzing retirement homes and contacted the company. He thought My LifeSite might help prospective customers gain objective information about the financial commitment they were about to make. The service also turned out to be a good way for retirement homes to better understand their industry and competitors. Eventually, financial advisors and consumers began to come on board, but if Brad hadn't been open to changing his marketing focus, the company might not have been able to stay in business long enough to win them over.

> **Hockey Stick Principle #35: Don't dis the market that shows up for you, no matter how unexpected.**

Some products that abjectly fail in their intended market can sometimes be adopted with wild enthusiasm by another. The inventors of bubble wrap intended the technology to be used for wallpaper. It turned out that people didn't want the kind of bubbly wallpaper they had in mind, but they persisted with other ideas and found a huge market when they thought of approaching IBM to use bubbly packaging for shipping a new computer model coming out in 1959. When marketed as a way to assure safe transport of fragile goods, bubble wrap boomed.[56]

A more recent story of finding an unexpected market in packaging is that of Packrite, founded in 2008 by Michael and Mary Drummond as the only firm in North America to manufacture specialized packaging for consumer-goods firms. The concept was that they would produce cleverly branded yet difficult-to-manufacture boxes for companies—say, for example, creatively designed boxes for special occasion cakes. But after investing all their wealth into purchasing millions of dollars' worth of expensive package manufacturing equipment and getting off to a good start with sales, when the 2008 recession hit, their sales dropped precipitously. They needed $7 million in sales to break even, and in 2008, they made only about $3 million. That's serious revenue, so they were right in thinking that there was a consumer-goods company market for their businesses, but without making more money, they were going to tank nonetheless. So Michael got scrappy and decided to go after a different market, the box-manufacturing industry, Packrite's competitors. You may think doing so was ill conceived, but he was thinking creatively and realized that while the box manufacturing firms wanted to keep their customers happy, these short-run, specialty boxes were difficult for them to make a profit on. He smartly sought to get the attention of the box manufacturers by drumming up coverage of Packrite and the opportunity it offered the large manufacturers in the trade periodicals that serve the packaging industry. Soon after a number of articles came out, box manufacturers started calling. In 2013, Packrite earned $18 million in revenue, and it's still growing fast.

Market-Building Can Be a Long Journey

The process of finding an optimal market can sometimes take many years. Listerine, which was created in 1879 as a surgical antiseptic, was marketed for all sorts of uses—as a cure for ailments from gonorrhea to the common cold—until finally in the 1920s it was pitched as a cure for bad breath, and its sales skyrocketed. It's important to emphasize that a product may find a certain amount of success before hitting the market sweet spot—Listerine chugged along for over forty years before finding its niche. As an entrepreneur, you want to discover that sweet spot, not settle for only serviceable sales.

So although you should absolutely identify and plan around a particular market while you're initially developing your product and model—and you should do some testing of that market—you have to be aware of the limits of advance research and keep an open mind about making changes, exploring other possibilities that may be off your charted course, and hanging very tough through lean times.

Sometimes It's Not the Product; It's the Positioning

In some cases, connecting with your market won't involve changing your product much, if at all. With First Research, Ingo and I didn't change the nature of our reports after discovering that while bankers weren't initially interested, CPAs were. The reports were just fine as they were, but it took us some time to figure out who would want them and how to convince them to buy our product.

Another great case study of this is the story of Febreze. Researchers at P&G had discovered a formula for an odorless liquid that, when sprayed on fabric, could completely eliminate any odors lingering in them, like cigarette smoke, not just cover them up with a perfumed scent. P&G marketed the product as a laundry freshener and expected it to take off. But when they launched it in test markets, sales were lackluster by comparison to their plan. P&G didn't give up on it, though. Some customers absolutely loved the spray, and P&G talked to them about it, looking for any possible clues they could offer about how to convince others to buy the product. In one of those interviews, a woman said, "It's nice, you know? Spraying feels like a little mini-celebration when I'm done with a room." That comment helped P&G see that it had to market Febreze differently.

It had been pitched as a spray for clothes. But spraying clothes that way wasn't an established cleaning routine, and people didn't want to pick it up. However, spraying a *room* with a nice-scented fragrance was a more regular routine in households. So the company added an appealing scent to the product and came out with a new set of commercials showing people spraying Febreze on bedspreads and piles of just cleaned clothes, positioning it as a refreshing finishing touch to add to their regular cleaning routine. When positioned this way, the product immediately took off.[57]

The bottom line is this: *The best way to discover a market is by selling to it—not by only researching it.* Of course, you should research a market before selling to it, but research alone won't tell you enough. The best way to learn whether or not a market will adopt your product is to sell to it and learn from both the good and bad experiences of that process.

> **Hockey Stick Principle #36: Early customers are the best product managers.**

Actual Buyers Will Tell You What You Need to Hear

Many companies invest a great deal in hiring specialists to anticipate customer interests and needs, such as the growing specialty of product managers, whose job it is to assess the market and guide the product to it, all the way from design through development and launch. But any honest product manager will readily admit how flawed even the best market research can be.

A key reason that advance market testing can fail is that people tend to want to please those who are asking for their responses to a product. And if they're not actually being asked to buy it, they're less demanding and forthcoming. I've experienced the same thing in product pitch meetings. A potential buyer seems to fall head-over-heels for the product and sends obvious buying signals. I leave the meeting feeling sure I've closed the sale. But the next day, next week? Nothing happens. The prospect drops off the face of the earth, never to be heard from again. I call this "good-meeting syndrome." This happens to me all the time.

When you're asking potential customers to actually spend their money, you get much more honest and constructive feedback. And this should involve some old-fashioned face-to-face or voice-to-voice conversation, not just analysis of user reviews, A/B testing, or ad-click analysis.

The Internet Doesn't Do Your Legwork

Because the Internet has provided such a powerful set of tools for marketing and sales—including crowdfunding campaigns; pay-per-click advertising; search engine optimization; remarkably refined customer targeting; e-mail marketing; and content marketing, as with Web sites, blogs, and through social media—it's tempting to think you can entirely forgo many traditional methods to market your product. All founders should carefully consider how to make optimal use of these tools. But watch out for falling into the trap of thinking you can just build a Web site, do some good SEO, buy some well-targeted Google AdWords and Facebook advertising, and forget about the traditional person-to-person methods of market building.

Primary among these market-building methods are cold-calling; face-to-face sales calls; working the floor at trade shows; and pitching to the media. Not doing any face-to-face or voice-to-voice sales and marketing is a serious mistake for most businesses. Booth School of Business professor Craig Wortmann stresses this: "I am very much of the school that we, as founders, no matter the product, should err away from pay-per-click and toward live contact. If I'm doing pay-per-click and all my selling is done behind the computer screen, I'm not getting a lot of rich feedback. People aren't going to e-mail and say, 'That ad you did stinks because . . .' That just doesn't happen. But in person, people will say, 'You know what, Craig? That just doesn't fit for us.' And then you can learn about why."

I know that for many aspiring entrepreneurs, this is not an appealing message, not only because the traditional selling methods are more time consuming but because they're not as comfortable with many of the requirements of marketing and sales, which are so different from those involved in tinkering with the idea. While building a new product requires concentration, alone time, sometimes engineering or programming, and hands-on creativity and project management, developing a market requires persuasive communication skills, the ability to make an emotional connection with buyers, lots of hustle, and a great deal of resilience. As Sageworks's Brian Hamilton says, "Starting a business is like creating a movement." It takes people skills and connecting face-to-face.

You've Got to Find Your Own Mix

Plenty of books and online resources offer what they pitch as sure-fire formulas for marketing and sales. Much of their advice is great, but the hard truth is that you cannot rely on any one formula for finding your market. A sales method that works well for one start-up may not work at all for another, and often it's hard to know why. Every founder has to figure out the right target, pricing, sales channel, marketing technique, and strongest value proposition for his or her own business by trial and error. This is the biggest difference between the sales and marketing operations of established companies and the approach an entrepreneur must take.

As Craig Wortmann points out, professional sales teams from established firms follow a well-honed process and have a deep bench of support: "There's this huge, wonderful infrastructure sitting under that [professional] salesperson. It's marketing and HR and training, and they have brochures, and you've been given a territory. And everything in that structure is built to support your ability to go close a deal with that customer. That's professional selling."[58]

You may want to build up a traditional marketing and sales operation, but way before making that investment, you should answer a number of difficult questions about the nature of your market. Is it broad-based or specialized? Are there multiple markets that may have quite different needs? Should you try to customize for those needs or choose one core market to pursue? What is the best way to deliver the product to them? Should you market and sell online, by phone, face-to-face, or all of the above? Are there companies similar to yours that are already selling to your potential customers? Might they be willing to partner with you in some way? How much would buyers in your target market be willing to pay?

To find these answers, you have to experiment with various marketing and sales techniques and be prepared to be surprised at the results. You may discover that your expectations about who will want your product and what they are willing to pay are way off. If you invest a great deal in a certain sales strategy before you've confirmed that it will work well by testing it out, you may end up wasting very valuable time and money. When you start selling, you must be in exploration mode and, always soliciting customer feedback, you have to be prepared to listen carefully to that feedback and make adjustments to your marketing and sales plans—and also to your product—according to that feedback. You should also be prepared to try lots of different methods for reaching your market. As you'll see from Schedulefly's story below, there are so many options for sales and marketing, both traditional and nontraditional. Most importantly, you have to be resilient. Some of the feedback you get is going to be harsh.

Schedulefly's Twenty Months of Trial and Error

A great example of founders who persevered and tried several approaches to build their market is the ultimate success of Schedulefly, the online restaurant employee scheduling software. The company now has more than five thousand customers who renew their subscriptions to the service every year, and it's growing fast. Let's use the story of the choices and many pivots they had to make in their approach as a basic example of the kind of process you should prepare for.

One of the smartest moves programmer Wes Aiken made in getting to the market-building phase was to bring in his partner, Tyler Rullman, to take charge of marketing and sales. Wes had no interest in outreach to customers, and he understood he had to partner with someone who would relish the challenge. If you're not going to be willing to throw yourself into the process—and I mean with real enthusiasm—then it's important to bring someone on board who is pumped up about it. Recall that at the time, in 2007, Wes just had two restaurants using the software for free. Tyler nonetheless agreed to take on the job of building the market, for a 40 percent stake in the business, and he committed to working full-time. This big step brings up an important point. To my mind, if a business is ever going to grow beyond the tinkering process, in nearly every case, it really needs a full-time founder committed to the challenges associated with figuring out how to market and sell its product. This process is just too taxing and difficult to do it part-time.

From September 2007 until May 2009, finding a market for the service was Tyler's entire mission, while Wes continued to make coding improvements during his spare time from his day job.

Wes believed the right market to target was restaurants rather than a wider range of companies that must deal with employee schedules, and Tyler agreed. They felt like they needed a niche; otherwise, they'd become overwhelmed with requests to specialize the product for different kinds of businesses. That meant Tyler was facing a real challenge because, as he told me, "There's no easy way to market to restaurants because the industry is just so fragmented." On the positive side, the market was well-defined, and Tyler knew that restaurateurs make up a community that talks to each other, so he expected that word of mouth would be a powerful engine of adoption. Getting word of mouth going, though, required first getting some customers, and he had a wide range of marketing techniques to choose from:

- cold-calling via phone
- selling face-to-face
- attending trade shows
- seeking referrals from centers of influence, such as consultants who advise restaurants

- e-mail marketing, such as offering discounts and promotions
- content marketing, such as social media, writing blog posts, and online articles
- soliciting media attention
- online pay-per-click advertising
- Web site SEO marketing
- selling through partnerships or resellers
- buying print advertising

He also had to choose from a wide range of business models:

- The low-cost model where you attempt to sell a product for a low price and spend small amounts of money to acquire a great number of customers. Video games sold on cell phones and tablets for $2.99 are a good example.
- The direct-sales model, which calls for hired employees to sell directly to customers. Many traditional, old-school industries, such as banking and insurance, use this model.
- The affiliate model, which pays commission to another similar organization to market and/or sell your product for you, normally through the Web traffic it produces. Commissions may range from 10 percent to as much as 50 percent or even more. Some commissions are also a set amount for each sale made. For example, iContact had good success with affiliate deals.
- The popular Internet freemium model.
- The subscription model.
- The advertising model, which enables companies to charge customers for advertisements based upon the amount of traffic the site generates. This model relies upon entertaining, useful, or educational content to drive people to the site.

Tyler and Wes agreed that the subscription model was the best way for them to go because they understood it well and also because it was the norm for selling new software products.

For marketing and selling strategies, Tyler initially focused on two key tactics: Web site optimization and an e-mail campaign. Selling door-to-door was an option he might have chosen, which often works with small businesses, but he thought it would be unproductive. "I just didn't think it was going to work to get us to any kind of scale," he told me. "You might get a one-off here or there, but you're approaching dozens of people and burning up gas, burning up time." But that wasn't his only reason; he admitted that another was that "it's not my nature, and it's embarrassing." He understood the value of building good relationships with the customers, though, and he was determined from the start to emphasize excellent customer service.

His first move was to tweak the Web site to make it suitable for search word optimization, and then he invested $1,500 a month to buy AdWords through Google. He also tried Facebook, MSN, and Yahoo! but wasn't getting the returns on those that he was with Google, so he stopped. For the e-mail campaign, he decided to try one of the most effective traditional methods of customer acquisition—offering free trials—which the Internet has allowed a small business to do on a much larger scale and at lower cost than with traditional giveaways.

I'm a big advocate of free trials, especially for SaaS businesses, because they help customers familiarize themselves with the offerings, generate awareness, and most of all, the feedback you'll receive is invaluable. According to a survey by Totango, a firm that specializes in helping SaaS companies improve their online sales models, 44 percent of SaaS firms offer a free trial.[59]

> **Hockey Stick Principle #37: Don't expect free trials to sell your product for you.**

One word of caution, however, is that if free trials aren't professionally run with good support and consistent follow-up, you could be wasting your time and money. At Vertical IQ, we offer free trials, but we also have a list of requirements for getting one, including full commitment from decision-makers, scheduled training, and providing survey feedback at the end of the trial. Schedulefly's e-mail offer was qualified, which means it allowed for one free month of service, after which a restaurant could convert to paying thirty dollars a month.

To push the offer out, Tyler sat in front of a computer for hundreds of hours, devoting himself to the mind-numbing grunt work of looking up the e-mail addresses of restaurants and contacting them one at a time, personally offering them the benefits of giving Schedulefly a try. Progress was slow. Tyler recalls, "I e-mailed thousands of restaurants. You know, when you spend a month, every night and all night long, sending e-mails and you're only getting two or three customers, it's like, 'Oh, man, c'mon!'" Eventually, a fair number of restaurants signed up for the free trial, but the conversion rate to paying for the service was low at first.

Here, Tyler made a brilliant move; he began making follow-up calls to restaurateurs who had taken the trial but not subscribed, which gave him lots of good information about why those potential customers hadn't decided to adopt the service. And he kept making the calls even though some of the responses were harsh. "When you introduce something that's totally different, they're either going to get it and say, 'Wow, this is cool; it makes my life a lot easier,' or they're going to say, 'This isn't how I did it before; I only know how to do it one way. You must be an idiot! You don't know how we do scheduling in the restaurant industry.' I got yelled at a lot," he told me.

The pushback you get from potential customers and some of the questions they ask about why they should try your product can seem foolishly shortsighted. It might seem obvious to you that they'd benefit from the product, but they're just not seeing it. I love the example Sageworks's Brian Hamilton used to address this issue: "Let's say it's the year 1300 in Europe, and an entrepreneur is selling a new invention, the spoon. He goes up to a man holding a bowl of soup up to his mouth to sip it and shows him how great it is to use a spoon instead. But the guy asks him, 'What hand do I hold it in? Can I hold it with two hands? Why is it round? Can I eat spaghetti with it? Why can't you make it work with spaghetti?'"

One of the biggest mistakes entrepreneurs can make is to look down on this kind of reaction to their products. The discomfort of such negative reactions can also lead some entrepreneurs to retreat from doing this invaluable person-to-person outreach. We love our products, and that can make us arrogant about them and make us think that their value ought to be perfectly clear. We can find ourselves thinking that potential customers who aren't interested are just fools, and that often leads to staying on one course, pushing the same product in the same way for much too long.

Hockey Stick Principle #38: Your harshest critics save you.

Nick Lowe's 1979 song "Cruel to Be Kind" is about relationships, but it also pertains to entrepreneurship.[60] Rejection, even when brutal, works out to be kind to the entrepreneur in the end. Wes and Tyler did a terrific job of coping with their negative feedback and using it to improve the service. Wes was able to make many key enhancements to Schedulefly, such as adding a feature that enabled employees to request time off and find someone to pick up their shift easily, saving both employees and managers lots of time and annoyance. As Tyler recounts, "The people who signed up for trials but did not convert, which was most of them, were sometimes brutally honest, and that kind of feedback was usually more helpful than [the pleasant generalities] we heard from folks who liked us."

This kind of product development is vital to continue to do after launch (and sometimes major pivots should be made, which we'll discuss in more depth later). By the middle of 2008, the number of restaurateurs signing up for Schedulefly's free trials was rising, and conversion rates were increasing from 5 percent to 10 percent and closing in on 20 percent. This is the beauty of free trials. Note that according to Totango, a firm that helps SaaS firms acquire customers, companies making offers that accept credit cards may convert as many as 50 percent of their free trials to paying customers.[61]

Keep Tweaking Your Sales Pitch

Improving the product is usually only part of the solution. The method of pitching, the actual content and style of the pitch, and the market being pitched to also must often be changed. Wes and Tyler smartly experimented with a number of other approaches. One thing Tyler tried was blogging, but he didn't get any traction with it. According to HubSpot, which offers online marketing and sales support for businesses, 82 percent of marketers who blog daily acquire a customer using their blog, as opposed to 57 percent of marketers who blog monthly.[62] So blogging requires a massive time investment, and it's difficult to be successful at it unless you're committing to it not only in terms of posting quality information often but also posting over a long period of time. Since Tyler was bootstrapping, he had limited time and needed to use it wisely, and he just didn't feel blogging would move the needle fast enough.

His next move was to sign the company up for memberships in a number of restaurant associations for the purpose of building connections so that industry influencers would know about Schedulefly and hopefully spread the word. But for Tyler, that was another goose egg. "You have to find what works for you," he says. He or Wes would have needed to actually attend the meetings and schmooze with people, but that approach wasn't appealing to them. Tyler also tried direct mail, which didn't work, either. "We found out restaurants are deluged with mail hawking every conceivable product, and we kind of got lost in the shuffle," he explains.

Direct mail can be effective for certain types of businesses, primarily ones where the recipient already knows what the product is and has a need for it. However, it's relatively expensive, because to do it right, you have to pay to design the mailing, and the printing and shipping costs are considerable. Furthermore, studies show that you need to send out more than one mailing; generally three or four at minimum to have an impact. Direct mail came with a lot of risk, so Tyler made the good decision to abandon the approach.

He next decided that they should give door-to-door selling a try, after all. His first idea was to hire salespeople on a commission-only basis. To find them, he advertised on Craigslist, targeting college towns in the South, like Tallahassee, Gainesville, and Columbia, because he thought college students might be interested, and they would be more technologically savvy than older, traditional salespeople. Unfortunately, that plan didn't work for Schedulefly. "Very few responded, and we stopped the experiment pretty early on, as we couldn't really find a compensation model that worked for both parties," Tyler recalls. This taught him that for their product, the door-to-door selling model was, as he put it, "a joke." The students found that they had to make about one hundred sales calls to close one sale, so they quickly gave up. They also needed training, which wasn't something either Tyler or Wes wanted to invest time in.

As I said earlier, I'm an advocate for face-to-face selling—especially during your first year because you learn so much from the meetings. But it's important to point out that in today's economy, unless your product costs several thousand dollars, face-to-face selling is often just too expensive to do at any real scale unless your prospects are in relative proximity to your salespeople. At Vertical IQ, most sales of $15,000 and below are conducted by phone, and sometimes sales much larger than that are, as well. Also, whoever you have doing your selling for you must absolutely be well-trained, which Wes and Tyler smartly realized.

They decided that a better approach would be to bring in a star salesman they'd gotten to know from First Research, Wil Brawley. I can attest that Wil is a brilliant salesman with a genial, outgoing personality as well as great knowledge of the full range of sales and marketing tactics, such as social media and other Web marketing, and he brought wonderful creativity to the process. For example, Wil began filming video interviews with founders of successful restaurants offering words of wisdom, which were posted on their Web site. He also made some videos of servers on-site at customer restaurants saying things like "I love Schedulefly because my schedule comes right to my cell phone. It's really cool!" These were refreshingly casual and unrehearsed, which was innovative at the time. Wil also produced educational videos about running and working in independent restaurants, and he distributed these to restaurant magazines that went on to distribute them to an even wider audience.

Wil even wrote a book titled *Restaurant Owners Uncorked*, for which he interviewed several owners of customer restaurants and told their founding stories. This was a smart form of content marketing, which not only enhanced the relationship between Schedulefly and its customers by showing that their insights were respected but offered real value to them and to prospective customers. Because it was also fun to read, it was a great brand builder, as well, helping to portray Schedulefly as a friendly, engaging company.

> **Hockey Stick Principle #39: Selling is not a game for amateurs.**

Get Expert Opinion Behind You

One of the decisions that Tyler and Wes made that can be quite difficult for founders is they committed much of their scant revenue to hiring a public relations firm to promote the company to the editors of trade magazines. If an editor is impressed by the pitch and writes an article, the effect can be catalytic. It's hard to beat the value of having your name in print in a recognizable publication. The problem is that hiring a public relations firm is expensive, often as much as $5,000 per month minimum. That money might well be worthwhile, because they have the know-how and connections to get the job done correctly. But I've also known many successful founders who have hustled hard on their own and landed some excellent press.

For Wes and Tyler, hiring a firm paid off nicely. An editor from *Nation's Restaurant News* thought restaurant owners could benefit from the product, and he wrote a front-page article about it. As Tyler recalls, "That was one of the biggest things that ever happened to us. The magazine is the bible for the restaurant industry, and tens of thousands—if not hundreds of thousands—of people read it." And the value of such press goes beyond people reading the piece and positive coverage in a curated periodical—whether in print or online; it also lends you a good deal of credibility. Tyler says that after posting the article on Schedulefly's Web site, he saw a clear increase in the conversion rate of those who came to the site.

Once You've Got Customers, Serve Them

One of the keys to Schedulefly's ultimate success in cultivating its market was that its customer retention was high. This was due in large part to Tyler's emphasis on customer service. Tyler recalls, "I took really good care of the customers that we got—answering calls at midnight, that kind of thing. They had a lot of questions; they had a lot of problems. But they always had somebody here to answer the phone or to respond within a few minutes."

> **Hockey Stick Principle #40: No one else can care as much about your customers and learn as much from them as you can.**

Good service is absolutely essential for successful start-ups. Some founders try to offload customer service as quickly as possible to an outside firm, and I think that's a mistake. As Tyler found, if you deal with customers yourself, not only will they be impressed, but you will also learn all sorts of ways in which your product or service should be fixed or enhanced. Tyler says those customer calls taught him about Schedulefly's true value proposition—which was saving time and aggravation for managers and employees—and that helped them to further hone their pitch.

With so many customers staying with the service, Wes and Tyler began to feel optimistic that the company could really take off, and with the push to offer free trials and Wil's salesmanship, sales started to accelerate more and more, and the word of mouth Tyler had anticipated started to kick in. They had found their growth groove.

The Best Mix Is Not Obvious

The Schedulefly founders discovered the sales-and-marketing approach that was right for them—the subscription model with e-mail marketing, online pay-per-click advertising, PR and media attention, and, over time, word of mouth. Of the seventeen sales-and-marketing methods listed on pages 119–120, Schedulefly ultimately honed in on four of them.

Some of the others *could* have worked, as well. For example, the affiliate model might have worked here. Some larger companies, trade associations, and consulting firms that advise restaurants or media firms might have been willing to promote the service, and if so, that would have lent credibility to the Schedulefly brand and greatly extended the reach of its marketing. But the downside of the affiliate approach is that it requires complicated contracts, management of day-to-day needs, and training, and all of that might have taken too much time away from Tyler making his direct calls to customers that turned out to be so informative and eventually produced good results. The Schedulefly founders figured out the balance that was right for their time, resources, and skills.

When you ask founders about how they managed to find their market, the methods they used to target that market, and what actually worked for them, the answers can be quite surprising. Take the case of Dude Solutions, a $40 million SaaS business that enables schools and governments to manage their physical locations and supplier operations more effectively. For example, if a school is having a play one evening, it's required to contact the local police department. How does it remember to do this? Dude Solutions to the rescue.

When Dude Solutions started in 1999, it was ahead of its time in going with a pure SaaS business model. It was innovative as well in being multi-tenant (meaning all customers used the same code) and in offering user-friendly training. Most Web-based firms at the time took a pure "build it and they will come" e-commerce approach, using Web advertising as the sole selling method. Dude Solutions took a different, surprisingly traditional approach for such an innovative product and model. Cofounder Kent Hudson told me, "We put up a Web site, tried to generate some interest, and we looked at some e-commerce stuff, but we just kept saying, 'This isn't going to work.' Everyone else around us was doing it, but we just said, 'No.' We thought it would be a long-term build-out."

I fully expected him to tell me that they cold-called all day long, as I did at First Research to get our first customers and which, though arduous and emotionally challenging for many people, can be a vital method of building an early adopter base. (We'll see the role cold calling played in doing so for Sageworks in a bit.) But that's not the route that Dude Solutions chose. "We never cold-called," Kent told me. "We started out going to trade shows. We'd show the attendees that we were specialized in small school districts." The trade show route worked well for Dude Solutions because it allowed them to teach customers how the product worked in a friendly, personable, even entertaining way. Again, it's important not to underestimate the potential power of the personal touch. With Dude Solutions, the customers that the company had to convince were quite new to SaaS systems, and the comfort of having an expert there to show them how to use the product was key to adoption.

Beware of False-Positives

Another founder who was creative and resilient in searching for a market is Brian Hamilton. Today, Sageworks is a big success, and Brian appears regularly as an expert on CNBC. Sageworks's first product, ProfitCents, is sophisticated software that provides easy-to-read, narrative-style reports about the financial performance of companies. The value proposition Brian banked on was that small business owners are often inexperienced in reading and using balance sheets, income statements, and financial ratios and that holds them back from using that information effectively to improve their business. With an estimated twenty-three million small businesses in the United States alone as of this writing, this would seem to be a huge pool of potential customers from which to get early adopters. But even so, getting the first of them to sign on was heavy lifting.

Along the way, Brian encountered one of the trickiest issues to manage in market development: a great sale that seems to indicate that adoption is taking off when, in fact, it's just a "false-positive." In fact, he experienced a false-positive twice.

> **Hockey Stick Principle #41: Don't hitch your wagon to one huge customer.**

Of course, it's great to get a large order from a big chain or a highly re-spected firm. Getting that kind of credibility does indicate that you're about to take off. The founders of Method products, for example, stress how important getting their big order from Target was for their eventual take-off. And the order from Kroger boosted Boogie Wipes into big business. But these big orders can be deceptive.

Brian had invested in creating a first-rate product but figuring out how to find a market for it took lots of trial and error. His business plan called for initially selling to small businesses. He built a good Web site, and he marketed online, but he ran into the limits of the Web-only approach just as Schedulefly had. The effort resulted in selling only a few reports to banks for fourteen dollars each. But then he did get a big hit: A manager from one of the largest banks in the United States who was looking for new ways to help the bank's small-business customers found Sageworks through a Web search. Two months later, the bank licensed ProfitCents for $250,000. Brian was ecstatic. If one of the largest banks on the planet wanted the product, it was sure to take off—and fast. Not so. For months, he made no new big sales to banks. But Brian was dogged and open-minded; he kept pushing, and he didn't let the rejection overwhelm him, even when he started to face serious financial difficulties. He spent about $300,000 in 2000 alone on operations and had only minimal revenue. At that burn rate, the clock was ticking loudly. But rather than buckling, he got even scrappier.

As Nobel Prize–winning physicist Ernest Rutherford once said, "Gentlemen, we have run out of money. It is time to start thinking."[63] Brian tried cold-calling franchises and small businesses. He also pitched to Web marketers and Chamber of Commerce offices, thinking they might help to spread the word to their constituency of business owners. He even got in his car and drove across the country making sales calls to all sorts of businesses, scoring meetings with H&R Block, American Express, Fair Isaac, several banks, and some small financial firms. Then he met with one of the largest accounting software providers in the country. The company indicated it was interested in a deal and wanted him to come in for a meeting with the company's founder. Again, Brian was ecstatic. The strat-egy seemed solid; the accounting firm was a good fit because its business mission was right in line with the Sageworks mission to make financial analysis easier.

But the meeting ended up being brutal. "It was the worst meeting ever—*ever*," he told me. "And I had a lot of meetings." The conversation was like an inquisition, with the firm's founder relentlessly grilling him.

"We're trying to make financial analysis easy," Brian opened.

"Why would anybody even want this?" the founder shot back.

"Well, it helps them understand their financial statements."

"Why would they want to do that?"

"To help them make better decisions."

"How would it help them to do that?"

"Because they'll understand their cash flow."

In the course of searching for a market, this exchange between Brian and the potential partner is common when approaching funders and partners, and you will need to precisely understand and communicate why your product will be successful to these groups.

Brian felt that he hadn't satisfied the founder with his answers, and he left the meeting sure that the deal was off, but before long, he got word that the accounting software firm wanted to go ahead with a licensing deal.

Licensing involves giving someone permission to conduct specified activities with your product (selling, promoting, publishing). It can be a great way to get more customers fast. The upside is that licensing provides you with a strong sales channel, but a pitfall is that you run the risk of losing control of your product's brand and reputation. Essentially, you have someone else selling and marketing your product. When licensing, you need a really experienced licensing attorney because the terms and conditions can make or break your success.

The accounting software firm agreed to pay $250,000 a year for the right to publish a free "lite version" ProfitCents report for each of its business customers. In addition to the fee, the deal was appealing because it seemed like a good way to get the accounting software's customers to buy into the full-version ProfitCents; the firm agreed to include in its marketing an offer to upgrade. Unfortunately, though, very few opted to upgrade. Then the partnership with the accounting software firm ended.

The first false-positive with the big bank had been tough enough; this was crushing. "The hardest part is the feeling of 'Where is this going?' I think that's why most people give up," Brian recalls. They can't come up with the answer before both their confidence and their money run out.

Brian had been trying to sell Sageworks for almost two and half years by this point, and yet he still didn't give up. He kept driving around the country making sales calls, and in 2002, about two and half years after starting the company, he had what is often referred to as a "small win." He sold a $500 subscription to a regional CPA firm in Knoxville, Tennessee. Here's where Brian made a crucial call; he made note of that small win and decided to drill into the possibilities of the CPA market further. He discovered that ProfitCents had a good value proposition for them: They provide the type of advice to small businesses that ProfitCents calculates, and the program could save them time—and of course time is money.

Brian had at last discovered a viable market, and it was big one. There are at least 132,645 accounting companies in the United States.[64] Now was the time to focus, so Sageworks turned its cannons on CPA firms. Building up a strong base still took some time, but they had found their market, and as we'll see in more detail in chapter 5, Brian then developed a method for drilling into it that ultimately paid off big time.

Don't Settle for a Mediocre Market

Another great case of a founder tenaciously hunting for a market is that of David Friedberg, the founder of The Climate Corporation, which he sold to Monsanto in 2013 for approximately $1.1 billion while staying on as CEO. Friedberg and his team had developed a truly brilliant innovative product, but when they discovered that the market for it was limited, they figured out how to please a market that turned out to be huge.

Friedberg was working at Google as a corporate development and business product manager at the time he came up with the idea for the company. It was a rainy day, and he made note that a bike rental shop on San Francisco's Embarcadero had closed up for the day. The thought occurred to him that the impact of weather on businesses must be a big problem. He was right: His subsequent research came up with the enticing statistic that 70 percent of businesses are adversely affected by weather in some way every year.

He thought he might be able to create a financial product for businesses based on statistical modeling of weather, which would allow him to calculate the likelihood of various kinds of losses well enough that he could offer to make payments to customers for whatever weather damage to their business they wanted coverage for. This would be a form of derivative rather than an insurance policy. They would pay cash up front in order to get a guarantee of payment of a certain amount in the event that whatever type of weather damage they wanted coverage for occurred. And he could agree to send payouts to customers automatically when those events did occur, because the system would monitor weather events through the masses of weather data available through data feeds from weather stations. There would be no claims process, as is such a hassle with insurance.

It was a bold idea, and to pursue it, he created a strong prototype that allowed him to raise $300,000 from a venture capitalist, at which point he went all in, quitting his job to develop the product. But when he pitched to venture firms trying to raise additional cash, they all gave him a pass. Persevering, he turned to the friends-and-family plan and was able to raise a very impressive $2 million that way. The idea seemed that good. That money allowed him to hire a high-quality team and to build the service. But when they launched the site, no customers came.

So this highly sophisticated data analyzer resorted to the time-tested tactic of cold-calling. The team called all sorts of businesses that were clearly affected by the weather—energy companies, agricultural companies, travel agencies, and ski resorts—and they got some takers, allowing them to bring in $2 million in revenue, which was again very impressive and allowed them to raise significant venture capital. But the problem was that serving their customers required a great deal of specialty work, tailoring to their diverse needs and teaching them about the product. That wasn't a scalable business model.

Still, working with those clients provided good funding for continuing the search for the perfect market. Finally, their research led them to focus on farmers, because they calculated that they would be the best group from which to get repeatable business that could be very lucrative. They made the smart decision to tailor the product to farmers' desires, which wasn't easy. It involved offering the product as insurance rather than derivatives, because that's what farmers wanted, and that involved learning the great many intricacies of the insurance business. But all that work paid off. They called the revamped product Total Weather Insurance, and in cold calls to farmers, they began making many sales per day. From then on, the business grew fast.

Hockey Stick Principle #42: Don't tell a market what it wants; give it what it wants.

It may seem that if Brian Hamilton and David Friedberg had done lots of up-front market research to identify the market segment to build their products for and approached lots of potential customers with a prototype, they might have more efficiently arrived at their solutions before having to invest so much money into the process. That could be true. But they might also have become so discouraged by negative responses before they hit on the market that expressed interest that they might have given up before they got there. For example, if David Friedberg had focused on farmers exclusively at the start, and they kept saying they wanted insurance, he might have been put off by the need to learn a business he had no interest in because he didn't have any real skin in the game.

Y Combinator's Paul Graham put it best when he said, "It's harmless if reporters and know-it-alls dismiss your start-up. They always get things wrong. It's even okay if investors dismiss your start-up; they'll change their minds when they see growth. The big danger is that you'll dismiss your start-up yourself."[65]

Both of these products were initially offered as just a basic prototype, the kind which might be an unconvincing model even to those in the markets that eventually became enthused. The fact that sometimes you really do have to build a product before customers come is one of the most difficult challenges at the crux of creating an innovative business. And often after you've done all the building, they still won't come, and you've got to build some more. My advice is that you aim at a target market segment and do market testing; doing so absolutely helps you to conceptualize how you should build your product and the benefits it will offer. But it's crucial to stay open-minded about whether you've targeted the right market or need to do some serious legwork to discover a different one, perhaps in another whole sector that might be interested for reasons you haven't anticipated.

You've Got to Find Your Market in Order to Be Able to Scale It

One of the many pernicious mantras about building a start-up is that you shouldn't engage in creating, marketing, or selling a product in ways that won't scale up, meaning that it wouldn't be viable at large scale, usually because it would be too time consuming or expensive. But time and again when you dig into founders' stories, you see that they did just that. Successful founders often engage in horribly arduous activities in order to get sales going. If David Friedberg from Total Weather Insurance hadn't been willing to do custom work for a first set of customers, he wouldn't have brought in the $2 million in revenue that allowed him to then raise substantial venture backing. If Schedulefly's Tyler Rullman hadn't been willing to devote many, many hours to personalized customer service, the early adopters he was able to sign up might well have drifted away. The high retention rate of customers was a vital indicator that the Schedulefly model might eventually work. If I hadn't been willing to drive four hundred miles round trip to make just one sale, I wouldn't have developed the confidence that I could make First Research work.

To quote Paul Graham again, "Do things that don't scale." And as he advises, "The most common unscalable thing founders have to do at the start is to recruit users manually. Nearly all start-ups have to."

> **Hockey Stick Principle #43: The way to scale up sales can only be discovered, not forced.**

Why Getting Sales Is Like Popping Popcorn

Here's a story I keep in mind to help stay the course when a company I'm building or backing is against the wall with the early adopter challenge. My wife and two young children and I have a regular family night for which we order pizza, play board games, or watch a movie, and—the essential ingredient to this night—make popcorn. One evening, we ran into a hitch; we'd bought a new brand of popcorn, and the kernels wouldn't pop. We use the old oil-in-a-pan stove-top method, and after my daughter and I had stared at the pot for what seemed like forever without a single pop, she said, "I think we bought a broken bag of popcorn." I wondered if popcorn kernels have an expiration date. Then, just when we were about to give up, there was a *pop!*

Finally, I thought. But then no more pops. We were about to give up again, when at last, there was another pop, followed by a rapid *pop! pop! pop!* but then nothing again. Really? That was it? Maybe it was a dud bag, after all.

Then all hell broke loose: *pop . . . pop . . . pop! pop! pop! pop! pop! pop! pop! pop! pop! pop! pop! pop! pop! pop! pop! pop! pop! pop! pop! pop!*

The erratic nature of sales and the long delays you may have between them is unnerving and can be deeply dispiriting, especially if you were convinced that sales would come fairly easily. Even when products seem to have sold themselves by riding a wave of enthusiasm and word of mouth, if you dig into the story of the launch more, you'll almost always find that a smart marketing plan and a great deal of rejection were involved.

So be prepared to try all sorts of things, some of which might seem outright crazy, and be prepared to do it for a longer period than you've been hoping for. And if you're not prepared to commit wholeheartedly to the sales effort yourself, then you must be prepared to bring in someone else who will.

Chapter 5

Fighting Your Way Off the Boards: Improving Your Model to Achieve Takeoff Growth

For some fortunate founders, once they've connected with a market, sales take off readily, and they hit their growth-inflection point shortly thereafter. But quite often, start-ups enter a phase of growth that can be especially vexing—they've got enough customers so that they can keep the lights on and pay themselves some salary and maybe even have a few employees, but they can't seem to break past that level. This is often after three or four years and at the $250,000–$750,000 revenue range. Rather than a phase of nicely continuing growth, this can turn into a period of stagnation and then often implosion. Founders can feel like they are pinned up against the boards. They're not making enough profit to invest much more in marketing, and because they're not making more revenue, they haven't been able to raise the capital to do so, either.

A typical (simplified) basic income statement for a start-up in this situation might look like this:

Revenue:	$650,000
Product Maintenance Costs:	($100,000)
Cofounder Salaries (for two founders):	($150,000)
Salaries for Staff (two employees):	($100,000)
Marketing and Sales Expenses:	($100,000)
Customer Service:	($65,000)
Travel, Office Supplies, Phone:	($45,000)
Health Insurance:	($40,000)
Rent:	($30,000)
Operating Profit:	$20,000

Maybe this seems just fine at first look, but then consider that the level of salary these two founders are able to pay themselves isn't allowing them to make substantial headway in paying off a good deal of personal debt they've taken on to start the business, so the cost of that debt keeps mounting. Meanwhile, that margin of profit could become razor-thin if a large customer switches to a competitor or if the rent is increased suddenly or the top-producing sales rep takes another job.

One of the most common mistakes made by founders in trying to get out of this limited-growth trap is to make more vigorous efforts to raise capital. Many founders throw themselves into creating a lavish pitch book and generating great financial projections, scheduling meeting after meeting with angel investors, or even trying to get venture firms to back them.

> **Hockey Stick Principle #44: Chasing investment capital is not a strategy for growth; it's a distraction from learning how to grow.**

There are three fundamental problems with devoting lots of time to fund-raising at this stage: It takes valuable time away from looking for *business* solutions to the problem; the odds of raising significant capital in this situation are not at all good; and even if you do manage to raise funds, doing so may well empower you to simply prop up a flawed model for your business for a period rather than pushing to discover a better one. Without having found a solution—or set of solutions—within your business model for achieving faster growth, often the returns from more investment in sales and marketing and even in product enhancements will not produce the increase in revenue you need.

At one entrepreneurial funding conference I attended, a panel of investors took questions from the audience, and when one founder asked what to do when you get stuck in this stage, the investors' advice was to spend lots of time with them so they can get to know your business and help you with their advice. While lots of the founders in the room seemed to like that answer, one brashly stood up and asked the panel, "Could any of you provide any advice about how founders should prevent themselves from wasting valuable time meeting with potential investors?" I felt like clapping. I've seen far too many founders spinning their wheels in the chase for funding just when they should be focusing on fixing their businesses instead.

One founder who shared his regrets with me about this is Brad McCorkle, who founded Local Eye Site, which is now quite successful. He found himself at this difficult juncture where he just couldn't get over the sales growth hump, and rather than meeting with angel investors, he met with lots of bankers, seeking to establish a $100,000 line of credit. He figured that because his results were better than breakeven, he would qualify fairly easily and pay comparatively inexpensive interest on a loan rather than have to give up any equity ownership as angel investors would demand. He also figured the process would be less time consuming. He was wrong. He met with five banks, and in the beginning, they all made bold promises, but they kept coming back with unreasonable terms or declining the loan request because he didn't have enough collateral or longevity of earnings. Brad pointed out that not only did the process take valuable time away from building the business, it was intensely stressful as he waited and waited to get word, and that cut down even more on his productivity. He was right to be stressed; he was in a danger zone that occurs in many start-ups.

Quite often by this point in the process, founders have used up most or all their savings. They may even have cashed in their 401(k) plans and taken on upward of $50,000 in personal debt. The last thing in the world they need to do is to take on more debt *until they have figured out how to generate faster growth* for their business.

Failure Is Grossly Overrated

Another unfortunate course taken by many founders at this difficult juncture is to fold things up and go back to a day job that pays a good salary. Game over.

I want to be clear that I don't think there is anything wrong, in principle, with failure in the start-up process. There's no question that sometimes things just aren't going to work out and that throwing in the towel sooner rather than later is the right choice. Launching a failed start-up can be a great learning experience that may allow you to have more success with a next venture. Indeed, most entrepreneurs I've spoken to about failed attempts at starting a business have described the experience as a step in the process of eventually achieving success. Brian Hamilton of Sageworks expressed this view when I interviewed him: "I know a fair number of entrepreneurs who have failed. Nonentrepreneurs ask them, 'Why did you fail?' or 'What did you learn from it?' Those people don't understand entrepreneurship. Entrepreneurs say, 'I tried it, and it didn't work. So what? That doesn't define me. I'm just going to try something else.'"

If you're aiming to create the next hyperfast-growth Internet phenomenon, then moving on to the next idea quickly may well be the way to go. Ben Horowitz, the founder of Opsware, a software firm that improves server and network performance, knows a thing or two about this. Not only did he sell Opsware to Hewlett-Packard for $1.6 billion, he is now a partner in venture firm Andreessen Horowitz. He says, "Ideas are like lightning in a bottle, so if the company is small enough and didn't seem to capture lightning on their first try, it makes sense to try again."[66] Indeed, *huge* ideas that have the potential to create billions of dollars in revenue are rare and difficult to come by, so if that's your goal, then maybe Horowitz is right. I totally agree that if it's the idea that makes the business, and if you're only interested in making an idea work in a really big way, then once you've determined the idea isn't going to take off, you should move rapidly on to a next effort.

Bradford Shellhammer and Jason Goldberg are two entrepreneurs who made the right judgment call when they decided to shut down their Web site business Fabulis, which was a review site and social network geared toward gay men. After they hosted an event in London to which hardly anyone showed up, they decided Fabulis was a bad idea. They shut it down and six months later launched Fab.com, an e-commerce site, completely unrelated to Fabulis, which a year later had a near $1 billion valuation.

There is no question that too many start-ups limp along as what have come to be called the "walking dead," operating almost entirely on debt financing and not making truly significant improvements either in their products or their marketing until they go into a death spiral.

That said, as I've stressed before, most successful companies become successful not so much because of the big new idea they're premised on but because the founders have engaged in a fruitful process of discovering and optimizing a good business model. And doing that usually requires a great deal of tenacity. The popular mantra out of Silicon Valley to "fail fast, fail often" is sometimes misinterpreted as suggesting that failure in the start-up world is a badge of honor, when in fact it's really about being persistent, resilient, and constantly trying new things *so you don't fail.*

> **Hockey Stick Principle #45: Do not tell yourself to be okay with failure; tell yourself to keep trying every single thing you can so that you don't have to be okay with it.**

I believe the balance has tipped too far toward being okay with failure when the emphasis should really be on working furiously not to fail. What's more, failure has not only been overrated, it's been significantly overstated. My research shows that successful entrepreneurs do absolutely everything they can think of to avoid failure. My research into the studies of failure rates also provides strong evidence that founders who don't give up on their idea when they encounter market resistance and who keep trying to build a better mouse trap succeed more than they're generally being given credit for. So my advice is to not quit on your idea until you've tried every way to make it work that you can think of—and to pay no mind to what you read or hear from pundits.

The fact is that there is nothing glamorous about failing, no matter if it is fast or slow. While many entrepreneurs show great resilience in coping with failure and great resourcefulness in learning from it, very few, if any, who have experienced a failure will tell you that it was anything but brutal. Ralph Waldo Emerson wrote, "Artists must be sacrificed to their art. Like bees, they must put their lives into the sting they give."[67] Entrepreneurs who have had a start-up implode tend to feel very much like those bees that gave their lives.

The 90 Percent Myth

An often-quoted statistic is that 90 percent of start-ups fail. I've searched and searched for proof of that, and it isn't available. Many studies of start-up failure rates have been done, though, and lots of statistics are available, all of which suggest a significantly lower failure percentage. One widely cited study was performed by Harvard Business School professor Shikhar Ghosh, which the *Harvard Business Review* described as showing that "75 percent of *all* start-ups fail" (emphasis added).[68] I tracked that study down and found that, in actuality, the 75 percent figure is of start-ups *that were backed by venture capital didn't return the amount of money invested.* That's quite a qualification. Keep in mind, only one-tenth of 1 percent of start-up firms are VC-backed. So this sample in fact represents just a sliver of "all" start-ups.

According to the United States Bureau of Labor Statistics, new firms show about a 50 percent survival rate after five years and a 33 percent survival rate after ten years.[69] According to a study conducted jointly by the Kauffman Foundation and the Bureau of Labor Statistics, 60 percent of all firms survive until age three, and 35 percent survive to age ten.[70] Techstars, an organization that provides seed funding and mentorship to start-ups, says that since its beginning in 2006, 79 percent of their 660 firms are still active, 12 percent have been acquired, and 9.6 percent have failed.[71] Another study, titled "On the Lifecycle Dynamics of Venture-Capital- and Non-Venture-Capital-Financed Firms," conducted by the National Bureau of Economic Research in conjunction with several highly regarded business schools, including Harvard, MIT, and Duke University, notes that "the cumulative failure rate of non-VC-financed firms by the end of year five is 51%, and for VC-financed firms it is only 19%."[72]

These numbers all make one thing clear: Failure is in fact common. But what seems to be the best, rough overall conclusion is that slightly less than half of new businesses succeed. That's a much better percentage than 10 percent! Hopefully with time, research will uncover more and more refined insights about the causes of start-up success and failure. A key set of factors that needs much more attention in a systematic way: what the nature of the founder's commitment was; what his or her goals for the company were; and how persistent, open-minded, and creative founders were in searching for breakout success. From my experience observing and interviewing so many founders, I expect that many of the failures in these studies were of start-ups that were really "hobby businesses," which a founder launches out of a special interest of some kind and runs for some years but then loses interest in and decides not to keep at it. I expect many others were founded on ideas that weren't strong enough to have reached this "up against the boards" stage of significant but not breakout revenue. If you looked at their income statements, many of them would have been operating at a loss all along. For founders who have been able to generate significant revenue at costs that are manageable, I strongly advise that rather than "fail fast, fail often" as a mantra, they embrace the mantra of the *Apollo 13* mission control commander Gene Kranz that "failure is not an option."

Does that mean hanging on even after you have no more ideas about how to improve the business? No. But it does mean holding on as tightly as you can for as long as you can and, most importantly, being extremely rigorous and open-minded about coming up with ideas for improvement.

Ramen Profitability

A great way to think about the challenge of this stage before you've achieved growth takeoff is that it's a stretch of time of what's been dubbed "ramen profitability" referring to the point when a start-up is earning just enough income to pay its founder the bare minimum to live on—enough to afford inexpensive ramen noodles. Rather than attempting to grow primarily by spending more, you want to be doing all you can to contain your expenses in this stage—though maybe not by literally eating nothing but ramen noodles—until you identify a set of repeatable processes that will greatly increase your profitability. Once you identify them, it's time to spend some money in order to boost growth. As we'll explore more in chapter 6, scaling up must be done on the firm basis of repeatable processes that bring you reliable and profitable returns for the additional cash you're pouring into the business.

> **Hockey Stick Principle #46: Scaling up operations isn't real growth until you've proven you can scale profitably.**

I love the point Y Combinator's Paul Graham makes about this ramen profitability point. Rather than feeling like you're stuck, you should feel good that you've achieved something so difficult and that you are now in a position of strength, with time to keep working on perfecting your model. He writes:

> If you're already profitable, on however small a scale, it shows that (a) you can get at least someone to pay you, (b) you're serious about building things people want, and (c) you're disciplined enough to keep expenses low. This is reassuring to investors. . . . Another advantage of ramen profitability is that it's good for morale. . . . Now survival is the default, instead of dying.[73]

After all, in hockey, you usually get crushed up against the boards because you're in a position to make a good play.

Discover Your Strengths

As popularized by a number of bestselling books on career advice for individuals, sometimes success comes from focusing primarily on doing a whole lot more of the things you're especially good at.

The right thing to do in the blade years is to rigorously scrutinize all aspects of your business model, make a close analysis of what's working and what's not, and then step up the energy you put into the things that are working—exploring how you could make them even better—while also experimenting with tweaks to the things that aren't working. In the last chapter, the focus was on trying many things in order to identify a market, and in both the cases of Sageworks and The Climate Corporation, doing so involved paying attention to a relative glimmer of potential success: one sale to a CPA for the former and the realization that farmers might be an especially good market for the latter. If you're not investigating your results extremely closely, you may well overlook such clues about a route to better growth.

What you should be looking for are signs of potential for drilling into *highly profitable repeatable actions,* or repeatable actions that would become highly profitable at a larger scale. Maybe one of these actions is cold calls in which you make a limited-time offer. Another might be sending out e-mails to customers who subscribed to a basic level of service that incentivize them to upgrade to a higher level of service. Ideally, you're making at least a small profit from each action or from a good ratio of them—say, one out of every ten cold calls. But it does sometimes make good sense to step up such actions even if they won't be providing a good margin at first *if* that period of low returns is a bridge to higher returns. One famous example of this is AT&T Wireless's 2007 deal with Apple, in which it subsidized the cost of an iPhone for customers in exchange for a two-year monthly wireless contract. AT&T lost money in the short run in the hopes of landing millions of happy customers for many years to come, and the strategy worked well.[74]

Another example is the case of Sageworks. Once Brian Hamilton had confirmed the notion that CPAs might be a fertile market by having one of his reps focus on them, he created a sales operation dedicated entirely to drilling into the CPA market. He had hired five sales reps, and he tasked them all with cold-calling CPAs all day every day. Even with a clear market and evidence that the product had significant value for it, the going was tough. The conversion rate on calls was low. For every one hundred calls or so, they'd actually get through to about four people, and one of those would request a demo. But on the positive side, for every two or three firms that took a demo, one would sign up, which is a great conversion rate.

Kevin Gold, a specialist in market development at social media firm iNET Interactive, says that conversion rates for lead-generation campaigns "fluctuate drastically," but he estimates that rates of 8–20 percent are the norm.[75] Sageworks was clearly at the high end of that spectrum. So Brian decided to keep at it, and the effort became like a well-honed manufacturing process. "You could line them up," Brian recalls, "and predict that one out of one hundred leads we called would close."

Still, with five sales reps on the case and an average subscription fee of $1,000 per firm, each rep only brought in about $100,000 worth of subscriptions that year. Many founders would be discouraged by that revenue-to-overhead ratio and likely give up. Indeed, if they continued with that rate of customer acquisition to earnings, the company would be a bust. Here is where Brian's choice of sales model—which provided hands-on customer support and training—proved its worth. With a subscription model, one of the great positives is renewals, which are generally very low cost to service. Most of the CPAs who signed on paid to renew, and in the next year, all those subscriptions were highly profitable because the updating of the financial data was partially automated. As Brian says, "If we were a traditional software company, and we had to start the dial every year from zero, we never would have made it. Never. Never." So in this case, accepting a low return on ramping up the repeatable process was a great bridge to the high profitability needed for takeoff.

That year, 2003, revenues rose to $700,000 and then to over $1.6 million in 2004, and Sageworks was off and running.

To achieve your own breakthrough, you must carefully examine whether or not your pattern of sales, your customer feedback about a particular feature or benefit, or measurable key performance indicators (KPIs) offer you evidence that you might be able to crank up your business by focusing more on some key service, product, or marketing or sales tactic. Maybe you should limit your offerings to only one of a number of products you've been selling, or maybe you should focus on only one group of buyers who tend to purchase more instead of targeting several groups.

Hockey Stick Principle #47: Learn from what's working and lean into it.

Pivoting Is Not for Pivot's Sake

So much has been said about the need to make a "pivot" in order to arrive at a successful model, which might involve a change to a whole different product or substantially redesigning the product for a different use or market. It might involve a change as large as deciding that rather than selling a smartwatch, you're going to sell a smart home thermometer that uses much of the same technology. Or it might be that rather than a home thermometer, you end up selling temperature-control systems for industries. Sometimes a substantial pivot is crucial, which I'll further discuss later. Other times, though, growth takeoff comes not from an actual pivot regarding what your product, service, or model is but from more moderate tweaks to your offerings.

In building First Research, for example, we realized that we should tweak our industry profiles to highlight a section called "Questions to Consider." I had put the section in as an add-on, just a handy analytical shorthand for users. Ingo and I didn't think the section was an especially important part of the reports, and we certainly didn't think it would be the key to our success. But after the first year of sales, by taking a close look at anecdotal customer feedback from conversations, we discovered that early adopters gravitated to the section more than anything else. When we asked them about what they liked so much about it, they stressed that it saved them time, enabling them to get the information they needed fast because we offered short summaries below each question that explained why that question was relevant. If the users were in a rush (which they often were), they didn't feel they had to read the entire report; they could just go straight to the "Questions to Consider" section.

So we started focusing our energy on this feature, making it better by writing more questions and improving its organization, and we renamed it "Call Prep Questions"—a tweak to make the section stand out more to users. The fact that so many users loved how we presented this information taught us that our strongest value proposition was not in offering more and more information, but in how rapidly it could be digested. So it was a great discovery in two ways. For our part, focusing on these questions also made the writing of our reports a more efficient, repeatable action, and so our process became more focused and efficient at the same time that users became happier with what we were offering. Our sales started to take off.

Augment Your Offerings (and Prune)

Another path from ramen profitability to breakout growth is by continually enhancing your product and services until you have reached a critical mass of offerings that tips you over a threshold to a fast-growth rate of customer response. Much has been written about the pitfall of "feature creep" in developing products, in which more and more whiz-bang features are added that the customer hasn't asked for and doesn't actually want. One example is the customer relationship management (CRM) solution Salesforce.com. It's a terrific company that in the beginning set out to make CRM less complex, but it keeps adding features that make it difficult for the average small business owner to use without getting expert advice. This is to be avoided. However, adding features and more service offerings *that customers are saying they want* can be exactly the way to arrive at your breakout formula.

> **Hockey Stick Principle #48: Continually add features and services customers tell you they want, and ruthlessly jettison those that most don't respond to.**

Kent Hudson's Dude Solutions is an example of how a start-up should listen carefully to customers and continually augment its features to align more with their desires. The company started out selling its most basic, relatively inexpensive software to small school systems because they had less complex needs. All the while, he was calling on large school systems for many years—being rejected each year. "We called it the annual 'I love you, but . . . party,'" Kent recalls. "They would call and say, 'We really want to look at your software because we hear great things.' So we'd show it to them, and they'd say, 'Oh, this is so good. Oh, this is so much easier to use than what we have. Oh, man, we love these features. Oh, this works. Oh, gosh, this is beautiful, *but* we need blah-blah-blah.'"

At the time, Dude Solutions couldn't quite make the sale because it lacked several features big districts desired, such as sophisticated systems for managing inventory of maintenance supplies like lightbulbs and cleaning products. They would add a feature and try again the next year and hear the same exact story. But finally, seven years later, the bigger school districts finally started to buy.

"You've just got to climb that ladder one rung at a time. You can always sell someone slightly bigger. Every now and then, you get a breakthrough where someone is more of an early adopter."

Another method of augmentation is to add entirely new products or services to your repertoire. A good case of this is the way the founder of Lattice Engines achieved breakout success. In 2006, Ph.D. data scientist and consultant Shashi Upadhyay started the company with what he describes as "a vague idea to bring science-based techniques to sales and marketing to improve performance." Eventually, he found his way to creating the company's successful product, salesPRISM software, which enables salespeople to access valuable data about their potential customers all in one place. Staples, DocuSign, and EMC are a few of Lattice Engine's customers.

Shashi's first product attempt was a set of dashboards that offered intelligence on sales performance and product management. He found no takers for it. His second product attempt used mathematical models that took into account the territory size, market opportunity, and other metrics to figure out individual sales quotas. Enough customers purchased this one that the company reached ramen profitability, which allowed him to learn that there was a third product that might generate much better sales. "While we were [marketing the sales quota product]," he recounts, "we realized people were less interested in quota problems and that what they were really looking for was a recommendation engine that would help salespeople make better targeting decisions and have better conversations with their customers."

Lattice Engines released this third product in 2009, three years after launch, and that became its flagship offering.

A key to Shashi's success with adding the new product was that he also did away with the old. In his case, he decided to stop offering the sales quota analysis product even before he launched the recommendation engine. As he recalls, "What was hard was that we had an ongoing business, but we chose to shut it down and go after a bigger prize." This is the solution to the problem of feature creep, or the related hazard of becoming overextended with too many product lines, which can not only overstretch your attention and resources but cause customer confusion about just what your business is.

"Killing your babies," as this is sometimes called, can be very difficult, especially if a product or feature played a big role in your initial success, as was true for Shashi, who says, "That was a very hard decision and gave us a lot of sleepless nights." This is not only due to your attachment to these creations but also to the fear that some customers who love them will be annoyed. Doing a good job of pruning requires as much open-mindedness and rigor of analysis as adding features and products does. Even when some customers still want the offering, and even if some of them are quite vocal about that, you have to be tough-minded about where you're taking the business. As Shashi looks back on his choice, he says, "Five years later, it's probably the best decision we ever made."

A notorious case of killing off a product that was still beloved by some is that of Apple's decision to discontinue the OS 9 operating system, which many Web developers were deeply fond of, to replace it with the OS X system. Steve Jobs was well aware of how unpopular the move would be with some, so in making the announcement, he staged a faux funeral for OS 9, even bringing a coffin onto the stage. Jobs was a great role model for founders in the way that he killed off features that were preventing his product from being relevant to a wider audience. Apple has been very rigorous in constantly weeding out products so that it can put its energies most effectively into developing and marketing those that are most successful.

Pivots Big and Small

Sometimes, a pivot absolutely is the right course to take for your business, but this doesn't mean that the change you make has to be radical, has to involve your entire model, or that there is just one big pivot you have to make. Most pivots involve only a part of your model, and successfully pivoting usually involves two, three, or more such changes.

> **Hockey Stick Principle #49: When pivoting, it's best to start small.**

Take the case of Boardroom Insiders, which offers profiles of corporate executives and provides hard-to-find information about them and their management histories. Large enterprise sales organizations, such as IBM, Cisco, Citrix, and Microsoft, now pay substantial annual subscription fees to access these executive profiles. But when the founders, Sharon Gillenwater and Lee Demby, launched the service, they sold individual reports on the Internet on a per-report basis (pay-by-the-drink sales model) and soon realized they didn't have enough executive profiles to satisfy many of their prospective customers. So they invested time and more money into building up their profile base. After two years, though, they were still toiling along earning a paltry living, so they decided to start changing their model. The first move was away from their pay-by-drink sales model. They dedicated more energy to selling unlimited-use annual subscriptions. They also decided to offer the option of prepaying for a set number of "custom" executive profiles, prepared specifically in response to a customer's request. These new offerings helped to build some sales traction, but it turned out that the writing of the custom profiles was not cost effective, and on top of that, many companies didn't like having to determine how much they should be willing to pay up front before they knew exactly what profiles they wanted. What if it turned out they wanted to order more profiles than they had paid for, because their search for someone to hire was more difficult than expected? They'd have to ask for more money than was budgeted, which is never looked on well by corporations. With this model in place, Boardroom Insiders continued to limp along.

Then Lee and Sharon decided to take on some price risk in exchange for much higher licensing fees and started to offer custom reports to subscribers only but at no additional cost. They thought they might be able to meet that demand at a reasonable expense. When they started telling prospective customers, "If we don't have a report you need, let us know who you want, and we'll make it happen," the business suddenly took off.

You might be thinking that those are really just tweaks to their model. What's the dividing line between a tweak and a pivot? That's more a matter of judgment than of hard definition. The important point about the distinction is that it's probably best to start with tweaks—and only after these fail to do the trick should you try to make a bigger pivot. What does such a pivot look like? Two were mentioned earlier, but consider three more cases of substantial pivots that we've covered in prior chapters: The choice made by Red Hat to market to mainstream customers of commercial software rather than just to Linux users; the decision by Packrite to switch its emphasis from making deals with the manufacturers of goods for their specialty boxes to making deals with their prime competitors, the larger box makers; and the decision of the founders of The Climate Corporation to become an insurance company rather than selling derivatives so that they could target farmers. All of these involved fundamentally rethinking a major element of the business model.

Famous cases of other major pivots are Google's decision to start selling advertisements, which the founders had been strongly opposed to, and

Netflix's controversial decision to switch from a per-rental fee basis to a subscription model.

It's best to start with smaller changes for two key reasons. One is that by taking more radical steps, you may well pivot away from a model that could actually be made to work very well. The other reason is that making a big pivot can be very high risk and costly. The choice by the founders of The Climate Corporation is a great case in point. They had to invest a great deal of time and considerable costs in learning about the insurance business and becoming certified to offer insurance. The change worked well for them largely because they had become familiar enough with their new target customers by selling their first product for some time.

But pivoting can sometimes also lead to disaster. A real train wreck case is Fab.com's story of pivoting.

Recall that Bradford Shellhammer and Jason Goldberg shut down their start-up Web site business Fabulis to pivot and start e-commerce site Fab.com, selling carefully selected items from high-end designers all around the world, such as a chandelier made of martini glasses or a rhinestone-covered motorcycle helmet. Fab.com launched in June 2011. Key to their model was that they would be a platform for those third-party producers to sell through and that they would be a flash sales site, like the very successful Gilt and Rue La La. This model allowed them to sidestep the headaches and risks of inventory control. They wouldn't have to buy items up front, and they wouldn't have to pay for warehousing. The producers would determine how many items could be offered for sale, and they would ship them directly to the buyers. Bradford and Jason did a great job of marketing and reeled in 45,000 prelaunch signups for membership, and within just a few weeks of launch, the site had 250,000 members.

With booming sales and membership, a couple of months later, the company raised $7.7 million in a Series A round, and by the end of its first year, it had raised another $40 million in venture money from Andreessen Horowitz. All was looking good, right? Well, no. The founders made a number of unfortunate decisions thereafter, some of which we'll discuss in the next chapter on managing fast growth. The one that's relevant here is that they pivoted away from their flash sales, a model that didn't require them to hold inventory. A key issue with the sales fulfillment by the third-party producers was that it resulted in waits of up to a couple of weeks for goods to arrive, which had led to some customer complaints. They decided to begin holding inventory in their own warehouse, and they invested a great deal of money into building one.

Before long, they found themselves holding large volumes of unsold items. Rapid overexpansion led to many other problems, but this core pivot away from their successful model was one key to their equally rapid demise. Trying to grow their way out of the problem, Fab.com took on more and more staff and offered more and more items for sale. By October 2013, the company had to slash two-thirds of its staff, and Goldberg wrote in a memo announcing the dire straits the firm was in that "we spent $200 million and we have not proven out our business model. We spent $200 million and we have not proven that we know precisely what our customers want to buy." Nothing they tried could get them back on course, and in March 2015, having once been valued at $900 million, Fab.com was sold to design and manufacturing firm PCH Innovators for a reported $15–$50 million.[76]

More incremental tweaks to the model might have produced a very different, more favorable result.

Jason Goldberg learned from the debacle and started a new firm, HEM, which sells high-end specialty furniture, cutting out the middleman retailer, which allows it to offer items at favorable prices and still make a good margin. He's scaling it up much more strategically.

All of the emphasis on pivoting should not lead to the notion that there is some genie in a bottle that is the true business you should be pursuing instead of the one you've planned on, almost as though the whole reason to launch a start-up is to discover a pivot to make. You must be extremely strategic in making any changes to your model, big or small.

Investigate Your Entire Business Model

To decide about which tweaks, augmentations, prunings, or pivots to try, it's best to go back to the key set of questions you answered to formulate your model in chapter 1 and to systematically consider all tweaks and more substantial changes you could make to each of the answers you came up with. You want to rigorously challenge not only your original assumptions but also findings from market and customer research.

> **Hockey Stick Principle #50: Don't work on fixing only the part of the model you think is broken; think of improvements even for the parts you think you've got right.**

The purpose of this exercise is to take a step back from the rush of daily demands, which pretty much always has founders in the weeds, and to fundamentally rethink all aspects of the business.

So, say that you're someone like Bob Young and you're trying to get Red Hat to take off. Perhaps your initial set of answers to the set of questions in chapter 1 were as follows:

- **Who will your customers be?**
  High-level programmers who are using Linux.
- **What benefits will your product or service offer them?**
  Providing a version of the operating system that's easier to use and programming improvements that make Linux more beneficial.
- **What competitors will you have, and what extra value are you offering customers over and above your competitors?**
  Other small firms offer enhanced Linux versions, but they're not substantial challengers; there is plenty of room to corner the market. We're offering users a Web site platform for sharing experiences and tips directly.
- **What processes will creating and then continuing to run the business involve?**
  Programming more and more improvements to the software; creating a good enough value proposition that customers are willing to pay for an improved version of software that's free, largely through making the Red Hat Web site a vibrant enough community of users.
- **What financial, physical, and human resources will you need to run the business?**
  Programmers, marketing professionals, sales reps, and financial professionals.
- **How will you sell and deliver your product, and at a price—or prices—that generate a good profit?**
  Because Linux is free and is always being improved by the open-source programming community for free, we can make our improvements at a relatively low cost and charge a low price, which will convince our target users that purchasing our version is preferable to making their own improvements.
- **How will you market your product and build customer relationships and loyalty?**

We'll focus on building a community of users through our Web site, providing support and the opportunity for users to discuss Linux issues directly with one another.

If you were Bob Young and you went through the exercise of revisiting each of these answers in light of market feedback you were getting as you failed to make appreciable sales, you'd have to admit that your assumption that the Linux enthusiast market you'd targeted just wasn't convinced that it should pay even your relatively low price. The exercise would also force you to rethink who your customers were. A key question that you would be led to would be, are there any other customers besides the high-end programming crowd that like Linux that we can go after? That question would make you reconsider the potential of the much larger market of those buying Microsoft, Oracle, and Apple software. So if you now include this larger market segment in your customer base, you're contending with a set of much more serious competitors. The downside of that is that they're behemoth companies with incredible firepower. The upside is that this customer segment is so much bigger and that in trying to chip away at this massive pool of buyers, your key competitive advantage—lower cost— might be more compelling. This market might be more price sensitive. But if you're going after mainstream corporate buyers, you're also going to have to rethink the benefits to customers the model was premised on. For example, you're probably going to have to offer them the same kind of support that Microsoft, Oracle, and Apple offer.

This process has put you on the path to discovering, as Bob Young did in his own way, how to restructure the Red Hat model and tweak its offerings. In arriving at the notion that maybe you could go after the larger, mainstream market, you would be led to do some market research with potential customers, as Bob Young did, and that would lead to the realization that you probably really could get some of these customers as long as you provided the documentation and support that corporations need.

Forcing yourself to rethink every answer breaks down the assumptions you previously made. It also allows you to consider the cascade of changes you may have to make, rather than thinking about only one or another, randomly.

Take another example. Say that Brian Hamilton had decided to offer the Sageworks program as software to be purchased and installed by companies rather than on a subscription basis. When he discovered that CPAs were a good potential market and he started cranking up sales to them, he would have found himself in a quandary. The hit rate his sales machine was getting wouldn't have been profitable if he continued selling the program outright. Recall that it only became profitable once he started getting subscription renewals. When he discovered that the number of cold calls to sales was so low and that he'd never be able make that sales model work, if he really critically scrutinized his whole model anew and went back through each key question and really challenged his answers, the exercise would force him to rethink how he was selling the product; considering sales of subscriptions would be the main alternative for sales of software. That would allow him to lower his price, which might be a big incentive to potential early adopters, and it would also lead to the realization that a stronger customer relationship management service would be important, which is a key of the subscription software model. Strong customer service, has, in fact, been a hallmark of Sageworks's success. He would also identify another core repeatable action that, if he could figure out how to make it work, would be highly profitable and would make the whole business viable: the relatively low-cost process of securing customer renewals.

Open-mindedness and creativity in this analysis are vital. You want to free your mind of all your prior expectations and analysis and genuinely consider new ideas, even if they directly contradict your prior assumptions. Taking a hard, systematic look at how you will make, market, and sell your product—and to whom—allows you to see in a fresh way the evidence you may have been accumulating thus far. It helps you to step back and see your total operation with fresh eyes and formulate new hypotheses to test.

Expect Multiple Tweaks and Pivots

Don't expect to arrive at all the answers you need in one sitting. The process of interrogating your model this way and trying out tweaks and pivots is one step in the continuous buildup of insights and testing of ideas that you will make until you reach a breakthrough.

In the Hockey Stick Research Study, I asked each successful founder to rate on a scale of one to ten how similar their business is today to what they had predicted it would be when first starting, with one being exactly as they'd planned and ten being nothing at all as they'd planned. The average response was 3.7. The lowest response was 1, and the highest was 8.

Here are a few of their responses:

- **Jay Faison, SnapAV** (Distributes audiovisual parts): "The products are a bit different [from those in our original plan]. We didn't expect to be in the networking business or the surveillance business or the HDMI distribution business or the video distribution business. [But today we are.] We didn't see those things. The product world changes, and we've changed [with] it, so that's been different, but our underlying strategy has not."
- **Dinesh Wadhwani, ThinkLite** (Manufactures LED light upgrades that fit into traditional fixtures): "The concept of what I imagined is spot on with [what turned out.] The whole vision was to have any lightbulb that could fit into any fixture and be able to customize it. The concept of what was needed was always the same, but of course the actual product changed a lot."
- **Michael Drummond, Packrite** (Manufactures specialty boxes for retailers): "When we first started out, we believed we'd be selling 50 percent of our work [directly to manufacturers] and 50 percent of our work through the trade. But during the first year, we found out that wasn't going to work; we were going to have to work exclusively through the trade."
- **Neil Gloger, InterGroup** (Reprocesses and sells postindustrial plastics): "One major [difference] was deciding to focus only on two or three different market segments."
- **Henry Schuck, DiscoverOrg** (Sales and marketing prospect database): "We met with a sales chain company who told us, 'One of the most important things we need and that we don't see out there are direct-dial phone numbers.' And so we realized our customers want this, and this [would be] a clear differentiator for us. It was an expensive investment and a shift in focus. But it was really successful and that [change] actually opened a lot of doors."

I also asked founders how many pivots (or, as I said, major changes) they made to the business in their first three years. The average response was 1.8. The greatest number was 4 pivots, and the smallest was 0, which was the answer of only one founder, Ranjith Kumaran of YouSendIt, which enables individuals to send large files via e-mail. He elaborated, "In retrospect, it was a pretty linear journey. In the first three to five years, we did one thing, and we wanted to be the best at it."

That underscores a key takeaway for this chapter—when you're running into a wall in generating sales, you should quickly pivot, but be careful that you don't pivot away from a big success. Instead, systematically work through these three stages to make the model work:

1. Drill into what's working, and stop doing what's not.
2. Make incremental tweaks to augment and improve your product and model.
3. And if those efforts fail, carefully investigate your entire model and make a substantial pivot or set of pivots.

The Growth-Inflection Point

Chapter 6

Go, Go, Go!: Ramping Up Your Newly Discovered Model

The definition of the growth-inflection stage is that your revenue begins to surge because you have found repeatable actions that reliably result in sales. This is, of course, never really an exact point in time as it appears on a hockey stick graph; it's usually a matter of many months of strong uptick.

When you have honed your model and you hit the growth-inflection point, the excitement you feel from the burst of positive customer response is like the state of play that sports psychologists call being in the zone. Your formation is in sync, and you're finally making a good percentage of goals in relation to shots taken.

Or, to depart from the hockey metaphor for a bit, you feel like you at last have liftoff. The revenue growth you experience is like the phase of a rocket's launch after it's shucked its boosters and is bursting straight up to orbit. When iContact hit growth inflection in 2005, its revenue spiked to $1.3 million from $296,000 in 2004. For LendingTree, the spike was from $476,000 in 1998 to $8.0 million in 1999. Facebook's spike was from $394,000 in 2004 to $9.0 million in 2005. For Google, it was from $294,000 in 1999 to $21.5 million in 2000.

A start-up in this stage has the new power of momentum, and this period of sales takeoff can be outright exhilarating. Good things start happening without you and your team having to work so hard for them. Prospects start calling due to word of mouth; you close sales much faster and with less hardball pitching; product enhancements are easier to plan and execute because you've got so much more customer feedback and more cash to put into them; employees are easier to recruit because they are more confident in your future; potential partners are starting to return phone calls. It's like you've built up kinetic energy, the energy an object has because it's in motion. Once you have this liftoff, you really feel the power.

Ryan Allis of iContact beautifully described how empowering this stage of growth is: "You need all the same processes to get to fifty thousand in monthly revenue that you needed to get to ten thousand. But when you're at zero, you have nothing; when you're at ten thousand, you got a heck of a lot that you can take advantage of to get to fifty thousand." I can't resist also quoting one of my entrepreneurial heroes, Ben Franklin, on this point who wrote this about his printing and newspaper business: "My business was now continually augmenting, and my circumstances growing daily easier, my newspaper having become very profitable. . . . I experienced, too, the truth of the observation, 'that after getting the first hundred pound, it is more easy to get the second.'"[77]

> **Hockey Stick Principle #51: Don't spend lots of money to fuel fast growth until you're pouring it into a high-performance engine.**

This is a critical time in which to apply the wisdom of the physics of motion. When the speed of an object is accelerating, it's comparatively easy to further accelerate it, and that's just what you want to do. This is the *only* way in which you want to significantly scale up your operations—on the basis of a model that has proven it works and when it's clear to you *why* it works. Otherwise, you are pouring more and more fuel into a machine that can't sustain liftoff.

The Pitfall of Premature Scaling

Knowing when and how to scale is one of the trickiest issues for founders to manage, and much research has shown that scaling up too early is, if not the single-biggest mistake founders make, certainly one of the top few. The Startup Genome Project study of 3,200 high-growth start-ups in the technology sector, which was conducted by a group of researchers from the University of California–Berkeley and Stanford University, including Steven Blank, determined that "74% of high growth internet startups fail due to premature scaling," making it the number-one reason for failure.

One of the most intriguing findings in the report they issued about the scaling problem is that "startups that scale properly grow about 20 times faster than startups that scale prematurely." What's so remarkable about this is that so many founders scale up too early precisely because they're trying to spur faster growth.

So what exactly is premature scaling? And how do you know if you're doing it? The Startup Genome group defines it as start-ups "focusing on one dimension in their operation and advancing it out of sync with the rest of their operation." More specifically, the report identified three key mistakes: Founders decide to put too much money too early into growing "their team, their customer acquisition strategies," or they "over build the product."[78] The only thing I'd add to that is that sometimes they do two or all three of these things at the same time.

The classic horror story of premature scaling is that of Webvan, which aimed to be the FreshDirect of its day. It opened for business in the San Francisco Bay area in 1999, quickly raised almost $400 million in capital, and went into high gear with a plan to expand to twenty-six cities, most notoriously signing a $1 billion contract to build a number of highly sophisticated warehouses, all before it had worked out many kinks in its operations. The company declared bankruptcy in 2001.

A more recent case is that of Monitor110, which was a New York City–based start-up that provided deeply researched information for investment bankers. The idea for the company was a good one, and it raised $16 million in two financing rounds. But the start-up quickly ran out of money and closed down in 2008. One of its investors and board members, Roger Ehrenberg, wrote in a postmortem about what went wrong:

> Too much money is like too much time; work expands to fill the time allotted, and ways to spend money multiply when abundant financial resources are available. By being simply too good at raising money, it *enabled us to perpetuate poor organizational structure and suboptimal strategic decisions. . . .* We weren't forced early on to be scrappy and revenue focused. We wanted to build something that was so good from the get-go that the market would simply eat it up. Problem was, with all that money we hid from the market while we were building, almost ensuring that we would come up with something that the market wouldn't accept.

While in the blade years, following Paul Graham's sage advice that sometimes it's necessary in the early building period to do things that don't scale is a great best practice. However, it is crucial not to misunderstand this as a justification for scaling up a model that doesn't have true momentum. Doing things that don't scale is all about giving you more time to keep crafting a good working model that *will* scale up well, which you must achieve before you begin pushing for scale, such as by pouring more money into marketing or expanding your operations by hiring more staff. Scaling up in those ways before you've fixed your model is not a way to fix your business; it's a temporary crutch, and before long, it won't keep your business propped up.

This doesn't mean that you don't sometimes have to make investments well ahead of getting the returns from them. For example, when I hired my first salesperson at First Research, I had to start paying his salary well in advance of getting the revenue I hoped and expected he would bring in, which was one of the hardest decisions I made, because at that time, in the spring of 2000, I was still making very little revenue. But during the course of 1999 and early 2000, I had spent a great deal of time experimenting with selling subscriptions by various methods and to various markets, and I was beginning to reliably land sales with a combination of banks, CPA firms, and consultants. I had refined my selling process. I had learned to run successful free trials, figured out the best way to find warm leads, who the right people to call were, and how to convert a good percentage to customers. I had figured out my repeatable actions and honed a good machine. That's why I decided it was time to make the move, and I brought in Wil Brawley, the ace salesman who was later hired by Schedulefly to grow their market.

Wil needed some time to build up the pipeline, which is important to account for as you scale your sales operation—growing sales generally requires a significant lag time. By mid-2000, my sales were picking up as I had expected, and we earned $227,000 in revenue that year. For the first time, I paid myself some salary, though just $11,200, and I paid off the roughly $30,000 I'd borrowed to get started. I didn't then hire a big force of salespeople and try to move into overdrive. I hired one more salesperson, plundering Bank of America where I had worked from 1993 to 1999 to bring over Lee Demby, a sales guy I knew was good and would make a good fit for us from my days working in sales at the bank. I also personally kept selling, and selling with Wil and Lee in 2001 was for me the best of times for First Research.

As Wil recalls fondly, "Each prospective customer was like a new game of chess. Some of them left the king, the decision-maker, exposed relatively quickly. But most made you work hard to get to that king. I knew we'd win every single game if we stuck with it long enough. People saw it in our eyes and heard it in our voices. We sold a great new product with fire, passion, energy, enthusiasm, confidence, love, and honesty. We were genuine. Our product was unique." I knew that we now had a scalable model for just these reasons; we knew where we were aiming, and we were scoring much more often. We were working hard to make sales, yes, but they were coming in reliably. In 2001, we earned $726,000 in revenue, and I paid myself a salary of $74,700, and in 2002 we nearly doubled our revenue, broke the $1.5 million barrier, and were in growth inflection.

But I continued to scale up incrementally. I brought in more sales-people in carefully measured steps that coordinated with our increases in sales, and I made sure that they all understood and could execute on what I came to call the "Wil and Lee method." That was the linchpin of our success; we drilled into the Wil and Lee sales method by training people in it well and steadily adding more of them.

> **Hockey Stick Principle #52: Scale up only in step with the success you are already generating; don't try to force the machine.**

Big Bangs Can Lead to Big Busts

The growth-inflection stage may seem "all good," but the challenging decisions you have to make about ramping up in this period can all too readily lead you to crash and burn.

One big pitfall is that the surge in growth you're seeing may be a fluke. Strong upticks in sales can be another kind of false-positive. The lift turns out to be a one-off occurrence, or it may be premised on market and sales pitches that are too good to be true and therefore are not repeatable.

A striking example of this is the meteoric growth and spectacular crash of Amp'd Mobile. For a time, mobile virtual network operators—which offered cell phone service plus content, such as streaming videos—seemed like the big new thing in mobile, and in 2006, Amp'd was hot. It targeted a particularly desirable niche, the high-use eighteen- to thirty-five-year-old market, and attracted $360 million in investor funding, including backing from MTV. That year, Amp'd had 100,000 customers, and with all of that newfound investment money, they poured fuel on their fire, running a series of ads on MTV starting that November and continuing for several months. The effort seemed a fantastic success; they soon had 175,000 customers. That sure looked like classic hockey stick growth. The problem was that huge numbers of those new customers never paid their bills. By June of 2007, the company filed for Chapter 10 bankruptcy and reportedly had just $9,000 left in its coffers.[79]

Until you've seen strong growth for at least several months and you can identify whether or not the fix or fixes you've made to your model are working well and exactly why they have helped you grow, it's premature to conclude you've truly taken off.

The popular mantra to "go big fast" can lead founders into all sorts of traps in this stage. One of the great ironies of start-ups reaching the inflection point is that faster growth can have revenge effects, meaning that it can lead you to believe certain new investments are required in order to sustain it or to take it to a whole new level, and those outlays can come back to bite you, sometimes badly.

Veering from the Game Plan

In chapter 5, we discussed how pivoting and tweaking are important elements of success during the blade years. It's true that the blade years are a time of trial and error and open-mindedness. But as a start-up is beginning to experience success and hitting its growth-inflection point, a common mistake made is that rather than drilling even more into what's working, founders instead make a change or set of changes that actually violate their model. At this juncture, you should still go with what's working well and build upon that. Of course, that doesn't mean you should never pivot or tweak after the growth-inflection point, but do so without sacrificing what's working well for your business.

> **Hockey Stick Principle #53: Once you've achieved takeoff, focus on accelerating with what's working; now is the time to scale up, not to keep making changes.**

In the case of Amp'd, the founders decided to relax strict credit requirements for new customers, the result being that rather than drilling deeper into their successful customer base, they extended into the high-risk sector, which was a violation of their model. In hindsight, this seems an obviously crazy thing to have done. But in the heat of the takeoff moment, founders make such ill-conceived decisions all the time. Sometimes, they make many of them.

Go back to the case of Fab.com. Recall that the founders decided that in order to continue growing, they needed to begin building up inventory of items for sale so that they could offer faster delivery. To do that, they determined that they should build their own warehouse, one of the highest ticket expenses for a company to take on. They also assigned themselves one of the hardest of all business feats to pull off when they took on the burden of estimating in advance what customer demand would be for items. But there was more. They decided to expand into Europe, which proved a fiercely competitive market. Perhaps most problematic, though, was that they veered off the path of offering truly distinctive, beautifully designed items, broadening their offerings so wide, that, as an *Inc.* article highlighted, "the company had strayed so far from its commitment to design that it had begun selling steaks."

To his credit, cofounder Jason Goldberg wrote a blog post about a number of lessons he learned from these mistakes, and he sums up well by saying, "We had started to dream in billions when we should have been focused on making one day simply better than the one before it."[80]

Operating at a Loss Is Overrated

One of the biggest factors for founders to consider when they are deciding which is the best course to take after they've reached takeoff is whether or not the surge in earnings is accompanied by a surge in profits. Sometimes you've crafted a model that begins to pump out more and more profits for only a marginal increase in expenses. But just as sometimes in order to get your sales to take off you've got to invest in efforts that aren't profitable in the shorter term, sometimes once you've hit sales takeoff, you face a similar challenge. In order to sustain growth, further investment in no- or low-profit growth may be required.

> **Hockey Stick Principle #54: Losing money on sales is not a growth strategy.**

If you do need to operate at low or no profitability for a time, you must have a strategic plan for growing out of that situation and into good profitability by a predictable time. If you can't see the way forward to making good profits, it's imperative that you seriously dive back into examining your model and come up with an answer for how you'll do so.

The notion that it's okay for start-ups to spend more on growth than they're earning has gained popularity due to some famous cases of companies that have taken a low- or no-profit approach to growing, such as Amazon. The company has poured its revenues back into investments aimed at gaining additional market share and launching new products and services to further fuel growth, and in order to fund these investments in growth, it has not shown profits on its annual statements. But Amazon can sustain its lack of profit because it's earning an enormous amount of revenue and demonstrating year after year that its revenue is growing. The notion that a start-up shouldn't even expect to be making profits for many years is dangerous. Amazon is an exception; very few start-ups make anywhere near the revenue it generates, and the path of their future revenue is much less predictable.

Just what level of profitability you should be aiming for is a tricky issue. The fact is that certain kinds of business models simply have higher profit margins than others, for various reasons. For some, competition is negligible, which gives them pricing power, the extreme case of which is a monopoly. For others, once the up-front costs of designing and producing the product are paid, each sale is made at very low cost, as is the case with many software products. Every copy of a new version of Microsoft Office sold costs the company a negligible amount to produce, so the company achieves a very high volume of sales with effectively no additional expense required. That is essentially why Microsoft has maintained profit margins ranging from 20 to 30 percent or more for years. Another high-margin business was razor blade maker Gillette that had 60 percent gross margins before being acquired by Proctor & Gamble.[81] The Apple iPhone has practically printed money for the company since the day it was launched. Businesses with such strong profitability can achieve phenomenally fast growth.

Examples of low-profit-margin businesses are construction and certain types of retail, such as grocery stores, which have little pricing flexibility because of such intense competition. Many of these businesses are perfectly viable, even highly lucrative, and they can be managed well because the reasons why they are low margin are clear. The same is often not true for start-ups. A low margin of profit can be more difficult to justify and can leave you vulnerable to market changes. So if you haven't reached good profitability even though you're seeing surging sales, you've got to carefully scrutinize where your costs are going, what benefits you're seeing from them, and what the trajectory of your profitability will be if you continue growing in this manner.

One example of a low-margin business that has a compelling rationale for how it will grow its way out of a lack of profit is marketing software firm Marketo that was started in 2006. In 2014, the publicly traded firm had revenue of $150 million, a 56 percent increase above 2013, but it lost $54.3 million in the process.[82] This has been a trend for Marketo for years. Its SaaS business model is one that's often profitable, but Marketo is deploying the adage that you have to spend money to make money. In a February 2015 investor presentation, its executives showed how from 2011 to 2014, its net income from operations has improved from negative 65 percent to negative 19 percent, respectively.[83] Gross margins are also improving. In addition, while in 2011, Marketo was spending 32 percent of revenue on R&D, that had dropped to 17 percent in 2014, and the company projects it will drop to 15 percent or lower in the future. As Marketo highlighted, its target profit margin is a healthy 20 percent, so in that regard, the company is on the right track.

The point here is that Marketo appears to have a clear plan for becoming profitable. While the plan does involve risk, the company has established that it can reliably increase revenues and improve margins. If you can't similarly anticipate attaining better profitability in the future and identify exactly what you'll be able to, you've got to take your low profitability very seriously. You don't want to become a victim of "We lose money on each sale, but we'll make it up in volume." That almost never works.

It's also important to be intensely aware of economic conditions and any trends that may affect your business. This is always true, of course, but for money-losing models, it's particularly important. If the economy turns downward and sales drop, while at the same time investors aren't investing, you're in a very precarious situation. Keep in mind that US recessions tend to occur every seven to ten years, and even though this has been so well established, they always seem to arrive when you least expect them. If you're profitable, but at a low rate, you may well be able to sustain strong enough growth to get you through such a squeeze by rigorously watching your expenses. But plan ahead and make sure your business is ready by maintaining relationships with key investors and keeping cash on hand to get you through a rough patch.

Invest in Profitability or Growth?

What if profits are in fact beginning to pour in? Many pundits argue that you should continue to invest all, or most, of your new cash into growth in this stage rather than banking it as profit, if you're indeed a growth business. That same argument is used to advocate for raising a big infusion of venture capital at this stage so even more money can be pumped into growth. However, operating with razor-thin margins and raising outside growth capital are sometimes fraught endeavors, with so many ins and outs to delve into that the next chapter is dedicated to it entirely. For now, let's stick with just the scenario of reinvesting most or all your profits.

Lots of founders go this route, pursuing market share generally either by jacking up sales and marketing efforts or investing in launching a wider range of products. This is a key reason why operating losses are common for several years for start-ups rather than their model just not being profitable. Facebook lost money until 2009, but by 2014, it earned $2.9 billion, so this strategy worked just fine for it. And its profits are the envy of all other social Web companies.

> **Hockey Stick Principle #55: If you invest all or most of your profits in growth, the growth must be worth more than the profits.**

There are many good strategic reasons for investing most or all your profits in further accelerating growth. One is that you are seeking to solidify first-mover advantage, meaning that you're the first company to the market with a product of your type, which can give start-ups a lead that competitors may never catch up to. But solidifying that lead may require investing in building brand recognition and customer loyalty. According to Boston University's Professor Fernando Suarez and Professor Gianvito Lanzolla of Cass Business School, the three reasons first movers have an advantage are: (1) gaining a technological edge, (2) being first to obtain scarce assets, such as location or patents, and (3) gaining an early base of customers.[84] You can be outflanked on each of these all too quickly by competitors if you're not investing in continuing to improve your technology, expanding into good locations and obtaining new intellectual property IP, and aggressively leveraging your customer base to reach new markets.

On the flip side, if you're up against a competitor with first-mover advantage, the best strategy for growth may be to invest more heavily in initiatives to take market share away from that leader. All founders should always keep in mind the possibility of being outflanked by competitors and also the opportunities they might have to be the one doing the outflanking. You might realize that your key competitor has a vulnerability, and it might make great strategic sense to invest in building up your own operations or improving your product or service in order to capitalize on that vulnerability. Maybe the market leader has offered a streaming service, but it's plagued by glitches. You might invest in offering your own streaming service with better technology. It's important to always be making proactive strategic moves vis-à-vis competitors and looking for good opportunities to either solidify your advantage over them or get a leg up on them. Perhaps your customer research has indicated strong demand for additional services or a wider selection of products. Investing in that kind of improvement to fuel growth is great business. You've also got to be willing sometimes to invest in improvements if you want to remain competitive. In a different category, your growth may have reached a point that substantial additional investments are required to sustain it, such as additional warehousing or server capacity.

But even when your rationale is strong for forgoing profits, you want to be able to see the profitability at the end of the tunnel. While for superfast-growth businesses with potentially enormous markets, going five to ten years before reaching breakeven and starting to bank profits or pay dividends is often just fine; for more niche businesses with smaller markets, I recommend no more than three or four years. And if you do opt to forgo banking profits, it's vital to continually scrutinize the course you're on very closely, asking really tough questions of yourself like:

- Is the growth I'm generating worth the cost because it is setting me up for even stronger growth to fend off the competition? Will I clearly generate larger profits in the future?
- Do I really have to worry so much about competition? Is the market large enough for several leaders? Or is my market segment specific

enough and deep enough that I can rely more on word of mouth and the quality of my product, customer relationship management, and marketing rather than on pouring more and more cash into marketing and advertising?

- Is there a critical window of time in which I've got to capitalize on the market opportunity, or can I opt to grow more steadily and slowly?
- Are there any ways that I can introduce greater efficiencies in our operation or optimize economies of scale in order to produce at least some profit as we expand?

In making these evaluations, you should systematically weigh all the pluses against the minuses. In other words, do the best cost-benefit analysis you can. In doing so, an important factor to consider is how you are compensating your staff. If you've got fast growth and yet your employees aren't sharing in that wealth, you can undermine their morale and their trust that you value their contributions.

> **Hockey Stick Principle #56: Your employees should not be asked to forgo banking profits; reward them commensurate to your rate of growth.**

Let's face it: In the early growth stages of a start-up in particular, the work hours and the responsibilities heaped on staff can be daunting. Using some of your profits to show them you've appreciated their hard work and sacrifice is a great way to boost motivation and strengthen the company culture. Some founders go way overboard, offering lavish bonuses and paying exorbitant salaries, but others make the mistake of being perceived as Scrooges. I'll offer advice about how to get compensation right coming up in chapter 8, which covers building your team.

Fixed or Variable, Most Costs Are Significant Commitments

We've all read stories of start-ups hiring too many people and moving into expensive new office space, quickly bankrupting themselves. The dot-com bust in 2000 and 2001 was replete with ghoulish examples, such as the appropriately named Boo.com. The founder of the online clothing retailer,

Ernst Malmsten, once notoriously said, "After the pampered luxury of a Learjet 35, Concorde was a bit cramped."[85] These cautionary tales have raised awareness of the danger of scaling up too fast. However, with the availability of so many inexpensive business support systems, there's now a lot of help for you to contain costs from scaling. But even so, keeping control of your finances is a challenging feat.

One of the common ways in which founders get their start-ups into a profitability bind is by investing too heavily and too soon in fixed costs. An important distinction in operating expenses is between fixed costs, which are those you have to commit to in advance and that you won't be able to increase or decrease readily—if at all—and variable costs, which rise and fall with your sales volume. For example, your costs of manufacturing enough smartwatches to fill demand will vary by volume, while your costs to warehouse your stock of them will be basically fixed—you pay for warehouse space by the space you rent or build, not by the space you fill.

> **Hockey Stick Principle #57: Achieving fast growth is not a license to spend.**

Scrutinizing your fixed costs especially rigorously is vital in plotting all stages of growth, but it can be a very tricky issue at this juncture because, with such fast growth, the tendency is to err on the side of spending too much too soon to sustain that growth. That's one of the biggest pitfalls for fast-growth start-ups. For all these costs, it's best to seriously consider if there are any other options, or even to test those options, before committing to the expense.

A better choice for the Fab.com cofounders in entering the business of inventory management, for example, might have been to contract for warehousing services until the change in the business model proved successful. While over the long haul building your own warehouse may be more cost effective than leasing space or contracting for warehouse services, you should carefully consider whether the additional cost of leasing for a year or two would be worthwhile because leasing would give you time to evaluate whether or not you really needed the space and wanted to potentially build your own space. Of course, very few start-ups face this particular decision at this stage of growth, but even working out the amount of warehouse space to lease—or for SaaS models, the server capacity and cloud services you choose—is a calculation that has to be made with great care.

Even with retail space, you may have alternatives that let you test the benefits before locking into leases that turn out not to be profitable, which is another of the very common revenge effects of fast growth. Say you're thinking that you need to expand from online-only sales into some brick-and-mortar retail locations. Perhaps you should try some "pop-up" stores first to test response and verify best locations for your business.

Fixed costs are hardly the only tricky part of getting expenses right. Variable costs and discretionary costs, such as your marketing and sales expenses, can also be extremely challenging to make good decisions about. For example, with variable costs, there's often a time lag that can bite you. The classic case is overordering of inventory and then facing a drop-off in sales. As for sales and marketing costs, many start-ups fall into the trap of pouring a great deal of money into higher-ticket campaigns that don't produce a commensurate increase in sales. In fact, the Startup Genome study of start-up failure found that this is one of the key differentiators between those who scale up well and those who falter. The study found that start-ups that failed due to premature scaling were more than twice as likely to "spend more than one standard deviation above the average on customer acquisition"—meaning that most of those firms were spending a great deal more than the average firm.[86]

Be a Smooth Scaler

The core issue here is whether you have a model with scalability. This is so vital to the success of start-ups that Steven Blank, a professor, author, and entrepreneur, makes scalability part of his definition of what a start-up is: "A startup is a temporary organization designed to *search* for a repeatable and scalable business model."[87]

But what exactly is the definition of scalable? Many explanations are deceptively simple, such as that offered by Investopedia: "A scalable company is one that can maintain or improve profit margins while sales volume increases."[88] Or consider this explanation from the cleverly named Divestopedia: "Scalability . . . refers to a company's ability to add significant revenue and not be constrained by its own structure and resources."[89] One puts the emphasis on profit margins, the other on revenue, and one emphasizes sales growth while the other stresses organizational issues and costs. All these issues combine in determining scalability.

I think there are two key ways to evaluate whether you've achieved scalability. One is when you're able to grow your revenues without having to increase costs as quickly. The other is when you can grow your revenues without making major modifications to your business operations. My favorite expert quote about this is from scalability expert at Siemens Corporation André B. Bondi, who says that scalability is "the ability of a system to perform gracefully as the offered traffic increases."[90]

> **Hockey Stick Principle #58: Scale up operations only as fast as your team can skate and still stay in well-coordinated formation.**

Whereas in the prelaunch to early postlaunch phase, you're scrambling as fast as you can to move forward on all fronts and you often can't help but operate in a state of controlled chaos, when you've reached growth takeoff, you want to be vigorously focusing on fine-tuning your operations. My advice is that rather than making any substantive changes to your model during this growth-takeoff stage, you work hard on continuing to maximize the performance of your model.

In Doug Lebda's office on his whiteboard, he showed me a calculation that revealed the profitable machine behind LendingTree's strong sustained growth. He knew the math of his model cold, with an exquisitely tuned understanding of the relationship between how much money it costs LendingTree to obtain a marketing lead (e.g., $50 per new lead), its lead conversion rate (e.g., 10 percent of those leads became a customer), and how much revenue it would get from each closed sale (e.g., $500 per closed sale). His key advice about honing for scalability is this: "Keep driving down your marketing cost to get a customer; keep driving up your revenue per lead."

During the growth-inflection point, founders should have a firm understanding of the mathematical reasons their business's growth machine is working or not. At its most basic level, having a successful business ultimately requires earning a healthy profit on sales. That's why on the TV show *Shark Tank,* the sharks always ask the founders, "How much does it cost you to make your widget, and how much do you sell it for?"

The founders of iContact also paid extremely close attention to honing a scalable model in this phase. Ryan Allis explained the beauty of this process this way: "The appeal is that the return from the cost-per-click model is predictable and scalable. By gathering data over several years, iContact was able to show that, for every dollar they put into marketing, they got back a customer who would spend a certain amount of money with them over a number of years." So iContact knew exactly how much to spend on additional advertising in order to generate a precisely calculated amount of new business. Because sales growth was so predictable, the company was able to confidently scale up rapidly. In the next chapter, we'll see how iContact used this predictable model to raise funding that resulted in surging growth.

Calibrating the Machine with Metrics

The right way to manage a start-up in the growth-inflection stage—and really from here on out as you grow—is, metaphorically speaking, like calibrating a machine: the process of configuring a machine to ensure it's working properly. To calibrate something, a calibration specialist (that's a real job) conforms or adapts a noncalibrated machine with a *standard* machine, meaning one that has been known or proven to be accurate. The process of calibration is important because if a machine isn't calibrated, the parts it produces will drift toward lower and lower quality. Food will be packaged with the incorrect mix of ingredients, or tools will be forged at the incorrect length or weight.

Founders must be like calibration specialists. And you can't calibrate well if you're not keeping close tabs on your metrics and making sure you're measuring the right variables.

Some of the most obvious measurements to keep your eye on are monthly revenue, revenue run rate (annual revenue divided by twelve), gross margin, and operating margin. After the obvious ones, there are hundreds of key performance indicators (KPIs) to choose from depending upon what type of business you're managing. For example, if you're an online SaaS firm, some of your important marketing and sales KPIs might be the number of new leads generated per month, the number of prospect demos provided per month, Web site traffic, renewals and churn rates (or the percentage of customers that discontinue their service), and prospect to customer conversion rates. Some KPIs are quite specialized by type of business. If selling products online, for example, a key KPI should be how many prospective customers fail to actually purchase after having put items in their carts.

Not all founders are data people, and that is fine; you don't have to be. But you absolutely need someone who is. I recommend you hire a top-quality, experienced manager who has a deep knowledge of how to identify and track results for KPIs. This person doesn't have to be a CPA or accountant, but he or she should have demonstrated experience with this process. And creativity is important; this is not just a matter of following preestablished rules. You need someone not only to track what's happening but to help with the tricky costs and benefits calculations involved in making decisions about future growth. This requires not only a quantitative assessment but a qualitative one, as well.

> **Hockey Stick Principle #59: Do not let numbers make decisions for you; the qualitative must be paired with the quantitative to make good choices about growth.**

Say that you've hit $1,350,000 in annual revenue, and for simplicity's sake, that your income statement looks like this:

Revenue:	**$1,350,000**
Product Maintenance Costs:	($200,000)
Cofounder Salaries (2 founders):	($200,000)
Marketing and Sales Expenses:	($397,000)
(Salaries, Commissions, Web	
Marketing, etc.)	
Customer Service:	($50,000)
Travel, Office Supplies:	($20,000)
Health Insurance:	($40,000)
Rent:	($50,000)
Operating Profit:	$393,000

Suddenly, you've got a good pool of profit to work with and are in a nice position to make some investments in accelerating last year's growth. How should you allocate the funds? Some payoffs from expenses are much more quantitatively obvious than others. One example from above could be the affiliate marketing program into which you paid $40,000 to get referrals for sales. Let's say you earned $250,000 in revenue from the affiliates. That's a very clear return and a pretty good result. So you'll want to increase your number of affiliates.

Figuring out which of your marketing programs are leading to sales can be trickier because marketing requires a great deal of time and measurement in order to see if it's working or not. That's why using such tools as customer relationship management (CRM) systems and lead tracking is important from early on, which large providers like Salesforce.com and Microsoft Dynamics offer. They are also provided by some less expensive start-ups, such as Zoho and Insightly. These tools give vital information for making this difficult assessment. But even with these diagnostics, you often can't know the return on investment (ROI) of various efforts, such as new product enhancements, product upgrades, packaging tweaks, and hiring new salespersons, until months or years after you've spent the money. This is one reason why qualitative judgment is also so critical—you have to make your best evaluation based upon what you're hearing and learning in the marketplace in order to know what marketing methods to invest in.

Take the case above again. You've learned that increasing your number of affiliates will produce good results. But doing so will take a fair amount of your time because you have to build a partnership with each affiliate, including convincing them on the idea and—if you're successful—entering into an agreement. You might determine that hiring an additional rep for direct sales is a higher priority than investing more money into your affiliate marketing program. Maybe you've noted that in the last few months the ratio of deals to calls has ticked up, and the size of deals closed has also been improving, so you're convinced that more person-to-person selling will produce increasing returns. Also, you've still been working on sales yourself, as I was in First Research's takeoff year, and hiring another rep will free you up to focus more on strategic planning and implementation.

For me with First Research, in 2001, having invested more in the sales operation allowed me to refocus my time, largely on two key tasks: analyzing the customer feedback we were getting in order to prioritize product improvements and targeting some new, potentially lucrative markets. Both worked well for us. We added more frequent industry updates, industry news features, additional financial data, e-mail alerts, and training, and we developed a system for investing new customer payments into product features. I was also able to land a number of important new accounts with large outsourcing firms, such as ADP, and software firms, including Microsoft, as well as their network of value-added resellers, and dozens of others.

Our revenue increased from $797,000 in 2001 to $1.8 million in 2002, in large part due to the combination of my new efforts and the sales brought in by the new rep.

Developing good metrics and keeping close track of them is only the baseline of start-up management; metrics don't make the most important decisions for you. In fact, an interesting finding from the Startup Genome report is that "Google Analytics, homegrown solutions and spreadsheets are the top 3 three tools that are used by more than 90% of all startups to track their metrics and make decisions. . . . There are slight differences between consistent and inconsistent companies but we didn't interpret it as significant." Note that the report refers to start-ups that are scaling prematurely or dysfunctionally as "inconsistent" and those that are scaling up smartly as "consistent." The important point here is that the type of data analysis being used was not a key factor in whether start-ups were scaling correctly or not. This underscores that it's the quality of the decisions you make in light of the data that makes the difference, and these decisions must be made according to judgment calls based on your intuition, your assessments of the talents of your team members, and your deep understanding of your customer base and why and how you can grow it.

As only a very general guide to prioritizing outlays, I advise that in this growth-inflection stage, you allocate profits in this order of priority:

- keeping at least five to ten months of cash in reserve to cover overhead expenses should need be (I often say to my partner in Vertical IQ, Bill Walker, "We need to store up nuts for winter!")
- employee raises and bonuses
- new sales and marketing expenses
- new expenses associated with maintaining and improving your product or services
- founder salary increases
- debt repayments

From Early Adopters to Early Majority

One of the great challenges of sustaining growth in this phase is that it generally involves what marketing specialist Geoffrey Moore called "crossing the chasm," in his classic book of that title, meaning moving from a customer base of early adopters into the larger pool of what he calls early majority and late majority customers. The fact that this can be so difficult to do is the main reason that spending too much on customer acquisition is such a common error. With some cash in their coffers, many founders decide to make a big marketing push involving an expensive advertising and PR plan. Sometimes doing so can work very well, but there is one big caution. Before you make such an investment, you must be sure you really understand the needs and desires of the majority. Ideally, you want to build a bridge to the majority by leveraging the knowledge you've gained from your early adopters and by making as many of them as you can into brand evangelists.

> **Hockey Stick Principle #60: Nothing can bring in more new fans better than your early fans.**

A great case of a founder who discerned how his early adopters were the key to bridging to the wider customer base is Bob Young. For Red Hat, the early adopters were computer programmers who mostly called the 800 number or ordered on its Web site. The majority adopters the company wanted to reach were corporate technology directors who could decide to make larger orders for departments or whole corporations. But when Bob first pitched them, they were having none of it. They would respond with one or another version of "You've told me that there are only fifty of you working away in the tobacco fields of North Carolina and by your own admission are writing maybe 5 percent of the code that I would buy on your disk. And the other 95 percent of that code you have only a good guess where it's from, but you really don't know. Just how long do you think my career would last in front of either that bank inspector or my board of directors?"

But Bob knew that many server administrators, often from the same company and many levels below the technology director, would approach Red Hat's trade show booth and buy a copy. Those customers were buying Red Hat to satisfy a specific yet unbudgeted need. For example, an HR manager at a firm needed to send internal announcements, so she would ask for help in doing so. If she didn't have $10,000 in her budget to buy the necessary software, the server administrator would suggest an inexpensive workaround—paying $49.95 to install Red Hat. These first corporate purchasers had heard good things about Red Hat from the early enthusiasts who were avid participants in the user community Red Hat had worked to create through its Web site. The decision to compete on price combined with this quality service to early adopters created a bridge into corporate purchasing. Over time, the company had sold so many copies to firms that the technology directors would realize that Red Hat was in fact an inexpensive, flexible, workable solution and that they needed to account for hundreds of Red Hat applications already running on their servers. They'd need to prove they had a license to use it, and they also needed support to keep Red Hat up-to-date for them. So more and more technology directors started calling Red Hat asking to purchase site licenses and make deals for ongoing support rather than Bob having to do a hard sell on them.

This is why Red Hat's growth curve has two points of distinct uptick. Its growth-inflection point occurred only a year after it got started, after Bob had worked out the innovative sales model, and then three years later, growth really took off when large-scale corporate sales kicked in.

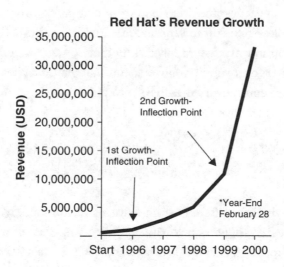

Red Hat's Revenue Growth

Build a Community, Not Just a Customer Base

Red Hat mobilized its early adopters so well in large part because it stayed closely engaged with its users and created a vibrant platform for their needs. The Web site became a hub for Linux discussion groups in addition to downloads of the program and applications. And this was way back in 1999, before even social media had been born, let alone Facebook brand pages morphing into platforms for offering ongoing "brand experiences," as Red Bull, Coca-Cola, and others have become such masters of. At the time of writing this book, Red Bull has forty-three million likes on Facebook and two million followers on Twitter, and its Web site is chock-full of entertaining, extreme sport videos. Red Had was a pioneer of community creation. In March 1999, RedHat.com had 2.5 million page views.

INSEAD Professor Jean-Claude Larréché highlights in his book *The Momentum Effect* that the "'customer' is much wider than simply the product purchaser," and Bob Young understood that important truth about customer relationship building.[91] Red Hat customers really did become part of a community. Bob understood the culture of the community and its ethics and aspirations, and he communicated that in all his marketing to them. In speeches and interviews, he compared proprietary software companies like Microsoft to "feudal lords," which was exactly how so many in the IT community felt. He was skilled at connecting *emotionally* with both customers and potential buyers, and that played a vital role in turning more of those community members into purchasers.

> **Hockey Stick Principle #61: Customers don't just want a product; they want a relationship.**

One of the key differentiating features of founders who successfully rally their early adopters, creating brand evangelists and establishing a strong and appealing brand identity that acts as a magnet to draw in more and more and more customers, is that they convey an authenticity of connection and communication with customers. They don't rely only on traditional techniques like listing benefits in their marketing. They understand the point that Harvard marketing professor Youngme Moon articulated well in her book *Different: Escaping the Competitive Herd*:

Marketing is the only function within the organization that is expressly designed to sit at the intersection where business meets people. Real people.[92]

Rather than launching a high-ticket marketing campaign to stoke growth at this stage, founders should focus on connecting in real ways with those real people and being creative about ways to do so, many of which are relatively inexpensive.

Grasshopper, a firm whose product lets you run your business using cell phones, mailed twenty-five thousand chocolate-covered grasshoppers to five thousand influential bloggers, reporters, politicians, CEOs, entrepreneurs, and TV anchors and then posted the media attention they received (which was lots) on its Web site. This idea was a huge success. Ben Silbermann, founder of Pinterest, wrote seven thousand notes to users himself asking them about why they joined the site and what they liked about it.[93] That was clearly a considerable investment of time, but it was a low-cash, high-quality way to connect and also to learn. He credits the process with helping him to tailor Pinterest to users' desires.

Let Customers Know the True You

Though you will almost surely want to hire a professional firm to collaborate with you on your marketing, you should not simply outsource this function. Your marketing should be an authentic expression of your brand identity, and in this stage of growth—and ideally for many, many more years to come—your brand identity should be an authentic reflection of you and your mission. As talented as many professional marketers are—and they can truly be brilliant—they can't give you that, and if you don't develop your own deep understanding of your brand identity and what appeals to your customers, you might be led astray by the pros.

> **Hockey Stick Principle #62: Catchy taglines and clever ads are no match for an authentic brand identity.**

Joe Colopy, founder of six-time Inc. 5000 fastest-growing firms, Bronto Software, a cloud-based e-mail marketing provider, is a great example of a founder who has fashioned a strong brand identity and knows exactly how important it is to growing the company. He has built his firm's marketing around a playful green brontosaurus logo. When I visited with Joe at the Bronto headquarters, bright-green brontosaurus blow-up toys and stuffed animals were everywhere. He told me, "The brontosaurus humanizes our technology. It's approachable. We're regular, folksy people; we're open, transparent, and tell it like it is. We make business fun. And no one hides behind a title here. These are the core things as to who we are."

He went on to tell me, "Marketing agencies don't quite get why we have a green dinosaur representing our identity and want to do things with it or change it. They consider it is something that can just be used and changed for campaigns and that's all it is. But it's not all it is. It's way more than that. I won't cheapen it, ever."

Bronto's green brontosaurus is a perfect case of what marketing specialist Seth Godin advocated for in his influential book *Purple Cow*—it is marketing that is "*worth talking about, remarkable, new, and interesting.*"[94] Companies at their growth-inflection point are in a great position to follow this approach and stand out by having a lot of personality.

There is so much focus on social media marketing and content marketing being new ways of engaging customers and building community, and they are extremely powerful tools. But just as with the data from measuring metrics, they don't do the work for you. It's the quality of your marketing much more than the fact that you're broadcasting national ads or videos on the latest hot mobile platform that builds a community. And by building a strong brand identity and nurturing your customer community, if and when you do decide to launch a major marketing campaign, you will be much better equipped to make sure it speaks in your company's voice.

Doug Lebda of LendingTree did a great job of this when he decided to launch a prime-time cable television and radio campaign during the company's growth-inflection stage. He and his marketing team chose to work with a small, creative, and entrepreneurial advertising agency, Mullen, located "in the woods" near the north shore of Boston. They worked closely together to craft a tagline and approach to the ads that brilliantly expressed empathy with the frustration of trying to get a mortgage loan, the very frustration that was Doug's motivation for starting the company. The tagline, "When banks compete, you win," clearly conveyed the customer focus, and the ads struck right at the heart of the customers' pain point with irreverent humor. The first television commercial, titled "Rejection," featured a casually dressed couple in their middle-class kitchen interviewing bankers in three-piece suits. The couple speaks to two bankers at their kitchen table: "Your rates are a little high. What's the word I'm thinking of? . . . *No!*" And the couple laughs gleefully.

Doug attributes much of LendingTree's success at scaling to the effectiveness of the campaign.

Partnering and Licensing to Expand Your Reach

Another important approach to scaling up your customer base in this stage is to pursue licensing deals and partnerships with large brands. These deals can provide a start-up with massive leverage for revenue growth because the reach of these brands to customers is on such a large scale. And at this stage of growth, you are a much more attractive partnering prospect than you were before takeoff, so making deals will be a much more efficient process.

Many of the founders profiled in the Hockey Stick study had great success with scaling up through such deals. Red Hat negotiated a whirlwind of product integration, co-marketing, and distribution partnership deals with such global software and technology companies as IBM, Dell, Intel, Compaq, Oracle, SAP, Netscape, Hewlett-Packard, and Novell. When Bob called on them, it turned out that their customers were already asking for a Linux solution, and by that time, the big firms wanted to figure out a way to capitalize on the potential, or at least not miss out on its value to their customers.

Another firm that benefited from deals like this is Shashi Upadhyay's start-up Lattice Engines. It has struck partnership deals with Oracle, Salesforce.com, Microsoft, SAP, and DemandGen, just to name a few.

The types of deals you should look into are:

- **Product integration paid partnerships** that license your product, patent, or technology to other firms in exchange for a set license fee. Oftentimes, start-ups may license only parts of their intellectual property. For example, a start-up may embed its product into another company's core product to make a more compelling offer.
- **Free product integration partnerships** wherein you license a portion of your product for free to other firms to enhance their offering, and in exchange, you receive brand awareness and marketing

prospect leads. The goal is to enable your brand and product to reach a broader audience and attract interested buyers who become sales leads.

- **Revenue-sharing sales and marketing partnerships** with companies that promote your product within their existing channels. There are many ways to do this, such as media deals, affiliate marketing arrangements (discussed in chapter 4), and resale arrangements.

> **Hockey Stick Principle #63: Big firms don't have all the power; they want your innovation and hustle as much as you want their market muscle and customers.**

I've heard founders say that they worry that big companies will push them around if they partner with them. Well, they might if you're not tough, but that's up to you to stand your ground. Keep in mind that if they're interested in a deal, they may need you as much as you need them. Sometimes these partnerships do lead to merger discussions because they enable larger firms to learn firsthand how well a start-up's product fits into their larger offering—such as how it sells and for how much. This outcome could be a good thing or a bad thing, depending upon your goals. Moreover, it's important to keep in mind that whatever revenue the larger company is producing for you, their portion of the revenue may be discounted when the valuation of your company is being calculated by the investment community, should you decide to pursue venture funding. That's not necessarily a problem, just an important thing to be aware of and account for yourself.

One thing that is a real risk to be cognizant of is that if a large company becomes your largest revenue producer, it may have more leverage over you in future negotiations than you'll be happy with. In order to mitigate this concern, I encourage founders to diversify their revenue as much as possible in most cases. You don't want to be in effect owned by any one other company.

When it comes to making these deals, the devil is in the details, so my advice is to lawyer up. There are dozens of considerations to be aware of. Are you providing them pricing control? Who will handle customer support—you or your partner? How much control does your partner have over your trademarks, if any? What is the deal's duration or term? One year or five years?

The term is a really important provision to pay close attention to. If you wind up not liking the deal, and if the term is for many years, you're stuck with it. I've seen long-term partnership deals severely hurt the profitability of a start-up. Negotiating these agreements is no time to try to save on legal bills by using an inexperienced attorney.

Whatever methods you use to scale up successfully, as your momentum builds and the power of your model is confirmed, you'll be in a good position to raise growth capital, if you choose. Firms may now even be calling on you. Getting an infusion of growth capital can be the boost that pushes you solidly onto a long-term growth trajectory. But there are many cautions, so in the next chapter, we'll closely investigate the pros and cons.

Chapter 7

Playing in the Big Leagues: Raising Growth Capital

Though scaling up by investing only your earnings into growth is a good way to calibrate the process of gaining hockey stick growth and helps assure that you don't get way out ahead of your revenue generation, there are also many good reasons to decide to seek substantial outside investment. As I said in the last chapter, sometimes raising substantial capital is the key to allowing you to grow fast enough to secure a dominant market position, especially when you must outflank a competitor who's either coming on strong or threatening to take market share from you—or whose market share you are gunning for. A good example is the market battle between next-generation taxi services Uber and Lyft, which offer essentially the same product with the same business model. In order to secure their future, each has no real choice but to expand rapidly, and each has raised many millions of funds from outside investors in order to do so.

Even if you aren't facing competition that threatens your market share or your future survival, you may want to gun for the fastest growth possible, the best reason for doing so being that you've confirmed that your model can reliably scale up much faster and capture a much larger market. A great example of founders who made a good call on this is that of Ryan Allis and Aaron Houghton of iContact. Though they had bootstrapped so successfully to reach growth inflection, their in-depth analysis of the market and the speed with which their sales took off—hitting $1.3 million in revenue in 2005, just three years after launch—assured them that they had a huge additional market to grow into.[95] Roughly thirty million small businesses operate in the United States, but only a few hundred thousand had adopted e-mail marketing tools at that time. At that point, they could likely have sold the company for $3–$5 million, if not more, but instead, they opted to raise outside funding and shoot for even more accelerated growth.

They started by raising $500,000 from nonprofit accelerator NC IDEA. Then between 2007 and 2010, they went on to raise $53 million in six different rounds, continuing to pour that money into their scalable model.[96] Raising funds in measured increments based on their well-honed ability to generate revenue was the key to their smooth road to success even while growing so fast.

As Ryan explains, "The whole business is based upon a mathematical model where we invest $500 to acquire a customer and can get $2,500–$2,600 in lifetime revenue. So it takes about eleven, twelve months to pay back that up-front investment. And then that turns into three years of gross profit after that." The precision, reliability, and profitability of their sales model convinced funders to continue offering infusions of cash. By 2010, sustained fast growth provided a strong case for a much larger infusion, and they hired Allen & Company, a New York City–based investment bank with a rich history of helping successful online businesses, such as Google, raise capital to help secure a larger deal. In August 2010, JMI Equity, a Baltimore-based growth equity firm, invested $40 million in the company. In 2012, publicly traded marketing firm Vocus acquired iContact for $169 million.

You may also need to raise funds in order to make the major capital investments required to sustain growth—things like equipment, space, or systems, which simply can't be covered by current earnings. For example, when Julie Pickens and Mindee Doney of Boogie Wipes secured a very large order from the Fred Meyer grocery chain for placement in about 120 stores, they hadn't been in business long enough to have banked enough revenue to cover the costs of fulfilling that order. They needed to get a good dose of cash to pay for inventory and for shipping to the retailers, who wouldn't be paying for many months. They successfully raised a strong cash infusion that carried them through this critical growth juncture.

Hockey Stick Principle #64: Raise capital to boost or sustain strong growth, not to search for it.

The most fundamental mistake founders make when seeking substantial outside funding is trying to do too much too soon—before they can make a strong case for the firm's growth potential or, even better, have a proven record of that growth. They waste a great deal of time and experience enormous frustration—and often disillusionment—because funders just aren't buying their pitch. Once you've got fast growth that you can clearly demonstrate is based on a solid and scalable model, attaining significant outside funding is much more viable. Investment firms may even come calling on you and compete to do business with you. That was true for Dude Solutions, for example, which completed its first fund-raising round in 2014, obtaining $100 million from private equity firm Warburg Pincus.

Founder Kent Hudson waited fifteen years from launch to seek this infusion, preferring to be in a strong growth position. "We didn't run a [fund-raising] process with twenty private equity firms," he recalls. "We said this will be a 'by invitation only' party." He didn't even write a five-year business plan, which is generally a baseline requirement when approaching funders. He recounts, "We told them, 'Here's our market analysis. Here's the market potential as we see it and the opportunities. Here's the competition. Who would like to team with us to exploit the position we're in? Now let's jointly talk about how best to exploit it.'"

Capital Is a Form of Control

One of the primary cautions about seeking funding is that it generally involves some loss of control over the company to the outside investors. Waiting until you're in a strong growth position before raising money can give you the negotiating leverage to maintain more control.

> **Hockey Stick Principle #65: Venture capital always comes with strings attached; make sure they don't bind you.**

While most angel investors offering seed money act primarily as advisors and don't seek a controlling share of your firm, the venture capital and private equity investors who offer more substantial investments require a good deal of control over the future course of the company, including seats on the board. If performance isn't meeting the standards they have set, you are in danger of them hijacking the company and taking it in a different strategic direction or of being forced out of your leadership role. Much too often, founders find themselves in a mighty struggle, or even outright war, with their backers.

One founder who went through such a battle wrote a thoughtful and cringe-inducing account of the ordeal, which is a great cautionary tale for all founders to consider. Philip Greenspun and partners started ArsDigita, a provider of open-source software for online learning communities, with just a $10,000 investment. The company had made many good deals with major firms, including AOL, Hewlett-Packard, Levi Strauss, Oracle, and Siemens. By 2000, the firm was making $20 million in annual revenue, with good profitability, and it had become a strong prospect for venture funding. The partners decided to go for it. Greenspun recounts that they made a combined deal with a venture capital firm and private equity group for $38 million in funding in exchange for a 30 percent stake in the firm and, as Greenspun describes, "veto power over certain kinds of big transactions, such as the buying of expensive capital equipment, the selling of the company, the acquiring of another company." The terms also included a stockholders agreement, which Greenspun discloses required him and co-founder and fellow shareholder Jin Choi to elect a board of directors that would include one representative of the venture firm, one of the private equity group, three senior officers from ArsDigita—including the CEO—and two outside directors.

This arrangement gave the funders two seats out of seven. But shortly thereafter, the founders decided to bring in an outside CEO, and they chose a person who had been recommended by one of the funders. This person came on board before they had brought in the two outside directors. Suddenly, the weight of authority on the board had shifted to the funders and the new CEO, who controlled three out of five sitting directors. As plans for rapid growth were pursued, the company expanded, and Greenspun recalled in a case study on waxy.org that the new board more than doubled the number of employees from eighty to two hundred. Furthermore, they paid those employees much more than Greenspun had, increasing salaries to more than $200,000 for executives and programmers base salaries of $125,000. He reports that he began to disagree about the course in which the company was headed, but because candidates he put forward for the two open board seats were not approved, he could not regain decision-making authority.[97]

You can avoid such a painful scenario by understanding the three basic means by which founders lose control: 1) allowing someone else to own more than 50 percent of the voting stock; 2) losing majority control of the board of directors; 3) entering into contracts that override voting control on how certain functions are governed. For example, if you own 51 percent of the shares, you can normally elect the board of directors, but not if you contractually agree to give certain shareholders the right to elect a majority of the directors. That's one way that VCs gain more control.

This can happen to even business-savvy founders. Doug Lebda was a highly professional business manager, and yet he ran into trouble with his board and feared he might be ousted after he had made a significant deal for additional funding. That deal was premised on a financial forecast, but LendingTree missed those numbers by a significant amount. He had predicted that sales would grow considerably in the fourth quarter of 1998, from the third-quarter revenue of $100,000, but the fourth-quarter number was only $116,000. The funder had obtained a seat on the board as part of the deal, and he said in no uncertain terms that the performance wasn't acceptable.

As is true with virtually all business projections, LendingTree had run into unforeseeable setbacks. One was that the banks weren't converting leads to closed mortgages at the rate predicted, which was a problem that, as we discussed earlier, took Doug time and intensive work to solve. Another problem was that spending more on advertising didn't equate to the higher proportion of leads that had been forecasted. When the company spent $1,500, they got three hundred leads, but when they spent $150,000 they didn't get thirty thousand leads, not even close. Meanwhile, the cost of buying keywords from Yahoo! and other search engines had increased significantly. And finally, a Web site relaunch was delayed. These are all problems that are entirely typical for founders to run into but also entirely unpredictable.

Because he had offered seats on the board for not only the most recent investment but earlier ones, as well, Doug had lost voting control, and now suddenly he was at risk of losing the company. The board didn't immediately make a decision about whether to keep Doug on as CEO or fire him; they decided to put him "on watch." He smartly decided to pursue a transparent, team-focused atmosphere with the board by scheduling weekly meetings to update them.

> **Hockey Stick Principle #66: Managing your relationships with the board is as vital as managing your relationship with customers.**

"After the January board meeting when I thought I was going to be fired, I quickly went from being scared to being completely determined to prove myself," he recalls. "I wanted to be totally transparent with the board. I wanted them to believe in the business the way I did. I didn't want to hide anything or be defensive. Also, I needed their advice and buy-in." By solving the problem of how banks could get higher conversion rates, later in 1999, LendingTree was turning its business around and had made deals to work with an impressive number of heavy-hitting banks, including Bank One, Bank of America Consumer Finance, Citibank, First USA, and JPMorgan Chase & Co.

Doug also didn't let the experience deter him from raising the additional capital needed to continue the new surging growth. On September 20, 1999, LendingTree closed a $50 million financing round by selling convertible preferred stock to a group of investors, including Capital Z, GE Capital, Goldman Sachs, Marsh and McLennan Risk Capital, and Priceline.com. "We went out targeting twenty million and ended up raising fifty," Doug says. "As long as we can raise money, we said, 'Let's keep trying to go big.' If we had failed to raise the capital, we would have retrenched."

The lesson isn't that pursuing outside capital is too risky; it's that it is inherently risky and that you must be highly cognizant of the predictions you're making and the strings attached to them. If you do decide to seek substantial outside funding, you must be extremely vigilant about the terms you agree to and highly strategic about your approach.

Why You and VCs May Not See Eye to Eye

It's important to understand the fundamental goal you are committing to in taking VC funding and to understand how VC firms themselves are funded in order to appreciate why tensions sometimes develop between founders and VCs.

VC firms manage pools of investment dollars that they raise from large institutional investors—predominantly insurance companies, university endowments, and banks—as well as high-net-worth individuals. These investors are made limited partners of the firm, or LPs, while the partners inside the venture firms are called general partners, or GPs, and they make the investment decisions and run the firm. The investment money from LPs is pooled into funds of, say, $100 million, which are used to invest in a portfolio of start-ups—say, ten or fifteen—and a VC firm will generally be managing a number of these funds. GPs typically also invest some of their own money in a fund and have a stake in its returns, and they also draw a salary. A fund may have $50 million or up to $1 billion, with the typical fund having about $150 million.

Over a three- to five-year period, the VC firm will invest a fund in outlays generally ranging from about $1 million to $15 million per start-up, with the typical investment traditionally being about $3 million to $5 million. The minimum investment is normally $500,000, but occasionally, VCs may invest as little as $100,000 in a seed round, as discussed earlier. The series of VC investments made into a single firm are referred to as "rounds." The first round is the "seed round," followed by the Series A Round, Series B Round, Series C Round, and on. These rounds are typically eighteen to twenty-four months apart, and the amount of investment tends to grow larger and larger. The median amount raised in the A Round by the forty firms that I studied in the Hockey Stick Research Study that raised venture money was $5 million. Big ideas that experience really explosive growth may obtain rounds faster. Uber's A Round was $11 million in February 2011; its B Round was $37 million in December of that same year; its C Round was $258 million in August 2013. By April 2015, it has raised $4.9 billion total through several more rounds.[98]

Venture firms typically invest in later-stage start-ups that can be underwritten based on well-founded revenue projections. In 2014, of the $48 billion invested by VC funds, only 1 percent, or $718 million, in 192 deals was invested in seed stage deals. The balance was invested into early stage—also called growth stage—at 33 percent, when the business is less than three years old; expansion stage (41 percent), when the business is experiencing rapid revenue growth and in business more than three years; and later stage (25 percent), when the company is growing revenues and its product is widely available and may have positive cash flow. The later stage may also include a mezzanine financing round, or a loan that can be converted to ownership if not repaid, also called bridge financing because it's invested with the express understanding that it is being used to help get the company to a public offering or an acquisition.

These investments in start-ups are not for perpetuity; the express intent is to assist them in achieving fast growth for the purpose of "exiting" from the investment at a strong profit, ideally either by the start-up going public or being sold in a merger or acquisition deal. The VC firm charges a fee for the amount invested, generally of 2 percent, plus a significant percentage of the funds raised either by the IPO or the sale. The VC is generally looking for all the start-ups invested in by a given fund to exit within five to ten years of the fund's creation so that the fund can then be dissolved and the profits distributed between the GPs and LPs.

> **Hockey Stick Principle #67: Once you accept venture capital, you're on a ticking clock to either acquisition or IPO.**

The first rule of seeking venture funding is not to do so unless you want to either take your company public or sell it and unless you want to do so within the time frame of five to seven years—or usually at most ten years. The second rule is that if one or the other of these exit strategies is your goal, you examine very carefully—and with the guidance of experienced professional advisors—what will be required to make your company ready for a successful exit and what growing pains that will entail. You cannot rely on the VCs to make that assessment for you, no matter how experienced they are.

It's vital to appreciate that while the venture firms' GPs take considerable risk in making their investments, the fees they earn and the portfolio methodology of creating the funds insulates them from much of the risk of the individual investments. This in no way means they don't make decisions carefully; they are extremely judicious and selective. They are also generally highly disciplined in focusing on a particular type of company and sector, such as biotech start-ups or start-ups that are on a clear path to IPO in the relative short term. A 2014 study "Specialization and Competition in the Venture Capital Industry" by professors from Northwestern, Duke University, and Rice University reveals that only 14.3 percent of VCs are generalists; most specialize in sectors such as medical (12.7 percent), or computer-related (19.4 percent).[99]

They are absolutely investing in a start-up with the strong incentive and the fiduciary commitment to help it achieve great success in exiting. But they are also doing so on a predetermined, though somewhat flexible, time line for achieving the best possible exit from the investment. This means that the pressure for the level of growth that will make the start-up appealing either to market investors or to possible acquirers can become extremely intense. And given the portfolio structure of funds and the comparative insulation from the risk of failure the VC firms are exposed to, it can also lead firms to choose to cut their losses if a start-up isn't performing up to goals. In this event, because they've taken on so much debt from the firm, founders are forced to either sell on unfavorable, fire-sale terms or shut down and liquidate—that is, if they haven't been forced out before this point.

Many, many start-ups have benefited enormously from both the infusion of cash they received from VCs and their guidance, like Google, Facebook, Uber, and iContact. The point is not to ward off all founders from pursuing it but to stress that it is higher risk than other kinds of outside capital they can target, even though no interest payments are involved, as with a bank loan, because of the time line imposed on hitting benchmarks for growth. The good news about how difficult it is to obtain VC and how risky it can be is that VCs certainly aren't all-knowing entrepreneurship masters who you need to guide you to success, and there are many other good options for outside funding, such as super-angel investors or debt financing, which I'll discuss later in the chapter.

The Wrong Reasons for Seeking VC Money

The fact that so many of the most successful start-ups in recent times have raised enormous sums of venture capital along the way to their ascent means that there is a popular myth about venture firms that exists today. For example, VCs make a higher return on investments than typical market vehicles, like stocks and bonds, and they steer start-ups away from dangers and give them the sage strategic advice that lifts them to runaway success.

> **Hockey Stick Principle #68: Venture capitalists do not lead start-ups to success; they bet on them being successful.**

It's true that many VCs have been successful entrepreneurs themselves or have learned a great deal about the process of growing a firm due to their experiences working with many successful ones. VCs also have lots of connections with people they know who can help your firm—such as access to key personnel, sales leads, future investors, and partnership opportunities. But the degree to which a start-up can expect to benefit from their experiences and connections may be exaggerated. For example, the average investment rate of returns for VC investing over the past ten years in 2013 was 7.8 percent, compared to the S&P 500 of 10.6 percent over the same period.[100] That's not good, considering the fact that venture capital attracts greater risk.

Yet VC-backed firms do grow much faster. My Hockey Stick study shows that firms that raised VC grew larger faster than those that did not raise VC. After the second year, for firms that didn't accept VC investment, the median revenue was $358,000, while for those that did take VC money, median revenue was $463,000. By the seventh year, median revenue for those that raised VC was $29.6 million versus $11.6 million for those that didn't. But whether this means that the VC cash and guidance helped accelerate growth or whether the VCs did a good job of choosing firms to back because they were well equipped for growth can't be determined.

The graph below is the growth path for *VC-backed firms* and shows revenue increasing from $0 to $29.7 million in seven years.

Firms using Venture Capital

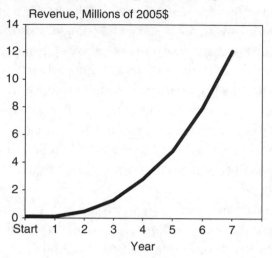

Firms not using Venture Capital

Revenue, Millions of 2005$

The graph above is the growth path for *non-VC-backed* firms and shows revenue increasing from $0 to $11.6 million in seven years.

The Kauffman Foundation's Diane Mulcahy, herself a former venture capitalist, made the case that venture capitalists have struggled to earn returns commensurate to the risk they take in an influential *Harvard Business Review* article:

> The story of venture capital appears to be a compelling narrative of bold investments and excess returns. . . . The reality looks very different. . . . Numbers [show] that many more venture-backed start-ups fail than succeed. And VCs themselves aren't much better at generating returns. For more than a decade the stock markets have outperformed most of them, and since 1999, VC funds on average have barely broken even.

She also highlights that while some VCs do give substantive guidance, others hardly get involved at all.

> If you asked the CEOs of 100 VC-funded companies how helpful their VCs are, some would say they're fabulous, some would say they're active but not a huge help, and some would say they do little beyond writing checks.[101]

In fact, Shikhar Ghosh, a senior lecturer at Harvard Business School who has held top executive positions at eight technology-based start-ups and has conducted extensive research into how companies that have raised VC have performed, warns about the odds of success when going the VC route. While the National Venture Capital Association says that 30–40 percent of venture-backed start-ups fail, which is a high percentage, according to Ghosh, the failure rates are actually much higher than that. This isn't better understood, he says, because the venture capitalists "bury their dead very quietly."[102] What's more is that failure often follows fast on the heels of a VC round. CB Insights, a venture capital database company, conducted a survey of VC-backed failures and learned that on average firms fail or get "acqui-hired" (meaning a start-up is purchased for dirt cheap, but its founder is hired by the acquiring firm) only twenty months after receiving financing and raising on average $1.3 million.[103] So the window for success is short-lived.

Venture Capital Is Not the Only Game in Town

So much of the coverage of funding for start-ups is focused on VC deals, but there are other less risky ways to go that will result in less intense pressure for faster growth. These other sources of capital have been gaining ground, and all founders should seriously consider them, especially in light of the fact that the odds of making a VC deal are, at any rate, quite slim. Entry into the VC club is still an exclusive affair. In 2014, $48.3 billion was invested in only 4,356 deals[104] out of the three million firms working at the time on high-growth-potential start-ups in the United States.[105] That computes roughly to one-tenth of 1 percent of founders having received venture capital! And 2014 was a big year for VC. In 2013, venture capital firms invested only $29.4 billion into just 3,995 deals.[106] Also, some firms raise multiple rounds of VC, so the number of firms raising capital is less. In fact, according to one recent study, it was discovered that angel investors actually fund sixteen times more deals than VCs do.

You might think that the percentages are actually higher if you limit the firms included to fast-growth companies, eliminating the many lifestyle businesses and less innovative, slower-growth firms. But research by the Kauffman Foundation indicates this is not true. A survey of the 479 fastest-growing companies in the United States from the Inc. 500 / 5000 database in 2013 showed that only about 6.5 percent of them had raised venture capital.[107]

So while the media talks a lot about venture capital, in reality, very few firms actually raise it.

> **Hockey Stick Principle #69: Think of accepting outside capital as investing your equity; take a portfolio-management approach.**

A great way to approach obtaining financing is to raise it from several sources at the same time, which allows you to distribute the stakes funders have in your company and is less dilutive of your control. Daniel Isenberg, professor of entrepreneurship at Babson College, and pharma executive Daniel Lawton describe the pluses of this approach.

> When you scale up, it is faster, more feasible and less dilutive to cobble together your financing from a combination of equity investors, banks, public funds, suppliers, credit cards, customers, and even employees who will take stock options in lieu of some cash. . . . It doesn't make as glamorous a story as "raising $5 million from top-tier Valley VCs," but this is how growth financing typically works in reality.[108]

Lawton offers one example of creative funding opportunities. For instance, a retailer he knows "discovered that the $100 or so penalty to defer California sales tax by a month was actually a cheap source of financing." The retailer discovered that paying the relatively inexpensive $100 penalty allowed it to keep large sums of cash on hard to pay for inventory, rent, and other expenses for the business. This only applies if you live California, but his point underscores the fact that you have to be creative and consider as many options as possible to improve your cash flow.

Another option is to approach so-called super-angel investors, who have been increasingly blurring the traditional line between venture funding and angel investing. Super angels may either be high-net-worth individuals who invest substantially more than the traditional angel investment of between $50,000 and $100,000 or formal groups of angel investors who do so, which are also sometimes referred to as micro VCs. One founder who went the high-net-individual route is Red Hat's Bob Young. He was repeatedly rejected by venture capitalists during the company's first four years. They just didn't believe in Red Hat's innovative model, telling Young, "Well, you can't make money in the software business if you give your software away." His explanation of why Red Hat could in fact do so and wasn't likely to make good money any other way simply didn't sway them. When he did eventually raise substantial capital, it was $2 million in funding from angel investor and businessman Frank Batten, Jr., who decided to take a chance on the unique model.

The super-angel investment groups are something of a hybrid between angel investors and VCs, and they bridge the gap for many start-ups between seed funding and the larger commitments of the VCs. These groups pool the investment money of a number of individual angels, and the investment decisions are made by the management, which differs from the groups described in chapter 2 in which angels make their own decisions individually about investments, though many of them may decide to join together in doing so.

A study by the Center for Venture Research at the University of New Hampshire showed that angel investors now fund sixty times more companies than VCs do, and much of that is from super-angel groups.[109] They typically offer funding between $250,000 and $500,000 and attach fewer strings to the offer, generally not requiring, for example, a seat on the board. Such a force have they become that it's been putting pressure on VC firms to begin making more investments earlier and in this range between seed funding and the traditional Series A offer.

Prominent super-angel groups include SV Angel, started by Ron Conway, a leading angel investor who has backed many of the most successful start-ups in the past couple of decades, such as Google and PayPal; Founders Fund, started by PayPal cofounder Peter Thiel, which has invested in Facebook, Mint.com, and Spotify; and 500 Startups, founded by Dave McClure, which has invested in Udemy and SlideShare among many other successes. You can get good information about many more of them easily through a Web search.

Another possibility to explore is finding a strategic corporate partner. These are larger companies, which may be private or public, that have created investing arms, such as Intel Capital; Steamboat Ventures, a part of Disney; Bloomberg; Microsoft; Qualcomm; Salesforce.com; and Samsung. Key advantages here are that the partner may become an appealing buyer and that these partners can provide access to much wider sales and distribution capabilities. But keep in mind that they are only going to be interested if your business makes a good strategic fit with their own, and they are sometimes criticized for trying to impose too much influence over developing in ways that align with their mission and may not be as appealing to founders.

A founder who raised funding from two different strategic partners, which was instrumental in getting to strong growth, is Doug Lebda of LendingTree. He had traversed the country pitching to top-grade investors and though conversations with a few notable firms advanced promisingly, nothing came of the efforts. He got all the way to the last step with SoftBank Capital, a Japanese VC that had invested in Yahoo!, but that deal also vaporized.

Then in the spring of 1998, Phoenix Insurance Group invested $3 million because it could leverage LendingTree's technology to reach more customers. This is a great example of the kind of strategic fit firms will be looking for. The jolt of fresh capital allowed Doug to hire twenty more employees and significantly grow the company's customer base. Later in 1998, LendingTree raised an additional $7.5 million more from pension fund Ullico, the Union Labor Life Insurance Company.

Another option that's been gaining traction is revenue-based funding (RBF), which is being offered by a growing number of firms that specialize in these deals. The firms offer a fixed amount of money, as with a bank loan, but rather than charging interest on a fixed schedule, they take a percentage of the start-up's revenue over the term of the deal, which is limited to a "cap" amount negotiated as part of the deal. Once the cap is reached, the deal is completed. Harvard professor and specialist on innovative start-up growth Clayton Christensen referred to this as "royalty capital" in a discussion of the benefits of these deals, in which he highlighted that they involve no award of equity, so are not dilutive. They also put no pressure on a founder to either go public or seek a sale.[110] According to Thomas Thurston, the president of research group Growth Science, which analyzes reasons start-ups succeed or fail, the royalty percentage charged is generally 1–10 percent of monthly gross sales, and the cap on the amount to be paid is generally between two to five times the amount of capital awarded.

Thurston advises that this is only a good option, though, for start-ups with healthy gross margins, as with smaller margins, such cuts into revenue could quickly become problematic. He recommends, "This kind of funding only tends to work for startups with 50% or higher gross margins, or otherwise flexible margins so that the royalty doesn't choke the business."[111]

A Portfolio Approach Is Diversified but Highly Selective

While raising funds from a range of sources is advised, you should also be cautious about the risks of taking on too many financial investors from too many different backgrounds. This was one challenge Doug Lebda faced when he was in trouble with the board. He recalls he had a "motley crew of investors"—an insurance company, a pension fund, and a hodgepodge of super angels with different backgrounds. Addressing all their concerns took a good bit of his time.

Another case of conflicting investor demands is that of Trax Technologies, a fast-growth B2B firm that automates the process of finding and correcting errors in freight shipping invoices. Its founder and CEO, J. Scott Nelson, raised money from a few different VCs, and he recalls, "Interests weren't always aligned." He also cautions about the time spent on investor relations, pointing out that he "had to spend a lot of energy helping the investors understand the company. That took away from strategy and other opportunities."

> **Hockey Stick Principle #70: Choose your investors as carefully as they are choosing you.**

How VCs Will Value You

If you do decide to pursue VC funding, it's important to understand the complicated set of factors they will use to calculate their valuation of your firm, which is a large determinant of the terms that they will offer. Valuations are an art rather than a science, but this is a good basic set of factors that will go into the equation:

- **Revenue and earnings for comparable firms:** How have closely related firms been performing?
- **Growth rates of revenue and profit:** Firms that are growing 300 percent are generally going to be perceived as higher future value than those managing only 10 percent, of course, but absolute size of revenue and profitability also factor in.

- **Scalability and profitability of the business model:** Does this business model make money? What are the potential gross margins and operating margins? How expensive is it to service customers? Are there big economies of scale to be had?

- **Management experience and skill:** This is a major consideration. In negotiating with VCs, it's important to show them you are in command of your business and have the required expertise to run it and that you have a strong management team. Particular qualities VCs value in founders are that they are open-minded and surround themselves with experts, as well as that they have already successfully started a company or two.

- **Intellectual property:** How much intellectual property do you own? Do you have any patents, trademarks, copyrights, or other assets that are difficult for others reproduce? Try not to overvalue your IP, because most VCs recognize that IP can only take you so far. But in some circumstances, especially with patents, the quality of your IP can significantly boost your valuation.

- **Size and hotness of the market:** What's the potential size of the market? How many potential customers exist in this market, and how much would they pay? How many of all the potential markets have you actually sold to? How much potential do as yet unexplored markets have?

- **Propensity for being acquired:** Is your firm the type that larger strategic buyers would be interested in acquiring? Can you name several large firms that would want to buy your company and have good reasons why it would make sense for them to do so? Have other firms in your market already been acquired?

- **Competitors:** Ironically, having lots of competitors in your market could be a good thing for VC negotiations, albeit that's mostly true if you have a big market to sell to. Competitors validate the worthiness of your idea. iContact had at least dozens of competitors when it was raising VC.

- **Competition from other VC firms:** If you're a hot commodity and have a great idea in a large market plus management skills, several firms may be bidding higher and higher to invest in your firm.

- **Market conditions:** Stock markets, the amount of money flowing into VC, the economy, and the condition of the market you sell to are all factors that impact how much a VC will value your firm.

- **VCs financial modeling:** VCs leverage elaborate financial models to estimate the returns they might earn on a deal. One well-known such formulation is the Venture Capital Method, created in 1987 by Harvard professor William Sahlman, which takes into account pre-money valuations (the value of the company just before an investment is made), post-money valuation (the value of the company just after the investment is made), and the terminal value (the value of the business when it is sold).

VCs run calculations based on these metrics and other models to figure out how much money they can return to their investors.

They're Investing in You as Much as in Your Model

While attending a venture capital conference, one general partner speaking on a panel summarized the key selection criteria of VCs with memorable efficiency: "We look for talent, talent, talent."

What does talent consist of, exactly? VCs are looking for many important management qualities. Experienced venture capitalist Ed McCarthy with River Cities Capital Funds, a Cincinnati-based VC with $500 million under management, says that some of the most-prized qualities are having a great start-up leader who is a team player and isn't defensive or controlling. He is driven; he can articulate the vision and what he wants to accomplish. He must be willing to—and want to—work with investors. He wants to get some outside viewpoints and assistance in terms of advice, governance, introductions, and different ways to approach things. And he's willing to give up some of the control.

"His motivation is to drive great value and take advantage of an opportunity in a timely way because time is of the essence."

> **Hockey Stick Principle #71: You must learn to sell your company, not just your product.**

VCs also want to know that you can do a very impressive job of selling your company because their goal is for you to either sell it to the market in a big IPO or sell it to a larger firm, and both are very picky and savvy buyers. As one VC partner expressed this concern, "We look for CEOs obsessed with how their product fits in with strategic buyers." They want to know you're just as intent on making a good sale as they are.

As iContact founder Ryan Allis, who was very successful at pitching the company, stresses, his job was to sell iContact *the business,* not necessarily iContact *the product.* And that is still his job today. "For the most part, I'm selling the company; I'm selling the future annuity-revenue stream and profitability that the company will generate if we execute on our strategy," Ryan says.

> **Hockey Stick Principle #72: Transparency is the foundation of investor trust; never engage in obfuscation.**

VCs are also drawn to candidness. They do not want you to hype your company to them. That is not the kind of salesmanship that impresses them. They prefer founders who can clearly articulate the challenges the business faces and have formulated good plans for tackling them. Instead of claiming, "Our projections are conservative," it's better to be more specific and up front about how provisional your numbers may be, saying, "As with any set of revenue projections, these are informed guesses based upon our current pipeline, lead flow, close ratios, current pricing, expected new salesperson hires, and marketing campaigns we plan to execute on in the next six to twelve months."

Hire a CFO and Lawyers for Preparation and Negotiation

This list of what drives the valuation of a firm is just a summary overview of key concerns. The complexity of information that VCs will want from you and of the negotiation process demands that you hire experienced professionals to prepare the figures and design a negotiation strategy. You need to hire experienced advisors who know the VC game and can therefore look out for your best interests. VCs are extremely tough and experienced negotiators, and they can be enormously intimidating.

> **Hockey Stick Principle #73: Don't show up for the investor negotiation gunfight with a knife; hire experts to join you.**

If you haven't already brought in a CFO with experience in the requisite financial analysis, it's vital that you either do so at this point or hire one on a consultancy basis. You may worry about the expense, but you can't possibly go into the process without one. Also, if you haven't developed one before this point, you must now create a very strong, persuasive business plan. This plan doesn't have to be one hundred pages long; those are generally overdone. What's more important is the quality of the content, not its quantity; that is what will impress investors. If you aren't an MBA or CFO yourself, hiring those skills at this point is critically important.

Bringing in trusted financial expertise will help you get your financial house in order and will verify that you are in the position you think you are before you enter the dragon's den. Working with highly skilled professionals with a strong track record also lends you clout. As Lisa Falzone of Revel Systems advises, "I think venture capital has a very firm mentality. I would say that it's about getting one person that is well respected to vouch for you rather than you vouching for yourself."

You absolutely must also hire an experienced lawyer with many successful negotiations to his or her credit. A venture capital firm's offer is described in a term sheet, and the agreed-upon provisions are detailed in elaborate final legal documents. But beware of the term sheet! The precise meaning of each provision could have dire implications for your business later on. In addition to describing the investment amount and ownership, a term sheet describes what legal terms you'll now share with your new financial partner, such as issuing new shares of stock, raising additional money, selling the company, appointing directors to the board, changing the articles of incorporation, entering into contracts that could materially affect the business, participating in legal actions, and settling a legal claim. Term sheets also often state that you'll devote 100 percent of your work time to the business.

When negotiating with VCs, you must not allow yourself to be bullied by the argument that certain terms are the norm. As Scott Edward Walker, a lawyer who specializes in representing entrepreneurs, says, "All terms are negotiable—no matter what anyone tells you."[112]

Pitch-Perfect Pitching

When it comes to doing the actual pitching, though, the focus is all on you. Getting it right is going to take practice, and it's best if that is not in front of friends and family, because for one thing, they're going to be inclined to be encouraging and may find offering criticism to you difficult. But more importantly, they probably have little or no experience with VCs. Instead, you need to pitch to real investors. Here are some key tips on how to pitch to VCs:

- **Start at the bottom of the list.** Try pitching first to VC firms that you already know probably aren't a good fit. That way, you get practice with real pitching and learn a great deal from your mistakes before you pitch to firms that you're really targeting.
- **Seek advice after each pitch.** More than likely, you're going to get turned down a number of times. Write a list of several standard questions to ask after these meetings to probe into how you can improve your argument and also to explore what connections they might help you make. Some questions to ask them: If you were me, how would you pitch my company to investors? What are the strengths and weaknesses of my pitch and company? Do you know other investors that might be interested in my company? Could you introduce me to them?
- **Limit your product demo time.** Unless requested otherwise, limit your demonstration to ten minutes. Even if you have an interesting product, do not overestimate the entertainment value of your pitch. These demonstrations quickly become boring, especially for people who attend so many of them.
- **Know your audience.** Do a great deal of preliminary research before the pitch meeting. Because most VC firms specialize in particular types of businesses, you can figure out a great deal about what they're going to want to hear from you. Study the start-ups they've invested in. Look for commonalities.
- **Pitching isn't a one-way street.** You need to select your investors just as much as they need to select you. Ask them questions too, and have some of these questions prepared ahead of time. They will respect you for this rather than be annoyed by it. This is one way in which you can demonstrate your managerial prowess and your basic confidence. Some questions to ask them: What is your culture and background? How do you interact with company CEOs in your portfolio? What were your key contributions to start-ups that were some of your greatest successes? And most importantly, what ideas do you have for growing my business?

- **Get them what they need when they need it.** As with any sales transaction, follow-up is critical. During a pitch, write down anything the firm asks you to provide and send it promptly. How quickly and completely you respond is a litmus test about how effective a manager you are.

Not only must you prepare well for making a pitch, you should seek the support of some allies when approaching venture firms. You do not want to go into these meetings relying entirely on your own merits. The best way to meet a VC is through an introduction by another entrepreneur or through an investor, banker, lawyer, or accountant.

One last thing to remember when you're trying to persuade VCs to offer funding for your business is that it isn't all about the quality of your pitch or even about how impressed they are by you. They know that the success of a start-up isn't really all about the founder; they will also want to know that a strong management team is in place and that you've created an organization that can rise to the occasion of surging growth. So in the next chapter, we'll consider the essentials of building up a strong team.

Stage IV

Surging Growth

Chapter 8

No Goal Is Scored Alone: Building and Managing Your Team

You've honed your model, and you've either raised outside funding or you're bringing in sufficient revenue to keep funding fast growth. It's all smooth skating from here, right? Well, not quite, because now you're at one of the trickiest junctures for most entrepreneurs—you're transitioning from scrappy creation mode into organizational development mode.

The development of an organization that's in the fast-growth stage slams you with many new challenges, some of which are extremely difficult for many founders. A year or so ago, you were fielding five customer service requests a day, and now over a hundred are flooding in daily. Your sales team was generating twenty or so good leads a week, and now it's clear that you could generate an order of magnitude more if you just had the people or the right mechanism. You've been planning, or even developing, most new product features yourself or with your partner, and now you have too many growing management responsibilities to do as much of that. But you don't want to lose control of quality. You also have a growing list of great ideas for new features and services as well as big fish customers to go after, but you just can't seem to find the time to pursue them. If you've got outside funders, they're demanding more and better financial reporting from you, and your board is starting to breathe down your neck about preparing for an IPO.

It's critical that you now bring in more direct reports, including a number of high-competency specialists. You need to become primarily a manager. Or, as Bronto founder Joe Colopy aptly put it, "To grow a business from $0 to $1 million, I had to be an entrepreneur. But to grow a business from $1 million to $10 million, I had to become an executive." Suddenly, the heady rush of the creation process is replaced by the crush of management responsibilities.

> **Hockey Stick Principle #74: Successful founders must either become equally successful managers or step aside.**

I call this apparent contradiction in the demands made of an entrepreneur the Paradox of Scale; in order to achieve fast growth, you had to be disruptively innovative and improvisational, and in order to sustain it, you have to become intensely disciplined and rigorously managerial. Some founders have no problem at all with this transition, such as Doug Lebda, who was comfortable in corporate life before he started LendingTree and is comfortable again in that world as the CEO of operations after having taken the company public and sold the company to IAC. But most entrepreneurs struggle with this change of pace, in large part because they worry that their firm will become just another corporate soul crusher. They also have no passion for management, not anything like the passion they had for creating their product. And even if they do relish the challenge of developing a larger, highly professional organization, they simply don't have the management or expertise needed. The aversion or inability to shift mind-sets is one of the main reasons why firms that have hit takeoff subsequently go into a death spiral.

> **Hockey Stick Principle #75: Good managers are made, not born.**

Most founders at this point face another moment of truth, confronting three key choices. Should they stay and learn how to manage the complexities of running a fast-growth firm? Should they stay but bring in an experienced CEO from outside and take on some other role? Or should they start looking for a buyer or take the calls of the companies that may well already be circling the waters? In truth, there really is no other choice but to learn the ins and outs of executive leadership. Even if your aim is to eventually exit, getting the company in good shape for either a successful sale or an IPO will require you to put in place a strong leadership team and develop a well-honed organization; otherwise, you'll end up selling at a fire-sale price.

So what does it take to transition?

The World May Be Flat, but Most Organizations Aren't

A great deal has been written in recent years about the need to dump the stultifying, motivation-sapping hierarchical bureaucracy of the modern corporation and create flat organizational charts. Some high-profile companies have made bold moves in this direction. Zappos, the intensely customer service–centric shoe retailer, announced that it was doing away with middle management and introducing a new, nonhierarchical organizational management structure that "replaces today's top-down predict-and-control paradigm with a new way of achieving control by distributing power," which is called holocracy.[113] Employees don't even have job titles.

In announcing the change, Zappos founder Tony Hsieh wrote in a memo to employees:

> In order to eliminate the legacy management hierarchy, there will effectively be no more people managers. In addition, we will begin the process of breaking down our legacy silo'ed structure/circles of merchandising, finance, tech, marketing, and other functions and create self-organizing and self-managing business-centric circles instead by starting to fund this new model with the appropriate resources needed to flourish. Functions that were previously silo'ed will be embedded inside these business-centric circles instead.[114]

Twitter cofounder Evan Williams uses this same structure for his online publishing platform Medium, as do some other relatively small firms, such as Morning Star, which is the world's largest tomato-processing company and was described in the *Harvard Business Review* by influential business author Gary Hamel as "the world's most creatively managed company."[115]

Another founder and CEO who has advocated for flat structure is Jason Fried of Web application provider Basecamp (formerly known as 37signals), who wrote in a blog post titled "Why I Run a Flat Company" that "one thing we've found is that groups that manage themselves are often better off than groups that are managed by a single person. So when groups do require structure, we get them to manage themselves."

Basecamp is still quite a small company, with only twenty-six employees at the time he wrote the blog post, and even so, the company was experiencing growing pains with this approach. Fried continued, "This has served us well over the years. But recently, as we've brought on more people, that model has been showing signs of strain. We're now at twenty-six people. And, as many entrepreneurs have learned, once your business reaches a certain size, matters you didn't have to consider before become difficult to ignore. In our case, HR terms like *departments, managers,* and *titles* have begun to pop up more often."[116]

Indeed, the Zappos announcement was widely covered in the business press because the company is so large, with 1,500 employees at that time, while generally holocracy is implemented by only fairly small firms.

The philosophy behind flat organizational structures is one that should absolutely be applauded, with the primary goals being to achieve more agility and efficiency by having fewer reporting processes and meetings, for example, and to give employees more autonomy and decision-making authority and also to make them feel more a part of the success of the company. But as Fried points out, this kind of organizational structure is tricky to manage and all the more so the larger a staff becomes. Flat organization isn't a simple structure. As Tony Hsieh wrote in his memo to employees, holocractic firms are "complex, participatory, interconnected, interdependent, and continually evolving systems, like ecosystems in nature."[117]

And even with such a radically nonhierarchical management system, leadership and expertise are vital. As Hsieh explained in his memo—under the headings "Misperception 1: No Structure, No Management" and "Misperception 2: Everyone Is Equal"—this approach doesn't mean that people have no responsibility of leadership; actually more take it on, and they must have the competency and the authority to get things done well and on time.

> **Hockey Stick Principle #76: A fast-growth organization without top-quality managers is like a team of star players without a coach.**

The late, great Peter Drucker stated that failure to create a solid team at the top-management level is the core reason start-ups go off the rails:

> The new venture has successfully established itself in the right market and has then successfully found the right financial structure and the financial systems it needs. Nonetheless, a few years later it is still prone to run into

serious crisis . . . it gets in trouble nobody seems to understand. . . . The reason is always the same: a lack of top management.[118]

In building a strong leadership team and setting up strong divisions of authority, there are a number of best practices that will allow you to achieve the greater agility, efficiency, and higher employee engagement and positive culture that the flat organization advocates aspire to. It is entirely possible to have a clear hierarchy of authority and to still make all employees feel valued and motivated. We'll discuss the ways to achieve both in this chapter. But first, it's important to address a question that vexes many founders—when should they set up separate departments and appoint department heads?

It's Not the Size of Staff; It's the Degree of Complexity

The nature of businesses varies too much for there to be a hard-and-fast rule about when a founder should create a leadership structure with separate departments. But a good rule of thumb is that you should do so once you have about fifteen to twenty employees. At that point, the complexity of processes to be managed generally begins to surpass the ability of you and your partner or a few key, trusted early employees to handle all tasks well. You don't have to create your leadership team all at once; you may want to bring in expert managers in a staggered fashion, perhaps first bringing in a chief financial officer to get you fully up to speed with all the financial reporting and analysis you should be doing, and then bringing in a chief operating officer, and then a head of sales, and so on.

In growing First Research, I moved incrementally at first, bringing in Tyler Rullman, who had an MBA from UCLA and had much more training in business management processes than I. He helped me manage four groups—finance, sales, marketing, and research—which freed me up to focus more on product development and managing the sales team. Not long thereafter, once we had twenty employees, he recommended that we bring in an experienced manager from outside to take charge of each department, and even though I had some trepidation about changing our culture, which was still quite informal, with key personnel operating with a great deal of autonomy, I agreed, and I was glad I did.

It's inevitable that making this transition will involve some bumps. Most founders will tell you that in one way or another, they made some mistakes when making key hires in this stage. To mitigate the damage, you must make these decisions with great care.

Your decision-making process about who you bring in to fill these spots will be one of the most influential factors for whether you continue to thrive or start to drift into the shoals of management dysfunction.

Building a Championship-Quality Team

No team in hockey can win the Stanley Cup without some star players and good coaching that ensures everyone is playing in sync. Likewise, you can't build a highly successful company if you don't hire some top-quality talent and make sure that your management team is working well together.

One of the biggest mistakes founders make is to continue to hire key roles by tapping their circle of friends and bringing in people they feel personally comfortable with rather than undertaking a more professional recruitment search. If you have a partner, he or she may well become one of these department heads or perhaps the COO who complements you as CEO or vice versa. You may also have one or two other employees who are well qualified to assume key leadership roles. But generally, many of your early employees either won't truly be qualified to perform at the level you need in these roles or won't want to. Managing finances or a team of salespeople or the marketing operations are all jobs that require specialized skills as well as hands-on experience at the speed and volume of business during this fast-growth stage. But many early employees are inexperienced in business, often having joined a start-up right out of college, and they have little if any management experience or expertise in business operations and planning. Many others are people who've chosen to work at a start-up in part because they wanted to escape the corporate style of management. Becoming corporate managers is the last thing they want, and they often wouldn't be good at it.

Hockey Stick Principle #77: Winning teams recruit star players.

For me, when building First Research, Ingo was a genius researcher, but he didn't want to manage the half-dozen people we needed to keep our content current or the relationships with our licensing partners. I also had an efficient, capable controller, Carolyn Beggs, to manage our finances, but once I had hired seven salespeople, I realized that I needed reports that provided key performance indicators (KPIs), such as the number of new customers gained, number of customers lost, cost per sale made, number of customer accounts managed per salesperson, and many other sales performance statistics on a weekly basis. Calculating KPIs was something Carolyn had no experience in, and her workload was clearly growing beyond what she could manage, so I brought in an experienced part-time CFO to complement her.

You should conduct a rigorous search to find people who can complement your skills with top-quality expertise. That may require working with a professional recruitment specialist. Bronto founder and CEO Joe Colopy told me that he realized he should have done that much earlier than he did because recruiting is difficult, almost like sales, and takes up lots of time. "If I had to do it again, I would have hired a recruiting expert much earlier on. Instead of waiting until we'd grown to [a staff of] fifty to seventy-five people, I probably would have hired a recruiting expert at like fifteen people." You may or may not need to work that way, but doing so can help with one of the most important mandates—that you go outside of your comfort zone of hiring people you feel closely aligned with or who are like you.

> **Hockey Stick Principle #78: Hiring only people who see things as you do means you'll have a blind spot.**

In a speech at Stanford Graduate School of Business, the founder of tech firm GO Corporation, Jerry Kaplan, offered some candid advice about the perils of entrepreneurs hiring people they like rather than people they need:

> I've got news for you, a company is not a social club. The problem is, if you hire people you like, you aren't going to hire the critical skills that are needed to build a venture. One of my greatest accomplishments over the past 20 years . . . is I have worked with people I truly detest and have done so successfully for long periods of time. You have to learn to respect people that you don't like.[119]

President Lincoln famously appointed to his cabinet three men who had run against him for the Republican nomination in the 1860 election: Attorney General Edward Bates, Secretary of the Treasury Salmon P. Chase, and Secretary of State William H. Seward. There was no love lost between him and them, but the reason he appointed them was to help bring a party together that was badly split by discord. He also knew they were highly competent. As the group took the country through the bloodiest battles in its history, they rallied behind the president and made a highly effective team. Each of the former rivals performed exquisitely. Seward was famous for his work in helping preserve the Union, though he also was famous for challenging Lincoln.[120] Chase smartly figured out how to finance the war utilizing paper currency to function as war notes.[121] Bates offered valuable counterarguments again and again for Lincoln to consider in making difficult decisions, helping him to weigh all options. Lincoln had decided that it was most important that he surround himself with the smartest people, not those who were in agreement with him or whom he liked.

The point isn't that you should seek out people you don't like; what you're looking for are people who are better at the functions they will perform than you are and who have different perspectives from you so that they can offer you healthy pushback and think outside of your own mental box. It is so important that you not surround yourself with an echo chamber. Stanford Graduate School of Business professor Lindred Greer, who specializes in the study of team power structures and dynamics, argues, "Ignoring the need for true complementarity is the number one mistake startups make."[122] The chairman of JetBlue Airways Corporation, Joel Peterson, also ranks this as the number-one hiring mistake and expresses well why so many founders fall into this trap: "Hiring yourself, over and over. . . . From the factory floor to the executive suite, no manager is immune from feeling comfortable with the familiar . . . we tend to like people who affirm our opinions and decisions."[123] This is a version of what's known in decision science as the confirmation bias. Extensive psychological studies have shown that we have a natural inclination to seek out confirmation of our views when we are supposedly seeking advice.

Having a homogenous management team can also lead to the problem of groupthink. Yale psychologist Dr. Irving L. Janis introduced this concept in his widely cited 1972 work *Victims of Groupthink*. A good definition of it is "the emergence of intense conformity pressures within decision-making groups that seriously restrict the range of options considered, bias the analysis of existing information, and promote simplistic and self-righteous stereotypes."[124]

If you can find highly competent people who are strong-minded and will speak up and make their case when they disagree with you yet who also share many of your personality traits, great—hire some of them. But also be sure to mix it up. If you find people who fit the first part of that bill who you don't have a natural affinity of personality and work style with, then you should become intent on learning how to work well with them. I like to say that these people rub me the right way. That was true for Ingo and me. He was a laid-back intellectual from the Northeast; I was a high-energy salesman from the South. But I appreciated how he complemented me. I needed his calm, cool smarts.

Your Lieutenants Must Share in Your Mission

Gino Wickman is the author of a popular management book for start-ups titled *Traction* and is also a consultant and entrepreneur himself. He stresses that it's important for founders to look for people "who share your company's core values. They fit and thrive in your culture. They are people you enjoy being around and who make your organization a better place to be."[125] I couldn't agree more that you want a good number of such people on your team and all through your staff. So what am I saying, exactly? Should you hire people you like who are also like you, or diverse people without any regard to how much you like them but who bring in new ideas? I believe it's essential to do *both*. And the point Wickman makes about sharing the core values is key here. You want to apply what economists call "bounded rationality" in bringing in people with different perspectives; you want a good dose of difference, but within the parameters of your business model and culture.

> **Hockey Stick Principle #79: The stars you recruit must be able to play with your team.**

While you want your management team to challenge your arguments on both your strategy and tactics for moving forward, they must be on board about the fundamental mission and about the culture and values that are the DNA of your operation. A great example of how a different perspective can be in perfect alignment with a company's culture and mission is that of IBM and Lou Gerstner. When IBM first hired Gerstner to turn the company around, the management had developed a plan for breaking the company into parts, but Gerstner, who had no prior experience in the computer industry and was coming on with a fresh perspective, wasn't wedded to that plan. He could see that integrated computing solutions was something that companies were going to need, and in order for IBM to offer these services, the company would have to keep its divisions together. Gerstner also appreciated that IBM was, in fact, a great company with an illustrious history and believed that it could rise to the challenge. He argued that the company should be kept whole. Gerstner turned out to be correct about offering integrated computing solutions, and IBM's revenue increased from $62 billion in 1993, the year he took over, to $87 billion in 1999. Profits also increased dramatically.

In this fast-growth stage, and in all likelihood for most of the duration in your company's future, you don't want to be making radical changes to your strategy or to your culture. You don't want to bring in people who are going to be overly forceful in pushing for a new direction or way of operating and who don't appreciate the value of what's working well. It's critical that senior executives you hire buy in to the basics of your business model and your style of doing business—your culture—whether you like them or not.

It's easy during this transition for a more professional organization to go off course. I know only too well; I fell into the trap of allowing a newly hired executive to lead me astray from our core culture and model at First Research.

Tyler and I had decided we wanted to hire someone from a technology background to help grow our sales operation because we knew that tech firms had innovated some great selling techniques that we didn't have experience in. First Research is not a technology or software firm, but we were a B2B start-up that shared some characteristics with those kinds of businesses. The catch was that technology companies tend to employ large inside sales teams and follow what's called a B2B lead-generation sales model, which drums up sales leads through a high-ticket, broad-reaching marketing operation that gets potential customers to click on a link of some kind—say, for a free whitepaper (an educational document to help improve business practices)—and then that potential customer is later contacted by an inside sales team member to get a potential conversion into a customer.

So the contact with the potential customer is "inbound," and the sales team has to follow up with calls to get conversions.

Our approach at First Research was fundamentally different. We employed mostly an outbound calling method that meant that our relatively small sales team focused on making well-targeted calls to potential customers and building relationships with them. This is a model that's widely considered old school in the tech sector, and that was the opinion of our new recruit when he came on to manage and grow our sales operation.

Tyler and I had reached into the depths of Research Triangle Park, which is home to dozens of venture-backed technology companies, to make the hire. As we began interviewing candidates, I started to feel uncomfortable because none of them thought our sales approach made sense. But I pressed on, believing that I had to be open-minded if we were to grow. Tyler thought we should hire someone who could get us up to speed with the B2B lead-generation model and manage an additional sales team that we'd bring in to implement it. I agreed to go for it, and so we hired Scott England, who had good experience with this model.

Not long after bringing him in, Tyler and I decided that it was time for me to step aside from the direct management of sales and focus on running the entire company by supporting all five departments equally. This was a big change for me to cope with, as from 1999 until then, 2005, sales had been my baby. The question of who should take over as sales manager was important. We had some great salespeople, but the best candidates all worked remotely, and none of them wanted to move to Raleigh. Tyler advocated that we give the job to Scott. I was leery at first about putting him in charge of all of sales, because his primary experience had been selling technology products using modern sales methods. Our sales approach had been more old school. But Tyler, with his MBA and VC work experience, thought that Scott's expertise with the new method would allow us to quickly make a success of the new method and evolve away from our old approach. I was told by new sales-and-marketing experts that in a few years we'd have 30,000 leads instead of 1,500 and higher conversion rates. I put my reservations about the change aside, still wanting to have an open mind about the best method for growing our sales, and I agreed to promote Scott.

We quickly began hiring employees for the new sales operation, which included not only salespeople but staff in marketing and customer service. This process was a very difficult jolt not only to the core team who had been behind our successful growth to that point but to our bottom line. The new hires and the technology needed were very expensive, and furthermore, the new system affected how the existing sales process worked in terms of cold-calling and finding new customers. For example, many of the tenured salespeople thought, *Should I be proactive and call or wait for leads to come to me?*

By promoting Scott and agreeing to such a rapid buildup of the new sales operation, I made several mistakes, none of which had anything to do with Scott or his abilities. First, I allowed a new initiative to severely interrupt our existing successful operations. Second, I asked a person with a different background to manage a group of employees who were aligned around our original model without assuring that the old was respected in the transition to the new. That wasn't fair to Scott, and it wasn't fair to the existing First Research sales team. Furthermore, I allowed myself to lose sight of the beauty of the model we had crafted. My original sales approach was, in truth, a great way to sell a product like ours—one that requires lots of explanation as well as pilot programs and follow-up customer attention. Finally, few potential customers were actively looking for what we offered; we had to teach them how industry call preparation could improve their sales process. Outbound calls to them were more effective than trying to drum up inbound leads.

So if I had it to do again, I would still implement aspects of a B2B lead-generation sales model, but I would do so gradually instead of transitioning full force into it all at once, and I would be sure to hire a sales manager with a great appreciation for my old-school sales model as well as the knowledge of how to run the new model.

The bottom line here is that when you bring in your executive team members, make sure to get their explicit buy-in to your culture and model. If they think you should be changing these two linchpins of your ways of operating, evaluate that advice very carefully. And if you do decide to make the change, move incrementally.

No Pain, No Gain

You cannot expect that bringing in new talent at the top will go over well with all your original team. Even as well as Ingo and I got along, when I started hiring new expert managers, he pushed back about my push for growth. He questioned the plan to build so much expensive infrastructure.

"First it was marketing, and then it was sales, and next it'll probably be finance," he once told me. And he was right; finance was next. He and Wil Brawley, my original sales master, began to feel shoved aside. When I asked Ingo about this, he responded honestly, telling me, "It was clear to me that Tyler quickly became your biggest influence, a role that Wil and I had shared before. That wasn't a bad thing because Tyler is a smart guy, but both Wil and I felt marginalized."

Some resentment by early members of the team toward outsiders coming in and taking over roles they've been filling is inevitable; it's fundamentally human. But given that this is the case, you should be aware and prepared to work hard to mitigate the friction. The way to do this is to communicate openly and honestly with your team about the changes you're making and the strategy behind them and to take their feedback into consideration and listen to their concerns. I could have benefited from heeding Ingo's caution about so much change in infrastructure so fast.

But even if you communicate and listen thoughtfully, some people may still choose to leave your company, and that may even be your partner. Paul Graham of Y Combinator reports that 20 percent of the start-ups the firm has invested in have had a founder leave.[126] This happens so often largely because of the changes to a start-up's management systems and culture that are required as the company gets bigger. You simply can't be as easygoing about management with fifty employees as you can be with five. You have to put in place more formal systems and processes, and while some people enjoy working in this kind of more structured organization, some of those who are drawn to working in start-ups despise it, often including the founder.

Delegating Does Not Mean Abdicating

As you build your executive team, you've got to start loosening your grip on every little detail of the business. Many founders hold on too tightly to too many responsibilities for much too long. I like the way Andreessen Horowitz cofounder Ben Horowitz discusses this transfer of responsibility. He wrote, "When you scale an organization, you will also need to give ground grudgingly." Horowitz uses the analogy of how football linemen protect their quarterback by backing up while they block. They're giving up ground to the defense, but for the common good of the team. If they tried to bulldoze defensive linemen, they'd probably lose too often, and the quarterback would get sacked. Founders have to do the same thing. They have to give up some ground that they've been taking the lead on or overseeing very closely, and they have to make some room for others on the team to step in and carry the ball sometimes. If they don't do this, their organization will break down, and the company will be sacked like a quarterback because the founder didn't give any ground. Managing this ceding of territory is another delicate balance.

Hockey Stick Principle #80: Keep your hands dirty with some details.

Think about what we know about how Steve Jobs managed Apple. He was a notorious stickler for details. Not only did Jobs conjure up many of Apple's best product ideas, he even went so far as to negotiate deals himself with partners to make products work. For example, he worked directly with many of the music companies to license songs for the iTunes store.

Steve Jobs isn't an anomaly. Many successful founders are very detailed as well and get into the weeds even as their companies are growing fast. Jeff Bezos is also characterized as a "devil in the details" manager; a 2013 *New York Times* article about him notes his "obsession with tinkering until he gets it right," and former employee Steve Yegge is quoted as saying, "He just makes ordinary control freaks look like stoned hippies."[127]

Another thing to stay detail oriented about is that you must stay closely in touch with what the executive team members you bring in are doing. Otherwise, you run the risk of discovering too late that their résumé-writing and interviewing skills are much more impressive than their actual business skills.

Founders bring in highly qualified experts all the time who underperform. I love the way Jessica Herrin, founder of WeddingChannel.com and more recently jewelry trunk sale firm Stella & Dot, talked about this problem in a Stanford Graduate School of Business publication. She recalled in an interview that one of her biggest failures was recruiting senior executives who had strong résumés but didn't do their jobs:

I made the mistake of falling for what I call a "job-shaped object." Those tend to be senior executives from big brands. They look like a job and smell like a job but they don't actually do a job. They tell people to tell other people what to do but they don't do anything themselves. . . . There are a lot of people with great functional skills but it doesn't mean they belong at your company.[128]

Despite the fact that you should delegate managing large portions of your business to others, you should still focus on your areas of greatest strength. It might seem that Steve Jobs was a control freak for not leaving the negotiation about terms for songs going into the iTunes store to others, but this was a vital component of the whole ecosystem Apple was building around the iPod, and the model they were developing was radical. They had to get it right.

In his intensity of personal involvement in the design of the products, he was also playing to his strengths. He had an extraordinary design sense. Yes, he had Jonathan Ive, his chief of design, who is one of the geniuses of design of our times, but Jobs knew that he also had a deep understanding of the aesthetic that he wanted to define Apple, and he knew that maintaining that extremely high standard was the lifeblood of the company's success.

The key takeaway here is that in delegating authority, it's a good idea for founders to keep direct responsibility, if not primary responsibility, for the key part or parts of the business that are in their core area of competence.

Another great example of someone who did this well is Jim Goodnight, the founder of software giant SAS. He is a brilliant programmer, and he could have delegated all programming responsibility to others since rigorous disciplines for managing software development had been created. And he could certainly afford to hire the very best programmers. But he knew his strengths, and programming was most definitely one of them. Even as SAS was growing into a behemoth, he continued to spend 90 percent of his time programming new features.

Had I rigorously followed this example when we scaled up the First Research sales operation, I would have kept a stronger hand in our strategy. Sales had been my baby, and as the saying goes, you shouldn't throw the baby out with the bathwater. We had a good core sales model, and I should have asserted my expertise about that.

Another key takeaway is that being an engaged, connected leader and being a delegator are not in the slightest bit mutually exclusive. One of the most compelling recent philosophies of leadership that is espoused by Harvard Business School professor Linda Hill is what she calls "leading from behind." As she wrote in the *Harvard Business Review,* she borrowed the phrase from South African leader Nelson Mandela. "In his autobiography, Mandela equated a great leader with a shepherd: 'He stays behind the flock, letting the most nimble go out ahead, whereupon the others follow, not realizing that all along they are being directed from behind.' "[129] This involves closely observing the team, communicating constantly with them, but not always being the one to set their agenda. One founder I talked with who described his role well in these terms is Joe Colopy of Bronto. He told me that he sees a key responsibility of his as the leader being to connect the dots between the teams by listening. "Most of my time is checking in on reoccurring meetings with the leadership team. A big part of my day is listening honestly. Soliciting feedback."

> **Hockey Stick Principle #81: Leading is as much about listening as directing.**

Don't hire good people and get out of their way; you should hire good people and get them together, communicate with them, and bridge communications among them. As Linda Hill explained:

> Leading from behind doesn't mean abrogating your leadership responsibilities. After all, the shepherd makes sure that the flock stays together. He uses his staff to nudge and prod if the flock strays too far off course or into danger. For leaders, it's a matter of harnessing people's collective genius. Doing so entails two primary responsibilities—and they are not easy to get right.
>
> First, leaders must ensure their organizations are willing to innovate. This is fundamentally about building community. Some leaders refer to this function as "creating a world to which people want to belong." In these communities, people are valued for who they are and have the opportunity to contribute to something larger than themselves. These communities have a common purpose, values and rules of engagement about how people should interact and problem-solve together. A shared purpose brings the people together and makes them willing to do the hard work of innovation.

Second, leaders must build the organizational capabilities necessary for engaging in the innovation process.[130]

We've just covered the building up of organizational capabilities. Now let's consider the shared purpose and create a world that your employees want to belong in.

Stock Options Are Great; Respect and Inclusion Are Even Better

So much emphasis in the discussion of how best to motivate a team has focused on financial rewards tied to individual performance, with stock options being the especially tantalizing incentives for employees at start-ups. This is with good reason; options for those who come on board a start-up that really takes off can turn into fortunes. I couldn't be a bigger advocate of good compensation, but all the stress on financial incentivizing has overshadowed what actually are the strongest motivators of employees. Backing up Linda Hill's assertion about the importance of community building, a great deal of research has found that employees are most engaged and productive when they trust that the management cares about their well-being and they feel connected in a clear and significant way to the mission and can see the positive difference they are making.

> **Hockey Stick Principle #82: Every team needs a deep bench; make all employees feel like key players.**

One of my favorite thought leaders on this issue is the former CEO of the hugely successful furniture company Herman Miller, Max De Pree. His book *Leadership Is an Art* is, to my mind, one of the most useful leadership books ever written because it skillfully articulates that the most important characteristic of leadership is caring about people. De Pree says, "Relationships count more than structure."[131] If you don't treat people well, it doesn't matter how well organized your leadership team is. De Pree advocates *inclusion* of all associates in the process of running a company, whereas most leaders are exclusive, sharing strategy and the rationales behind decisions and asking for input into them only from the upper management. De Pree stresses that employees want to feel needed, involved, and cared about, and, yes, also to be included in the monetary success of the company.

There's a phenomenal amount of evidence that treating employees really well results in a much more productive and profitable company. For example, studies have shown that paying above market wages leads to significantly higher productivity and profits. This is why they're called "efficiency wages." This isn't actually a new practice. The most famous example is that of Henry Ford increasing wages for the workers on his Model T assembly line as a way to combat high turnover and absenteeism. The increase—to $5.00 per day from $2.25 a day—led to a very good increase in productivity and profits.[132]

Paying efficiency wages has been found to be so effective that new businesses have sprung up based entirely on the premise. Chuck Wall's successful start-up, Freight Handlers, Inc. (FHI), is a good example of this. As an operations executive for a trucking firm, Chuck noticed his trucks were getting backed up for hours at distribution centers waiting to be unloaded. He observed that no one at the distribution centers seemed to care because they were not provided benefits, had low pay, and the management was lax. The people doing the unloading were oftentimes independent workers, and they didn't feel particularly committed to doing a top-quality job because the management was so unstructured and there was a lack of control and discipline about best processes.

Chuck had the idea of starting FHI to take over the unloading labor at distribution centers and deploy a business model where the treatment of workers was totally different. FHI more than doubled wages for those unloading trucks by paying them according to productivity. He provided them with benefits and training, and he treated them with respect. This was a win-win solution, and everyone benefited. The retailers that owned the distribution centers saw their costs come down, and the productivity of their distribution centers increased. The employees were not only paid more and given the security of benefits, they were happier and more committed to their work because they were treated with more respect. And FHI benefited by starting and owning a new great company that today is unloading more than a million trucks every year, or four thousand per day.

Jim Goodnight's SAS is another example of how efficiency wages pay off. Offering a well-above-market benefits package has been a fundamental management practice. But the company does much more to show employees that it respects and cares about them. In 2003, CBS's *60 Minutes* reporter Morley Safer noted, "If there is a heaven on earth on the job, it is at SAS Institute." The company offers a wealth of other employee benefits, including a more generous than usual 401(k) program, subsidized on-site day care, flexible work schedules, on-site massage, and free snacks and beverages. But more important even than the great benefits and pay, SAS also treats its employees with a tremendous amount of respect. When I interviewed him, Goodnight expressed the respect he has for his employees beautifully by saying, "Everybody's here because they want to be here, and they enjoy what they're working on and the challenge too." He continued, "[We] treat [employees] with lots of respect and let them do their best. I always operated that way, where you trust the people that you've hired to do a good job, and you don't impose any kind of childish nonsense on them. If somebody has to leave to go pick up their child or go to a school play or if it's the first soccer game, then we expect them to leave and go do that. I mean, we all have families, so we know that in being a parent there are many things that happen during work that you have to go take care of." SAS's workplace culture is so balanced, respectful, and healthy that turnover is only 4 percent per year, compared to 15 percent for all US firms.[133] Hardly anyone quits—and why would they?

Another great way of showing appreciation to your team is to offer performance bonuses. Start-ups are in an optimal position to pay bonuses, in part because they're subject to less regulation. You should set goals and reward people well for achieving them. The key is to make the goals realistic and your communication about them positive. Don't make people feel like this is really a way of holding their feet to the fire or that you're pitting them against one another. There are many ways of making sure everyone is inspired by bonus offers so they're a win-win, such as:

- **Variable Bonus:** Each employee receives a bonus if a goal is achieved, plus escalations if it is exceeded. But here is the catch: variable shouldn't mean that the percentage of the base pay differs from employee to employee. That can lead to resentment and backfire. Instead, institute a bonus structure with the same percentage of base pay for *all* employees. For example, if the company achieves its goal, *all* employees receive a bonus of 15 percent of their salary. This approach builds unity and teamwork.
- **Team Bonus:** Each employee receives the same amount of cash, plus escalations.

- **Profit-Sharing Plan:** Pay all or part of the bonuses into a plan that you then divvy up equally.
- **Add Attractive Benefits:** Invest some of the new profit into gym memberships, better health care coverage, more vacation, or an upgraded 401(k) plan.
- **Creative Benefits:** How about for the next year all employees quit working Fridays at 3:00 P.M.? Or upgrade your office space to be more employee friendly?

Whichever way you go, make the amount meaningful. Just think about how your team would feel if you gave them bonuses like those awarded to the whole staff last year by etailinsights. I spoke to founder Darren Pierce, who told me because the company exceeded its goal, each employee received a $5,000 check. The e-mail message he sent out announcing the payouts read, in part, "I'd like to issue a special thank-you. . . . Without an awesome team who creates a product with awesome data, we wouldn't have any sales."

A Failure to Communicate

A big mistake many founders make once they are so caught up in the process of building the management team is to become too exclusively focused on those direct reports and to become remote from the rest of the staff. A hallmark of founders that create a culture in which employees feel respected and cared for is that they communicate all the way through the organization about the mission and strategy. And they get out from behind their desks and interact with staff at all levels.

> **Hockey Stick Principle #83: If employees don't know you, they know you don't know them.**

One founder who has implemented many ways to stay connected to his staff and to keep open lines of communication with them is Joe Colopy. And as Bronto has grown, he has instituted more events so that he has scaled up his communication and his interactions with the whole employee pool in keeping with its growth. He told me, "Twice a year, we have some meeting of the minds with engineering and client services. In addition to that, every quarter, we have a half-day 'All Brontos,' which is a business meeting with everyone in the company in which our results for the last quarter are presented. Periodically, I have what I call fireside chats with a random assortment of Brontos, and we just talk about things not related to business." Colopy is sure to get to know his employees as people and to make it clear to them that this matters to him a great deal.

Another way in which he has stayed connected and approachable is by moving where he is working on a regular basis. He explained that Bronto doesn't have any private offices. "I could easily have a private office if I wanted to. But if I have a private office, then our VPs would want private offices. It suddenly becomes a thing. But by not having that, it sets that tone. We're all in the same boat. I change my seat every three months. I want to know different groups. Obviously, I can't spend time with everybody, but I can spend time with a lot of people, and that matters. I think it sets that tone for how everyone else interacts."

The Google founders famously established a once-a-week meeting that all employees are free to attend at which they take questions about anything employees want to hear about. One way I connect with my staff is to regularly go to a casual restaurant with an employee to have an open exchange and get feedback. Choose a method or set of practices that suit you and your culture, but be sure to do this in some way. The high-pressure demands on you in this fast-growth stage can make taking this kind of time for interacting with employees you're not directly managing seem impossible. The truth is that this step is simply essential.

One thing that can help make staying connected to your staff somewhat easier is keeping a very close tab on how fast you're hiring.

Beware Parkinson's Law of Triviality

In November 1955, C. Northcote Parkinson's *The Economist* article "Parkinson's Law" stated, "It is a commonplace observation that work expands so as to fill the time available for its completion."[134] The first example he cited was how an elderly lady of leisure can spend all day sending a postcard versus three minutes for a busy man to complete the same task.

Parkinson's Law suggests that if you hire too many people, they'll accomplish the same amount of work as a smaller number of people. For example, if you hire one person to manage sales operations—they'll remain busy doing just that. But if you hire three people to manage sales operations, then guess what will happen? They will remain busy doing just that. They'll make up stuff to do and create projects and reports, conduct meetings, and even still go home tired. So it's your and your leadership team's job to make sure you don't become like the elderly lady of leisure. You have to aim for optimal efficiency and be sure that the hires you're making are truly necessary.

> **Hockey Stick Principle #84: Understand the necessity of every hire you make.**

As with all things entrepreneurial, this is of course easier said than done. Calibrating how much staff to bring in trips up many founders, and they make mistakes both ways. Joe Colopy told me that he erred on the side of being conservative and should have hired more people faster. "You get in that middle stage," he said, "and it's like a 'tweener stage where you need a lot more people than you know." In this event, people are going to be overloaded and stressed, and more mistakes are going to be made.

A founder who erred in the other direction is Brian Hamilton, who went into high gear with hiring salespeople. In 2004, Sageworks faced a period of massive growth. What first caused the growth was when a much larger potential competitor, one of the largest information companies in the world, tried to acquire Sageworks. But after brief negotiations, the information company's executives tried to pressure Brian; if he didn't sell to them at a favorable price, they would compete with him. Brian refused the deal.

But in response to the threat, Sageworks raised $4 million in capital from investors to improve its product quality and gain market share.

"Here's what we did. We started hiring more people because we knew what their play would be. They would come at us with one product, expecting we'd go head-to-head. But no. If you're coming out with one product, I'm gonna have three. When you have three, I'm gonna have six. So where we really beat them was on the product side. They have one product, and we have like twenty that do different financial-analysis things."

Sageworks won the war against the information company, the larger competitor, in just that way. After a few years, the competitor's product fizzled out and began giving its product away for free. "So they had been a nuisance, but they haven't been a problem," Brian says.

But in response to the threat from the information company, Sageworks grew too fast.

"We started scaling the company real quickly. To compete, we weren't trying to get 30 percent-a-year growth; we were trying to get 500 percent! And our losses started really escalating because we were trying to grow too fast. We hired too many people, we fired too many people, and we lost money. I would never again overrespond to a competitive threat—even if they are a billion-dollar company."

While selling came naturally to Brian and his management team, they had little experience managing a telemarketing center—the sales method of choice for Sageworks at the time. They'd have to make up their strategy as they went along. For example, they thought that they could easily teach young college graduates to sell as capably as they themselves did, but that plan didn't go smoothly.

"We taught the kids the wrong way to sell. Like, 'I'm just going to just give it to you, and force it down your throat.' And that doesn't work. And now I realize why—because they never got the practice. And so we let those people down. I had been selling ever since I was a kid, and I couldn't understand why everyone couldn't sell.

"So, fundamentally, between 2002 and 2008, we made the massive mistake of thinking we could build a big direct-sales force with a lot of capable salespeople, when in fact, we learned the eighty-twenty rule—that we always had 20 percent of the people selling 80 percent of the deals."

There is the eighty-twenty rule again. Embracing this principle in regard to employees is a particularly difficult part of growth transition for entrepreneurs because many times the first employees are all productive. These first employees are likely hand selected, they often acquire ownership, and they embrace the new idea. But as a business becomes larger, it is inevitable that some new employees are less vested in the mission, and continuing to find such high producers becomes more difficult.

By 2006, Sageworks employed seventy salespeople, most of them young and inexperienced. Brian owns up to "letting many of them down," but says he was just trying things. "The thing is—we just didn't know. Everybody expects the boss to know. But we were trying a lot of things, and some of them didn't work. One of the things that definitely did not work is hiring a lot of salespeople, and therefore, we had high turnover."

Despite the high turnover and tough lessons, Sageworks more than doubled its revenue every year and created a successful company. "Now that

I look back on it with some perspective," Brian concludes, "the good news is that we were able to get revenue. But the bad news is that it was hard-fought-for revenue. Hard won."

More Hiring Inevitably Leads to More Firing

Brian Hamilton's experience with the eighty-twenty rule as it applies to employee results speaks to another of the most difficult aspects of this stage of growth, which is that pruning your staff of less productive employees—or those who turn out to be bad fits in other ways—is vital. This brings us back to Jerry Kaplan's sage advice that a company is not a social club. The widely respected former CEO of General Electric, Jack Welch, advocated and put into practice firing 10 percent of the lowest-performing managers working for him every year. That might be too strict a rule, but keeping close track of performance and weeding out those who just aren't meeting standards should be a core component of staff management. If employees are not meeting expectations, I believe in providing them with three specific actions they can take to retain their jobs and three to six months to make the corrections. This provides them with the option to either fix the problems or find another job. To my mind, it's the fair thing to do, and I've had some employees make good turnarounds.

> **Hockey Stick Principle #85: If you're not weeding out inferior performers, you're letting the rest of the team down.**

Always keep in mind that employees who aren't performing to a high standard are not only a hit to your bottom line, they're a blow to the energy of the rest of the team. I've found that they're a corrosive force, not only because other employees usually have to pick up their slack but because those who are performing well resent that it's acceptable for others not to.

To make good decisions not only with firing but with promoting and offering raises, it's essential to regularly evaluate performance. There are a number of commonly used methods for doing so, the most popular probably being setting annual goals that can be measured, which also allows you to calculate bonus awards. The annual review and bonus process can be a double-edged sword, however, and whether it cuts both ways or not has to do with the style in which targets are set and communicated and evaluations are conducted.

If the emphasis of creating goals for people is mainly on keeping tabs on their productivity, they can feel disrespected, as though you don't have faith in their commitment. It's more important to make sure projects that are set forth as goals are ones that employees are engaged by and with which the added value to the company is clear and compelling, so that attaining the goal not only allows you to measure the value they're contributing but allows *them* to understand that, as well. This should not be an exercise only in judgment; it should be a process that helps people see the important role they play in the organization. And if you're going to conduct formal annual evaluations, that's fine, but it's vital that communication with employees is ongoing, as well—that it's happening on a regular basis in a natural manner, not only at the end of a whole year.

Those end-of-year conversations tend to be awkward and often counterproductive, and the notion of summing up a person's whole contribution through the course of a year with a brief set of assessments or grades, such as the popular "exceeds expectations" and "meets expectations" responses, is misguided. I have disdained the use of such grades and instead conducted evaluations as a thoughtful, exploratory conversation. My favorite annual review recommendation comes from the wise Max De Pree, who in *Leadership Is an Art* advises that you have your employees who report to you give you their responses to these requests:

- "What is the most important achievement of your area?"
- "Please prepare a one-page or shorter statement of your personal management philosophy."
- "Describe your personal plans for continuing education and development for the coming year."

The answers will allow you to conduct a valuable discussion that results in meaningful outcomes.

Maybe You Just Don't Want to Be CEO

It's no wonder, considering all of these tricky management issues that slam founders in the fast-growth stage, that many choose not to continue as

CEO. Whether or not you do is purely a matter of your best judgment and your goals for yourself and the company.

> **Hockey Stick Principle #86: If you don't learn to love to manage, find a CEO who does.**

There's no question that sometimes bringing in an experienced CEO from the outside is a great option. One famous case is that of the founders of Yahoo!. When the Web site became so popular that the servers at Stanford were overloaded, which prompted the administration to request that the company find a new home, cofounders Jerry Yang and David Filo decided to seek advice about next steps from venture capital funds. With a commitment of $2 million from Sequoia Capital, they agreed to Sequoia's advice that they recruit a CEO with business experience to help them fulfill their vision for the company. They brought in fellow Stanford graduate Tim Koogle, who was at the time running a $400 million company, Intermec. Koogle helped them develop an online advertising revenue model, which in 1996 was a brand-new concept, and Yang and Filo became "Chief Yahoos" focusing on advancing the technology and promoting the brand.

Yang didn't want to be CEO. "People always ask me why I took myself out of the day-to-day operating responsibility," he says. "But that's never what I wanted to do, and besides, I knew so little about business that I didn't want to slow things down when the company began to scale up."[135] If you're not interested or don't feel confident about totally committing to learning the role, then you've got to step aside. No fast-growth firm can survive the intense challenges of this stage without a CEO who is passionate about tackling them.

Successful founders bring in experienced executives to take the lead management role all the time. Highly successful founders who've done so in just the last few years include Reid Hoffman of LinkedIn, Sophia Amoruso of Nasty Gal, and Jack Dorsey of Twitter. Red Hat's Bob Young helped hire Matthew Szulik to take over as CEO, saying hiring him was his single-biggest contribution to the success of the company, even though Bob was a cofounder and built and implemented the wildly successful business model.

Making this decision in no way means that you have to step entirely away from management. Most founders who do so remain deeply involved as board chairmen or product leaders.

There is of course a third option: selling the company and exiting. As said before, generally you will have had to build a strong management structure before you will be able to make a good sale of your business. Growing a firm purely with the goal of making a quick sale and departure before all the hard work of building a mature business has to be done is quixotic. Making a timely exit, though, once a strong foundation has been built may well be a great option. In the next chapter, we'll consider what to expect should it be time for you to sell your company.

Chapter 9

Leave the Ice or Skate On?: To Sell or Not to Sell

I was struck by an article by David Fleming in *ESPN Magazine* in which he describes how many hockey players used to make their own sticks. He quotes Washington Capitals star Alex Ovechkin as saying, "To a hockey player sticks aren't equipment. . . . They are a piece of your body."[136]

Fleming also shares the story of Canadian Bruce Boudreau, who was a star junior player in the 1970s. "Before games, the 20-year-old Boudreau would sit in his kitchen and customize the fiberglass curve of his weapon by carefully steaming it over a teakettle. Then he'd wedge it under a door hinge and bend it until it was perfect, race outside and plunge it into the snow to set the blade."[137]

For many founders, their start-ups also feel like part of their very beings. They have shed a lot of blood, sweat, and tears to build the company, and everything about it is a reflection of themselves. This makes the process of deciding whether to sell the company when potential buyers come calling extremely difficult, even if an irresistible offer has been made. For some founders, the decision to sell feels like the right thing to do or can sometimes even be a huge relief. They may be burned out from the daily grind, or they may be itching to get back to the scrappier process of initial creation and want start building a new company again. For other founders, selling is completely out of the question; they are determined to keep control of the firm and grow it according to their own vision. And for yet others still, they're left with no real option but to sell or to bring the company through an IPO because they have transferred so much equity to outside investors whose primary aim is to cash out.

When making this decision, only one thing is for sure: You will be barraged with all sorts of advice about what's the right thing to do, and much of it will be from experts who are highly persuasive and have a great deal of experience with the ins and outs of selling a company that most founders know very little about.

> **Hockey Stick Principle #87: Carefully consider whether or not you would like to sell your company well in advance of needing to know whether you have to.**

Many founders have not thought through the pluses and minuses of selling before they find themselves in the thick of the process. That can make it extremely challenging to get a firm footing in negotiations and to keep your focus on what your own objectives are. All founders should start thinking about these options well in advance of becoming a viable acquisition target and at the very least establish a set of guidelines about the types of offers they would seriously consider and the terms they want to make part of a deal. As was said earlier about negotiating with VCs, in mergers and acquisitions, all terms are negotiable, but good negotiation requires a cool head and a clear understanding of your interests and goals. Too many founders find themselves swept up in the heat of the moment and all the emotions that come with it and later regret the decisions they made.

As Ben Horowitz wrote in *The Hard Thing About Hard Things,* "One of the most difficult decisions that a CEO ever makes is whether to sell her company. Logically, determining whether selling a company will be better in the long term than continuing to run it stand-alone involves a huge number of factors, most of which are speculative or unknown. And if you are the founder, the logical part is the easy part." So let's begin to think of some of the issues to be aware of when navigating this emotional terrain.

Expect to Have Some Seller's Remorse

The words of one founder who made a great sale for his start-up especially resonate for me. Roger Bryan, who started Enfusen Digital Marketing, eloquently told mashable.com in an interview about his thoughts on the transaction, "I spent six years building the first company I sold. The day that I sold it was one of the greatest accomplishments of my life. . . . Then as each month went by, and the money sat in my bank account as I tried to figure out what to do next, the regret started to set in. I hadn't sold my company, I had sold my passion."[138] Many founders feel a deep sense of remorse once a sale is complete, even if they have made a truly great deal and even if as time passes they still feel that they made the right choice.

> **Hockey Stick Principle #88: When selling your business, you're selling your passion.**

With all the hype around technology start-ups that founders design primarily with the hope of being bought by Google, Facebook, or Amazon, the emotional difficulty of giving up your baby has been underreported. Certainly this will be a passing phase for many founders as they move on to a new challenge or they eventually realize that with the earnings from the proceeds they made they're now in a wonderful position to plot out their next adventure. But for many others, regret builds because of the way the acquisition ends up playing out or because with hindsight, they believe they could have achieved even more success if they had kept the company independent. Even with some of the sales that are seen as great triumphs, founders later express some regret.

Take the case of Waze, the real-time, social network traffic alert and map service, which was bought by Google in a $1.15 billion deal and which has now been folded into Google successfully. Cofounder and CEO Noam Bardin wrote in a reflection about the sale that "one of Waze's mistakes was the valuation of its A round which significantly diluted the founders. Perhaps, had we held control of the company, as the founders of Facebook, Google, Oracle or Microsoft had, Waze might still be an independent company today."[139] The acquisition made good sense, but the question clearly lingers whether the founders might not have been happier if they'd kept it independent.

In other cases, the remorse comes from the difficulties that arise during the merger of your firm with the acquiring company. Some mergers go fairly smoothly, but many are full of friction and are horribly frustrating for founders, even when they'll be staying on to keep running operations. One extreme outcome is that the acquirer isn't able to figure out a way to integrate your company's business into its own and simply dissolves your operations.

Such was the case with the acquisition by Google of Dodgeball, which was one of a hot new type of business at the time—location-based mobile social network programs—which seemed in good synergy with Google's plans for development. Google acquired the company in 2005 but shut it down in 2009. The cofounders, Dennis Crowley and Alex Rainert, made no secret about how they felt about the outcome, writing in a social network post at the time, "It's no real secret that Google wasn't supporting Dodgeball the way we expected. The whole experience was incredibly frustrating for us—especially as we couldn't convince them that Dodgeball was worth engineering resources, leaving us to watch as other startups got to innovate in the mobile plus social space."[140] Crowley, who went on to found Foursquare, the geolocation-based local search app, later reflected on the core strategic disconnect between what he came to understand was Google's motivation for the purchase and what he and Rainert had thought it was. He said, "We thought it was a product acquisition, and they knew it was an 'acqui-hire.'"[141] The concept behind an acqui-hire is that the acquiring firm is really most interested in bringing in personnel from the start-up rather than continuing the business.

This might seem a good problem to have; better for the acquiring firm to want to bring you and your team in because they value the skills and business savvy that allowed you to build your company so successfully than for them to want to cast you out, especially if the acquirer is a market leader like Google. For many founders, that would in fact be true. But for Crowley and Rainert, it was a great disappointment, and it might also be for you.

> **Hockey Stick Principle #89: The strategic fit of two companies cannot truly be known until they're put together.**

Rainert and Crowley's experience highlights one of the most important things founders should be prepared for should an acquisition be proposed: understanding the purchaser's strategy behind buying your company is not nearly as simple as it might seem, even when the synergies in your businesses are obvious.

Do Not Accept the Buyer's Plans for Your Company at Face Value

There are basically three major outcomes for your company when you sell:

1) **Your company remains intact and separately run.** Either a private equity firm purchases your company with the intent of either later taking it public or reselling it, or you are bought as a wholly owned subsidiary by a larger company. In this case, founders and key employees may well be asked to stay on to continue running operations, but this is never to be assumed, and significant changes in operations may be part of the terms of the deal.

2) **Your company becomes a division of the parent company.** While some of your operations may remain entirely under your team's management, other functions are taken over by the buyer to realize efficiencies, such as payroll, payments and receipts, marketing, HR, product maintenance, manufacturing, distribution, and warehousing. Becoming a division is the typical common outcome after a *strategic merger,* with the purchaser buying you with a plan for improving their company's products, services, and profits.

3) **The company is dissolved, and your product is folded into the buyer's product line.** In this case, even if you and a skeleton crew of key employees are retained, most employees will lose their jobs.

Knowing which of these scenarios you're getting into is only the beginning of probing into the buyer's intentions and the thinking behind the strategy. You must drill deep into their motivations, their expectations, and their analyses of why your firm is a good fit for their goals. You cannot take their pitch to you at face value, and you cannot assume that just because they're a big firm with so much more experience and with specialists in corporate acquisitions that they have a fundamentally good strategy for making the deal or one that you'll ultimately be happy with. You've got to challenge their arguments and vision.

Business author and *Inc.* magazine editor Bo Burlingham, who has researched and interviewed hundreds of founders of privately held firms who have sold their companies, warns that acquiring companies are intent on selling you on the advantages of the deal—basically telling you what you want to hear. "When you are in a situation where you weren't looking for a buyer, you seem to overlook the fact that [buyers] are actually giving you a sales pitch. In order to get you to agree to a sale, they've got to convince you that this is a great deal for you, and a great deal for everyone you care about. But once the deal is signed, you've lost all your leverage."

It's vital to keep in mind that some mergers work out much better than others, even when they're spearheaded by the same acquirer. Take the divergent cases of two high-profile acquisitions by online marketplace eBay. Since its founding in 1995, the company has made forty-nine acquisitions,[142] many of which have worked out as planned. One of these was its 2002 acquisition of PayPal for $1.5 billion, making the firm a subsidiary. PayPal's business fit so squarely with that of eBay's that eBay became extremely aggressive about the purchase. As PayPal cofounder Max Levchin recounts, "They would say, 'You need to sell to us because it's a natural synergy—and if you don't we will compete you out of the way and kill you.'"[143] In fact, according to Eric M. Jackson, at the time PayPal's chief marketing officer, 70 percent of eBay's auctions accepted PayPal payments.[144] Many pundits have argued that PayPal sold too early, leaving lots of money on the table. But as Levchin assesses the outcome, he stresses that the fight with eBay was getting "really, really bloody" and also that "eBay has been a fantastic steward of what we built."[145] Making the deal freed up the PayPal founders to move on and start a host of exciting new companies. Cofounder Elon Musk started the hugely successful companies Tesla and SpaceX, Peter Thiel has become a successful investor in start-ups, Reid Hoffman went on to found LinkedIn, and Jeremy Stoppelman founded Yelp.

In the end, PayPal's business was kept so well intact and developed so successfully that eBay announced in the fall of 2014 that it would spin the firm off into an independent company again.

However, eBay's judgment in making another premier acquisition proved less shrewd in September 2005 when they purchased online VoIP (Voice over IP) firm Skype for $2.6 billion, plus incentives that increased the deal to $3.1 billion.[146] The basic idea was that integrating Skype capabilities into its service would allow eBay buyers and sellers to consult face-to-face with each other, which would enhance the trust in one another when agreeing on sales. But the deal didn't work out as planned. "When we bought Skype, we thought it had synergies with our other two businesses, and it turns out it did not," recalled John Donahoe, eBay's CEO in 2009.[147] It turned out that not many eBay buyers and sellers in fact want to chat;

they prefer as smooth and simple a transaction as possible. eBay ended up selling 65 percent of its stake in Skype to investors in 2009 for $1.9 billion. This divestiture worked out just fine for both companies, as Skype thrived so much back out on its own that Microsoft bought the company in 2011 for a whopping $8.5 billion, in which eBay earned a $1.4 billion return on its investment.

There are a few key lessons here to keep in mind when companies are courting you. One is that the strategic thinking behind making the acquisition may be fundamentally flawed. eBay did not truly appreciate an aspect of the nature of the relationship that its buyers and sellers wanted to have, even though understanding that relationship is at the very core of its business. Another is that if the firm that wants to buy you has the ability to compete so effectively with you that you might well be put out of business by it before too long, a sale may be your best option. And a third is that it's extremely important to evaluate the timing of the sale and how long you might want to hold out on selling by doing a tough, rigorous assessment of your future prospects. This involves taking into account in particular the total potential size of your market and what share of it you might be able to claim, how much money you'll be required to invest into your product and how much marketing you'll have to do to remain competitive, and whether or not you can continue to grow or achieve profitability in the foreseeable future.

Some say PayPal sold too soon, but it fended eBay off for at least a year. Now consider that in 1999, roughly six months after founding Google, Larry Page and Sergey Brin almost sold out for $750,000 when a purchase offer was made by the Excite Web portal and search engine. Unbelievable. Now that's what you would call too soon.

The offer was spearheaded by Vinod Khosla, an investor in Excite as well as in Google. He thought the two companies would both be stronger if they were combined, and he had talked Page and Brin down to selling the company for $750,000. But the CEO of Excite, George Bell, who was a media executive and had been CEO since 1996, ended up rejecting the deal.[148]

The better way to think about the decision of the PayPal founders to sell to eBay is that they got the timing right for one key reason: They were still in a very strong negotiating position. The Google founders considered selling way before they were in a strong position to negotiate a reasonable amount for the firm, and they were totally unaware as of yet of the true magnitude of the company's potential.

Never, Under Any Circumstances, Be Afraid to Be a Tough Negotiator

When potential buyers are waving millions of dollars before your eyes, it is thrilling. Do not underestimate the power of this effect. However, on the flip side, the fear that if you don't take the money now you'll never have a chance to make such a good deal again can be terrifying. This is why it's crucial to keep in mind that it is almost always the case that no one understands the value of your company and has a more realistic assessment of its future potential than you. Mergers and acquisitions experts have elaborate formulas, and they have a great deal of wisdom from their experience, but the ultimate truth is that there is no one "right" valuation of a company. And the correct valuation for you can be quite different from the correct valuation for a potential buyer.

Your valuation should include not only the more pro forma considerations of revenue, profitability, market potential, degree of competition, current and future value of your intellectual property, and strategic value to the prospective acquirer but also your interest in continuing to control the direction of the company. Only you, of all the negotiating parties, can make this assessment, and doing so may put you at odds not only with the prospective buyers and their legion of M&A experts but with your cofounders and management team. You therefore must anticipate that you will have to negotiate not only with the buyers but with your partners, as well, when selling.

A great story of a founder who ended up realizing that continuing to run the company was much more valuable to him than he had understood when negotiations commenced is Gary Erickson, cofounder of energy bar company Clif Bar. His story of almost selling out to Quaker Oats is told in detail in Bo Burlingham's book *Small Giants: Companies That Choose to Be Great Instead of Big*.

The deal was worth $120 million, and Erickson would get half the money, but just minutes before closing, he had a change of heart. He started crying over what he was about to do. He changed his mind and called off the deal. Everyone—venture capitalists, lawyers, and other advisors—told him he was making the biggest mistake of his life by refusing to sign the closing papers. Clif Bar competitors PowerBar and Kraft had already been sold to larger competitors, and surely because of their size they'd crush Clif

Bar. Erickson's partner, Lisa Thomas, the then CEO, quit and demanded to be paid out. Erickson agreed to pay her $65 million over five years. He stayed on as CEO and has since increased Clif Bar's sales from $39 million the year he almost sold out to nearly more than $500 million in 2013.[149] In a demonstration of why it mattered so much to Erickson to stay in charge and that he had a particular vision for growing the company, in 2010, he sold 20 percent of the company to 239 of his employees through an employee stock ownership plan.[150] That is not a move that a corporate acquirer would be at all likely to support.

Another founder who considered a big deal but ultimately looks back with no regret that he instead ended up staying in charge—and who built the firm up impressively—is Jeremy Stoppelman, cofounder and CEO of review site Yelp. The first offer Yelp received, two years after launch, was for an impressive $100 million from an undisclosed would-be buyer. When three years later, Google came calling and offered $500 million, the deal was even more tantalizing, and so they entered into negotiations, but those fell through. Stoppelman highlights that this can be a disorienting experience. "It ends up feeling a bit like brain damage to everyone involved," he told *The New York Times*. "People start dreaming about paying off mortgages. Everyone had to shake off all those fantasies and get back to work, including myself." He accepted the challenge, dug in, and built the company very successfully, taking it through an IPO in 2012 that brought it a $5 billion valuation, a great deal higher than the $500 million Google offered. Despite a host of press that admonished Yelp for failing to make the Google deal work, the result has been stellar.[151]

No Regrets Are Necessary

Of course, one way to avoid any buyer's remorse is to be resolute about not selling and committing to developing your company for the long term.

> **Hockey Stick Principle #90: The value of the satisfaction of guiding the long-term success of your company cannot be quantified.**

A number of the founders I interviewed expressed a deep conviction never to sell, and the satisfaction that they feel from having stayed in charge of their firms and being able to drive the car on how fast to grow and in what ways is impressive and a factor that every founder should weigh heavily.

Schedulefly founder Wes Aiken makes a strong case for the pleasures of enjoying the controlled growth of a company whose model he has honed:

> I don't know why anybody would start a business that they wanted to sell, or for any other reason except to create a great life. Why would I ever say, "I want to sell my company?" I never want to sell this. I never want to have a different life. But my identity is not Schedulefly.
>
> We have an incredible business and life. The business is very profitable and has grown every month for eight years. The five of us work very well together—and know each other well and we are each great at specific things. For that reason, we rarely need to talk. I speak to Tyler a few times per year. We don't have meetings. We don't work in an office. We don't travel. This keeps everything extremely simple and low cost and free from things that don't really matter. I guess most go-getter business types enjoy the travel and the rat race and the meetings and the things that make up "doing business" because they feel like business is getting done. I don't. I never did well in an office setting—reporting to an office at 9am. I never liked team building events and doing expense reports and performance reviews. I hated conference calls.
>
> Instead, I now work only when I need to work and after eight years it's still fun and rewarding work because it matters to people. Staying simple and not overdoing it matters to people. It matters to my customers and to my family. And I never dread work. Monday mornings to me are every bit as great as Friday evenings. I spend more time with my family than anyone I know and our company still grows. Every morning I see my kids and every evening we play and I give them baths and read with them.
>
> Why mess with that kind of life? Why not do everything in my power to protect that along with protecting why people love what we do and want to do business with us? That's what I am doing. By saying no and by passing on the countless opportunities that I could pursue and focusing as hard as we can on those who think we matter, I am relentlessly protecting a life and a company that I had never dreamed could exist.

Another founder who speaks powerfully about the great satisfaction of continuing to run his company is Dude Solutions's CEO Kent Hudson.

When I asked him what he thought the chances were that he would sell the company in the future, he answered, "Zero. We had ten or eleven offers to be acquired along the way and turned them all down. It's our belief system about a year ago when we reassessed the business that the golden era of the Internet was just starting. We think that era was just beginning. We've done the hard part. Now comes the fun part." The way he describes his vision for the years ahead offers a powerful antidote to the mythology that to sell and move on is the ideal. "My goal is to come each day and build something so special that I can't give it up," he says. "I'm proud of it. The customers love it. They tout the customer service. They love the product. I'm going to build something that's so good I don't want to give it up."

If you are getting a good deal of satisfaction from running your company and feel that your results are providing you and your stakeholders with sufficiently rich rewards and that you can fend off competition and face the demands of the future, then making the determination not to sell, even when quite alluring offers are made, may well be the most logical thing to do, in addition to being the most emotionally rewarding.

You Likely Won't Have a Choice

All of the press coverage of acquisitions seems to suggest that they're quite common, but the fact is that successful sales of start-ups are much less common than the intense press coverage of sales suggests.

According to financial research firm FactSet, there were 11,994 mergers or acquisitions in the United States for twelve months ending February 28, 2015. This may sound like a lot, but considering there were three million high-growth-potential start-ups in the United States at the time, that number is actually quite small.[152] Moreover, many of the mergers are in mature industries, such as when one large utility or bank buys another, so the number of innovative start-ups acquired is even less than 11,994.

Even for VC-backed firms that are often *trying* to be acquired with professional investment behind them, acquisitions are rare. According to a study by Dow Jones VentureSource, "Of the 6,613 U.S.-based companies initially funded by venture capital between 2006 and 2011, only 11% were acquired or made initial public offerings of stock."[153] The hugely successful Y Combinator, which has helped launch some of the most recent successful start-ups, such as Dropbox, Reddit, and Airbnb, has also not made much headway against this basic math. By December 2015, only fifty-five of the 699 Y Combinator–backed start-ups had been acquired.[154]

Selling Is Not Always Selling Out

If you are one of the founders who does have to grapple with the decision to sell, another important step to take is to make a detached assessment of the opportunity costs of not selling your business.

Your vision and ambitions for the company may, in fact, be the best reason for selling, because by doing so, better capitalized players with greater scale than you will be able to take the company to a whole new level. A good example of this kind of sale is of Boogie Wipes. By 2012, five years after starting their venture, cofounder Julie Pickens had grown the company to $10 million in revenue, and the product was being stocked in fifty thousand stores. Recall from chapter 3 that when starting out, Julie and Mindee had shared their idea about their saline nose wipes online and face-to-face and weren't worried about a huge company like P&G stealing it. As we discussed, large businesses often don't take notice of such good ideas; but they do start to take notice when they see lots of customers buying another product and the serious revenue growth that comes with it.

Many big companies are constantly on the lookout for firms with such results. Jeff Weedman, P&G's VP for global business development, had Boogie Wipes on his radar for more than a year through its "Connect and Develop" program, which helps P&G generate revenue through its vendor relationships.[155]

P&G didn't want to buy the company itself, but Weedman referred Julie and Mindee to Dan Meyer, CEO of Nehemiah Manufacturing, which P&G had licensed the rights to market some of its products to, such as Febreze and Downy Wrinkle Releaser. Weedman thought Nehemiah might be a good manufacturer for Boogie Wipes. As things turned out, Nehemiah made Julie and Mindee an offer to buy the company.

"We had put a new concept on the market, and they were very interested in that technology," Julie recalls. "We went down the road to talk to them about doing it, putting it on an adult wipe, and ended up working with them for a short period of time on developing a wipe. In order to do it, they really wanted the company closer, in Cincinnati."

In 2012, Nehemiah partnered with Boogie Wipes and purchased a portion of key investors' shares. Julie still held her shares and moved the company to Cincinnati to help run the company. She sold her stock in August of 2014 and resigned to go work at another start-up. This was a win-win outcome, as it allowed the founders to not only preserve their creation, assuring it was managed by a major firm with good expertise, but also gave one of the founders a whole new adventure to pursue.

Doug Lebda is another person who made the decision to sell and is confident that he made the right call. In his case, doing so allowed him to put the company under more focused, aligned management. In February 2000, LendingTree completed a public offering, selling 21 percent of its stock for $43.8 million. That was a great result in terms of cash raised, but it also led to a very complex management situation in which Doug struggled to reconcile the competing demands of many stakeholders.

When in August 2003, IAC/InterActiveCorp, a $6.3 billion revenue media empire run by the famous business icon Barry Diller, made an offer, the sweetness of the deal brought the interests of all stakeholders into alignment, and IAC acquired LendingTree for $726 million ($21.67 per share) through a stock-swap transaction. The transaction cleaned up Lending-Tree's balance sheet and reconciled the complications related to having many different stakeholders with different objectives, allowing Doug and the management team to focus exclusively on the business rather than spending an inordinate amount of time on shareholder relations. The move also worked out well for Doug personally. He clearly made a good judgment call about the fit between his management style and that of IAC's, as shortly after the sale he was promoted to president of IAC.

If you do think that you would want to seriously entertain an acquisition offer, or if you've determined that all things considered, a sale is your goal, then there are a number of best practices for making sure you end up with a deal you don't later regret and helping you to keep your sanity during the process.

The Hockey Stick Rules for Good Mergers and Acquisitions

1. Don't Rush Into Discussions with Just One Party

Ideally, you want to be able to stoke competition and consider multiple offers. You should be proactive about identifying possible buyers and learning about their businesses so that if one company does come calling, you not only have a good basic knowledge of the businesses you think are the best strategic fits with your firm and how this potential suitor stacks up, but you can also readily put out feelers to competing firms.

As Manu Kumar, founder of seed start-up venture firm K9 Ventures, observed in one of his blog posts, "Most potential acquirers follow start-ups, and it's important to stay in touch with them. You want to have them know what you're doing and have those channels open. This should be well before the start-ups get to any acquisition stage."

You don't want to just be reactive or running as fast as you can to get up to speed on possible purchasers once a company tests the waters of your interest. As Bo Burlingham highlights in his book *Finish Big: How Great Entrepreneurs Exit Their Companies on Top,* one of the hallmarks of founders who made the best exits is that they planned well in advance the kind of deal they would want to make and with whom.

When I sold First Research, there were several businesses operating in our market—sales and marketing intelligence. Any number of them could have been suitable candidates to buy us, but instead of soliciting offers and discussions with them, I opted to negotiate directly with Dun & Bradstreet. I did this for a few reasons. I didn't want to invest the time to hire a broker and create a pitch book—a detailed information packet about our financial performance, business model, and operating plan. Putting one together is a great deal of work. I also didn't want to be distracted from the day-to-day business, which usually happens when founders are considering a sale or merger because so many meetings with potential acquirers are involved. In addition, I knew that D&B was acquiring sales-and-marketing Internet firms as part of a larger strategy, so they were probably the most motivated buyer. I didn't think I'd be able to get a better offer from anyone else. And finally, I enjoyed owning First Research, so if D&B didn't make an offer I liked, I would be happy turning it down.

The one problem with my process, looking back on it now, was that I really wasn't looking to sell First Research. Because I negotiated with only one party, the process went relatively quickly. If I had been negotiating with several other places, I would have had more time and spoken with more experts to better understand the broader implications of selling my company. And as I look back on the deal now, I think I might have decided not to sell.

2. Hire M&A Expertise to Work with You

Zappos CEO Tony Hsieh said wisely in a magazine interview, "Poker is very similar to business. Don't play if you don't understand it." Just as with negotiating term sheets with VCs, acquisitions deals are extremely complex, and founders are vulnerable to many pitfalls. The company that is negotiating with you may be extremely experienced at acquisitions, so you need experience on your side in the form of an experienced M&A advisor, accountant, and lawyer. Otherwise, it's like playing Texas Hold 'em in Vegas with millions of dollars. You're likely to lose—and maybe lose Texan big.

If you're thinking about selling your business, it's best to begin conversations with pros well in advance so you can take your time learning about the process. But be wary of hiring Wall Street investment banks that often put their youngest staff on deals that aren't huge in size. Furthermore, their incentives are not always matched well with yours. Instead, I advise that you hire experienced former business owners who successfully managed the sales of their own firms.

As Alan Smith, the founder of Advanced Medical Devices—which he sold to behemoth Johnson & Johnson for $22 million in 1998—attested in an entrepreneurship.org article about the value of an expert team, "Johnson & Johnson's initial offers were significantly less than the final offer. I attribute that to one factor: my decision to retain an expert in mergers and acquisitions to represent my interests. The leveling of the playing field between the two parties—J&J's sophisticated financiers were now dealing with a peer who they could assume was knowledgeable and credible—made all the difference in securing the higher price."[156]

This may seem glaringly obvious, but one of the things that comes up on list after list of big mistakes made by founders is that they try to take charge of the process themselves or get too far along in discussions before they bring in the pros. Professional M&A advisors know what acquiring firms will be requesting from you, such as financial statements audited by a top-five national CPA firm.

As outsiders, advisors can act as a neutral party to help you better understand the value of your business and how to market it best to a number of potential qualified buyers. They can also get you a much better deal. For example, when Pacinian, a keyboard technologies firm, was acquired by publicly traded firm Synaptics for $30 million, the advisor to the chairman of Pacinian, Basil Peters, helped drive up the price considerably. He recounts in exits.com, "You don't really want to negotiate one-on-one with someone and end up in a bear hug, with them telling you how much they love you . . . and how cheap they can buy your company."[157]

3. Expect Intense Competition for Your Time and Lots of Stress

From start to finish, including organizing information, having informational discussions, negotiating term sheets, helping with the buyer's due diligence process, and aiding lawyers with the sale documents, the sale of your company generally takes between eight and ten months, or sometimes longer. And during that time, you still have to run your company while you are going through all the elaborate and often very time-consuming processes of negotiation. You will also have to respond to seemingly countless questions and requests for information during the rigorous due-diligence process.

It's important not to underestimate how much time this will take. You may think you have a good idea of what to expect from talking to founders who've gone through the process—which you absolutely should do—and from reading about it, but trust me, until you're actually in the throes of it, you can't really appreciate just how many unexpected issues may come up and how much time responding to the requests from the buyer's attorneys and bankers will require.

I like the analogy used by Thomas Metz in his book *Selling the Intangible Company,* in which he writes, "Many CEOs think selling a company is easy. The process seems quite straightforward. . . . A founder typically enjoys a good challenge; that is why he or she started a business in the first place. . . . What they fail to consider is the tremendous amount of time and effort required to do the job right. . . . The situation is analogous to taking on your own home remodeling project . . . halfway through the project you uncover some unforeseen problems that are beyond your expertise."

Also know that the process is nerve-racking and often crazy making. People you don't know well and still aren't 100 percent sure you can trust to come through with an offer you can feel good about accepting are peering into every detail of your operations, your finances, and the quality of your management and staff.

Former investment banker Scott Moeller has written three books about mergers and acquisitions. In *Surviving M&A: Make the Most of Your Company Being Acquired,* he says, "Anything seems better than living through the hell of a merger or acquisition." From my experience, the process is indeed incredibly stressful. For a period of months, I had to shift dozens of hours each week to managing the sale. Here is how I spent my time:

- Explaining how the business worked to the buyer
- Reviewing legal documents hundreds of pages long
- Discussing the ongoing negotiations with shareholders and advisors
- Worrying about the implications of selling the business

Merger documents are complex, and because I'd never been through the process before, I had a lot to learn. I committed myself to understanding the basic meaning of each and every provision, and I was fortunate because I hired an experienced attorney who has a knack for explaining things very clearly—and providing just the right amount of detail and context to make all the implications of terms and conditions totally understandable. If the advisors you're working with aren't adept at this, you must look for someone who is. Understanding all the details and the possibilities about how the agreed terms might play out is crucial.

4. Expect Dissension among Stakeholders

If you have retained a majority share in your company, you normally have the authority to push forward with a deal, but even so, you will have to contend with the competing views and interests of various stakeholders. For example, you may find yourself in a very uncomfortable tug-of-war between you and your investors, who want to sell, and some members of your management team, who may object to the enterprise of working for the buyer or be rightfully concerned about their job security.

If you have awarded your management team stock options, they may well be incentivized to support the deal and to assist in making it happen. But sometimes when start-ups have raised substantial financing, particularly through venture funding, those outside funders will be entitled to so much of the cash from the deal that your management team stands to gain little from the transaction.

One very important thing you must do before selling your firm is you must gain an understanding of the impact of the sale on all stakeholders or those vested in your company. Basically, you have to make sure each group involved is treated as fairly as possible. This is your responsibility as a leader.

Fordham University professor Michael Pirson and Harvard professor Deepak Malhotra wrote a paper titled, "Unconventional Insights for Managing Stakeholder Trust," which says that most organizations don't do a good job of managing the disparate needs of stakeholders because "trust is multi-dimensional—and it is not obvious which dimension you need to focus on when dealing with any particular stakeholder group."[158] This is the core of the problem during mergers for the founder and CEO: trust to some people is "kind-hearted benevolence"; to others it is "fair-minded integrity." An incredibly important takeaway from Pirson and Malhotra's research is that they say during mergers, *building trust with one group can destroy trust with another.*

From my own experience selling First Research, I know just how difficult a balancing act this is. Pirson and Malhotra point out that each stakeholder has different needs, and therefore, when you build trust with, for example, suppliers, you can totally lose trust with your shareholders in the process or vice versa. An especially difficult period of time for me was the weeks leading up to the closing of the deal when I was obligated by the buyer to not discuss my possible merger with anyone outside of counsel, yet I was obviously very busy and distracted, so my employees knew something important was going on. I had always been transparent with the entire team, and keeping secrets wasn't how we did business with one another. So by keeping trust with the acquiring firm, I felt as if I was destroying it with my employees. This is just one example because when your firm is acquired, you're constantly facing this challenge with regard to operational decisions and communicating with customers as to what type of changes they can expect.

Shareholders, employees, customers, suppliers, and partners all have skin in the game, and how each group responds to the sale will inevitably be different. Your lawyers and CPAs will say you should pay attention to new regulations that are gray and unclear, but your suppliers will persuade you to ignore the regulations. Your employees will say that they want more benefits negotiated as part of the deal, but your most important shareholders will say that your staff expenses are too high as compared to other similar companies.

Furthermore, subgroups within a main group may have different objectives, as well. For example, one group of shareholders might desire to sell the company as soon as possible because they need the cash, whatever the price, while another group doesn't want to sell for any price. These disparate objections require that you balance out each subgroup's needs as best you can and try to see everyone's viewpoint clearly. Skills with regard to communication, listening, and understanding are at the core of helping form consensus.

5. Negotiate Every Point as Forcefully and in as Much Detail as You Can before Signing a Letter of Intent, and Don't Be Afraid to Say No

An important step in the process is signing a formal letter of intent, which spells out the terms that both the buyer and seller are agreeing to. After you've signed this, the balance of power shifts decidedly to the buyer, and you will also be excluded from continuing discussions with other buyers during the period of due diligence that will follow, which is usually between sixty and ninety days. You do not want to leave any substantive issues to be negotiated thereafter, so you should be a persistent pit bull regarding any big issues before you sign. This is one part of the process in which your team of M&A experts will prove of great assistance.

Too many founders feel overly pressured to sign the letter of intent. That is particularly true when venture capitalists and other investors have invested heavily in this exit. As M&A law expert and *Forbes* contributor Scott Edward Walker wisely counsels, "Entrepreneurs must understand that their strongest leverage as a seller is prior to the execution of the letter of intent (LOI). . . . Not negotiating the material terms of the deal in the LOI is the most common mistake I see from the sell-side. Once the LOI is executed, all the entrepreneur's leverage is gone because he generally won't be able to shop his company around to any other potential buyers . . . due to what's called a 'no-shop provision.'"[159]

6. Prepare for a Rocky Road in Integrating after You've Sold

Make no mistake: integrating your organization into another one is messy work. As the founder and leader of your company, you're constantly speculating as to what your new owner intends to do with your company. Will they fire employees? Will they change their pay scales? When will they implement their changes? How will mutual customers be handled? Will your product be integrated into the acquiring firm's product? Who's in charge of that process? I could list a hundred questions like these, and each one will weigh on you heavily. Employees and managers also want answers since their jobs could be in jeopardy. But during the first several months, no one has the answers about what will happen to most of their jobs because that will be decided as you go through the integration process. Communication often flows only awkwardly during this stage, with many parties being guarded about their next move.

Things became so tough for me during integration that I ended up suffering chest pain. There I was with a dozen red, black, and white wires attached to my bare chest and back as I ran on my doctor's treadmill. Though my heart was perfectly healthy, thankfully, I was in a good deal of pain. I like to say that the integration process just about broke my heart. Unless you've been through it several times and know just what to expect, you should expect it to be more painful than you're hoping for.

7. You'll Be Going through a Life Change

If you sell, just as with a divorce, the loss of a loved one, or losing anything you care about deeply, you'll go through something of a mourning process. This can become quite intense, and some founders fall into a deep depression. If you feel yourself sinking that way, I strongly recommend getting counseling. Don't assume *you* are the problem if you feel lonely or lost after the sale of your business. It's normal and in many cases should be treated.

Cashing Out through an IPO

While landing VC investment is rare, taking your company public through an initial public offering is much rarer. In 2014, there were 288 IPOs in the United States, and that was a banner year, up 27 percent from 2013. Health care was the largest sector, having captured 111 of the deals. The fact that 63 percent of the deals in 2014 were sponsored by VC or private equity firms underscores how driven to achieve a sale of their portion of a start-up's stock these firms are.[160]

For the most part, you have to be a relatively large firm to absorb the costs of regulatory filings and complex reporting required of public firms. Bronto Software, which had $27.4 million in revenue in 2013 and grew 40 percent in 2014, seemed like a good candidate for an IPO down the road, so I asked founder Joe Colopy what he thought of the prospect. His answer was insightful:

"It's not something we'll race to do because there are a lot of challenges. It's very hard to do any long-term planning and make trade-offs when, at the end of the day, you're living and dying based on that quarterly number above all else. It would be a wonderful financing event, but we don't need to [do it] because we don't have outside investors. If we were to do that, most likely, we would probably . . . take funding in there anyways because it would be like going from kindergarten to graduate school just like that. We don't really even have a board."

Going public requires managing a great deal of complexity. But the complexity can be well worth the effort, not only because you generally raise a good deal of capital but also because an IPO can help build credibility with customers. When Red Hat went public in 1999, its revenue increased from $33 million in 1999 to $84 million in 2001 in part for this reason.[161] Founder Bob Young recalls, "[Buyers from large corporations] genuinely fought this open-source thing all the way through the nineties. Not until Red Hat went public did Linux become safe for corporate managers to invest in."

> **Hockey Stick Principle #91: A founder should be the star player of an IPO, not sit on the sidelines.**

Some founders are naturals for the IPO process because they don't mind being in the public eye, and they're intent on greatly expanding their brand awareness. One of those is founder and CEO of GoPro, Nick Woodman, who in an interview with *Forbes* says this about going public:

> A lot of people who advised me asked, "Why would you complicate your life and your business this way?" I thought more about it and decided that as long as we had a strong vision—as long as we execute—everything's going to be ok. The team is only getting stronger every year. . . . I'm in my 12th year of [GoPro.] We're not suddenly going to start sucking at this.[162]

That's a good summation of the way I think founders should feel about the IPO process if they're going to take their companies through it. Founders are always following the lead from the firm's investors and investment bankers in an IPO, but their role is still vital. If you're not confident about playing the part, then I strongly advise that you work with your board to appoint a replacement CEO with good experience.

More Than One Kind of Great Adventure

When I've given speeches about entrepreneurship, I've often been asked, "Are you glad you sold First Research?" and "If you could do it all over again, would you sell?" Though I have moved on to an exciting and fulfilling new venture, as I have reflected on this question repeatedly through the years since the sale, I've realized that the answer is *no*. The reason is not that I think I should have held out for a better deal, though that might be true. Instead, it's that I enjoyed working at First Research so much. *What I had was already great—much greater than having money and options.* Moreover, because the business was already performing well financially, I already had more than enough money to be happy and have options. This is not to say that I regret the sale so much that I'm crying myself to sleep at night—not by a long shot. But given the opportunity again, I would think the decision through more carefully.

So why did I sell? The answer is probably best explained by J. M. Barrie's *Peter Pan* when he said, "To die would be an awfully big adventure."[163] I'm always looking for adventure and building First Research had provided that. When Dun & Bradstreet made its offer, I figured I was ready for a new undertaking, and the offer was a good one. All my partners wanted to take it, and I felt that the employees would be getting a good deal and would be mostly unaffected. I miscalculated, and that didn't turn out to be the case. Many were affected in the end, and that was difficult for both them and for me. I now realize that the greater adventure might well have been to keep building First Research into every bit the company it had the potential to be, and those employees were part of the reason why it was so successful in the first place. We were a happy business family, and I think it might have been best all in all if I'd kept us intact.

With that said, being with First Research prepared a number of the team members to go on and launch their own successful start-ups. So far, five successful firms have sprung up from employees of the First Research team.

I think the most important factor you have to weigh in making this decision is whether or not you are at heart a serial entrepreneur, one who finds the process of coming up with an idea and developing it into a successful start-up to be the most satisfying experience, or whether you're the kind of person who wants to bring your company through to maturity, continuing to grow it and guide it according to your vision and values—which, for some, is the greatest adventure.

> **Hockey Stick Principle #92: Founders grow companies better than outsiders.**

It's interesting to note that founders who do stay on may well be a generally more effective group of corporate leaders than the average. A series of studies have shown that founder CEOs of Fortune 500 companies that have gone on to take their companies public have led their firms to stronger overall results than those run by CEOs brought in from outside. A 2006 study showed that the average return on stocks of the twenty-six Fortune 500 firms run by founders was 18.5 percent annually from 1995 to 2005, which was seven percentage points better than the Fortune 500 average in those years. A 2010 study reported that "founding CEOs consistently beat the professional CEOs on a broad range of metrics ranging from capital efficiency (amount of funding raised), time to exit, exit valuations, and return on investment."[164]

So while it's certainly true for some entrepreneurs that running a large, mature company is neither their desire nor their strength, for others, making the transition to corporate management seems to be in their bones. Making a strong sale to a company with a good strategic plan for incorporating your firm into its own mission and staying on to keep building your company can both be great choices. You must decide which is the right one for you. Only you can do this.

Acknowledgements
and a Brief History

The Hockey Stick Principles project has been a seven-year journey—one that has been well worth the investment. In fact, this project has been strikingly similar to starting an innovative growth company because the reward truly has been in the journey and the people I have met during the process.

The Hockey Stick Principles front cover reads, "By Bobby Martin," but the attribution is a huge overstatement, like suggesting my own start-up was "First Research by Bobby Martin." The reality is that too many people contributed to the company's success to imply such a thing—and the same goes for *The Hockey Stick Principles*. Many of the project's greatest achievements came from people other than myself.

In the fall of 2008, while hiking in North Carolina's Pisgah National Forest with former First Research leaders **Lee Demby, Wil Brawley**, and **Darren Pierce,** I was pointing out that start-up books fail to acknowledge the haphazard, trial-and-error nature of starting a company. "That experimentation *IS* the formula for success!" I cried out. They encouraged me to write a book about the realities of building a start-up. So in 2009, I drafted a manuscript about lessons I'd learned from starting First Research. I might have given up on the project had **Pam Hurley**, my editor that year, not been so encouraging. I could have self-published it, but clearly critical details were missing, and Pam helped me fill in those gaps.

From 2010 to 2012, I improved the manuscript by interviewing successful founders and experts including **Brian Hamilton** of Sageworks, **Ryan Allis** of iContact, **Doug Ledba** of LendingTree, **Bob Young** of Red Hat, **Wes Aiken** and **Tyler Rullman** of Schedulefly, **Graham Snyder** of SEAL Swimsafe, **Ed McCarthy** of River Cities Capital, and **Joan Seifert-Rose** of Center for Entrepreneurial Development. These interviews resulted in a manuscript with seven start-up stories, emphasizing these companies' haphazard beginnings and their founders' vivid trial-and-error lessons.

From 2010 to 2014, I worked side by side with editor **Dr. Linda W. Hobson**. Linda is the ultimate encourager, an inspiring person, and a stellar editor. Together, we explored everything under the sun to help readers connect with the sometimes-unpredictable start-up process. Once, we even explored how famous children's stories such as *Peter Pan* and *Alice in Wonderland* could relate to starting a company. It was a wonderful time!

In 2010 and 2011, I attended writing classes at North Carolina State University where **Professor Dick Reavis** taught me how to write more clearly, and **Dr. John Balaban** taught me how to write creatively. Oh, how I loved their classes!

My primary writing venue has been Global Village Coffee, nestled in the academia-rich community near N.C. State. Owner **Mike Ritchey**, thanks for hosting me! While sipping coffee there, on a whim, I plotted numerous successful companies' revenue-growth curves and noticed each took the shape of a hockey stick. I embarked on a study to gather data about how hockey stick growth works. **Beth Ann Tidemann-Miller** and **Brian Gaines**, both graduate students in statistics at N.C. State, helped me devise how to gather, analyze, and interpret the data. **Kevin Bell** and **Drake Branson** assisted with gathering the stats.

In 2013, when I was soliciting an agent for the book, **Lisa DiMona** of Writer's House said, "Instead of sending me your proposal, why don't you just *tell* me about it?" So for an hour, I talked her ear off about the hockey stick–shaped revenue curves. Lisa is warm, hip, plugged in, creative, clever, and one of the kindest people I've ever met. Lisa has been my rock and has done way more than finding us a publisher.

Lisa suggested I collaborate with developmental editor **Emily Loose** to improve upon the manuscript. Emily has been hugely influential in making *The Hockey Stick Principles* what it is today by transforming its organization and style. She immensely improved how the stories relate to readers' interests. Emily is a relentless thinker and a highly skilled editor. She's been a joy to collaborate with, and I'm forever grateful for her patience and kindness.

In 2014, I interviewed several more successful founders and start-up experts: **Lisa Falzone** of Revel Systems, **Joe Colopy** of Bronto Software, **Julie Pickens** of Boogie Wipes, **Jim Goodnight** of SAS Software, **Kent Hudson** of Dude Solutions, **Darren Pierce** of etailinsights, **Shashi Upadhyay** of Lattice Engines, **Craig Wortmann** of The University of Chicago, **Bo Burlingham** of Inc. Magazine, **Shikhar Ghosh** of Harvard University, **Michael and Mary Drummond** of Packrite, **Scott Nelson** of Trax Technologies, and **Dinesh Wadhwani** of ThinkLite.

Several people along the way advised me to self-publish this book but doing so would have been a fatal mistake. My publisher, Flatiron Books in New York, has provided irreplaceable ideas, advice, and marketing that I never could have obtained without them. Publisher **Bob Miller** has been creative and thoughtful in conjuring better ways to present the material. Editor **Jasmine Faustino** has been encouraging, persistent, and hardworking during the creative process. Publicist **Steven Boriack** and marketing manager **Molly Fonseca** and the entire staff at Flatiron Books have been terrific teammates.

Since finishing the writing process, my fun, smart, and energetic friends **Karen Burke** and **Rachel Spensieri** have helped me spread the word about this book.

Lastly, I'd like to thank my loving family, my wife, **Gloria**, and children, **Jayne Beth** and **Sanders,** for encouraging me during this seven-year journey. It's been an unforgettable ride!

Glossary

Agile development process—a flexible, iterative product creation method that encourages input from customers throughout the project.

Affiliate model—when a business pays commission to another similar organization to market and/or sell its product for it, normally through the web traffic it produces. Commissions may range from 10 percent to as much as 50 percent or even more. Some commissions are also a set amount for each sale made.

Annual revenue run rate—what your future annual revenue would be if you were to extrapolate how much revenue you earn over one year. For example, if during one quarter you earned $250,000 in revenue, your annual revenue run rate would be $1 million ($250,000 × 4 quarters in a year). If during one month you earned $50,000 in revenue, your annual revenue run rate would be $600,000 ($50,000 × 12 months in a year).

Angel group—a group of angel investors that pools their resources and develops portfolios of companies they've invested in. You can find a listing of them online from Angel Capital Association (ACA), a trade association of angel groups.

Angel investor—an accredited individual investor who must have a net worth of at least $1 million and make at least $200,000 a year (or $300,000 a year jointly with a spouse).

Business-to-Business (B2B) model—when a business sells its product or service to businesses.

B2B lead generation sales model—a marketing method of attracting business customers through programs that offer some type of free, educational giveaway in exchange for contact information, which becomes "leads." The sales team later follows up with the leads to engage in a conversation to gain a new customer.

B2C model—when a business sells its product or service to consumers.

Blade years—the stage of a start-up when founders have launched their products and have fully committed to making the business work. During this stage, revenue and growth rates are low. This stage may last two to three years or longer.

Bootstrapping—the hands-on, low-budget method of starting a business that minimizes the amount of financial capital required. Bootstrapping entrepreneurs use creative methods for completing projects, such as bartering or completing tasks themselves that are often completed by professionals.

Brand identity—a customer's perception of your company and product. Brand identity is much more than a logo; it involves the customer's overall experience when dealing with your company, such as the buying process, customer service, and your employees' personalities.

Business model canvas—a visual map of nine essential elements—or, as they call them, building blocks—of making every business (customer segments, value proposition, channels, customer relationships, revenue streams, key resources, key activities, key partnerships, and cost structure). Placing all these elements next to one another on one page helps you keep them all in mind as you search for solutions to some of the most common problems as you begin to launch your business.

Content marketing—a type of marketing that uses sharing of educational written material, graphics, and other media to obtain customers.

Crowdfunding—raising money in small amounts from a large group of people, often through such online intermediaries as Kickstarter, Indiegogo, or Crowdfunder.

Culture—your company's style of doing business, such as its vision, personality, brand, beliefs, and habits.

Direct-sales model—when a business hires employees to sell directly to customers.

Discretionary costs—expenses that are not essential to a business's operations.

Early adopters—the first customers that choose to purchase your product, often before all the product features are completed.

Efficiency wages—above-market wages or salaries that lead to significantly higher productivity and profits because the employees feel that they are being compensated and treated well.

Eighty-Twenty Rule (or the Pareto Principle)—based on the work of Italian economist Vilfredo Pareto, this concept is a great aide for efficient decision making that posits that 20 percent of inputs generally account for 80 percent of outputs and helps you focus on how to use your time and energy most effectively.

E-mail marketing—a type of marketing used to remain connected with customers and prospective customers via e-mail with newsletters, special promotions, and educational material. Many businesses professionalize the e-mail marketing process with software from such companies as iContact, VerticalResponse, MailChimp, or Constant Contact.

False-positive—when you land an important customer or partner, and assume similar firms will follow, but few do.

First-mover advantage—when you are the first company to the market with a product of your type, which can give a start-up a lead that competitors may never catch up to.

Fixed costs—costs that you have to commit to in advance and that you won't be able to increase or decrease readily, if at all. Examples of fixed costs are rent, employee salaries, and insurance.

Flat organizational chart—a company with no, or few, middle managers so employees are empowered to take responsibility without being managed.

Free product integration partnership—a partnership where you license a portion of your product for free to other firms to enhance their offering, and in exchange, you receive brand awareness and marketing prospect leads. The goal is to enable your brand and product to reach a broader audience and attract interested buyers who become sales leads.

Freemium—a model that offers a version of your software or service for free, while simultaneously offering a paid premium version, similar to the models used by Dropbox and Skype.

General partners (GPs)—the managers of a venture capital fund responsible for raising money, investing it into promising companies, and organizing day-to-day operations of the fund. GPs are normally paid a salary in addition to a percentage of profits.

Growth-inflection point—a period of time—normally one to three years after product launch—when revenue turns sharply upward. During this time, you have made enough progress with your business model such that sales are coming in more easily.

Growth capital—money invested to help you expand your business after your product has matured and has established customers.

Holocracy—a nonhierarchical organizational management structure that does away with middle management and job titles.

Human capital—the founder's skills, knowledge, and expertise, including his or her work, school, and managerial experience, industry knowledge, and experiences from outside his or her schooling or work life, such as hobbies.

Incubators—groups that provide mentoring support, funding, grants, investments, and physical locations to work for entrepreneurs.

Independent contractor—a person or firm that is not an employee that you pay to perform a particular service. Hiring independent contractors is common with start-ups because work functions are unpredictable, so founders are wise not to commit to hiring long-term employees.

Initial public offering (IPO)—a company's first stock sale to the public. IPOs are used to raise capital for expansion and/or provide payments to other shareholders.

Intellectual property—an invention resulting from an individual's creativity and work that has a patent, copyright, trademark, or some other type of legal or business protection.

Key performance indicators (KPIs)—measurements of important data that help you manage your company, such as revenue per employee, customer retention rates, lead to closed sales conversion rate, inventory shrinkage rate, etc.

Letter of intent (LOI)—a document that outlines the terms and conditions agreed upon in a merger between two firms before the final legal agreements are finalized and signed.

Limited partners (LPs)—investors in a venture capital fund who aren't responsible for choosing investments, raising money, or managing and organizing the day-to-day operations of the fund. LPs' liability is limited to the amount they invest in the fund.

Low-cost model—selling a product for a low price while spending small amounts of money to acquire a great number of customers.

Love money—capital invested in a start-up based on the relationship between the founder and the investors rather than analysis of the business idea and its associated risk.

Matchmaker model—a business model where you don't have to hold any inventory or maintain an expensive product; you just connect two parties.

Mezzanine financing round—late-stage, high-interest-rate debt capital that is often a bridge loan between financing rounds. The debt may be converted into equity if not repaid.

Minimal viable product (MVP)—an inexpensive version of your product that includes only enough features to satisfy early adopter customers used to get on the market quickly and then learn from customers about improvements to make. The term MVP was popularized by authors Eric Ries and Steve Blank.

Nonbank lenders—firms that offer loans but do not have a banking license; they often charge higher interest rates than banks, and while some are reputable, others are not. It's best to ask an attorney, banker, or CPA for a trusted nonbank lender referral.

Noncore business functions—overhead activities, such as writing checks, managing inventory records, and processing payroll, that do not define a company's business model.

Nondisclosure agreement (NDA)—a legal agreement between two parties that protects confidential or proprietary information.

Online advertising sales model—an online sales model where your company charges customers for advertisements based upon the amount of traffic your Web site generates. This model relies upon entertaining, useful, or educational content to drive people to your site.

Opportunity costs—the amount of money or other kinds of payoff that you might have earned by doing something else with your time.

Parkinson's Law of Triviality—an idea conceived in 1955 by C. Northcote Parkinson that recognizes the amount of work people will do on a project expands so as to fill the time available for its completion.

Partnerships—business relationships with companies that can help you grow by marketing to their customer base or vice versa. Examples include product integration paid partnerships, free product integration partnerships, and revenue-sharing sales and marketing partnerships.

Pay-in-advance model—a business model where customers pay you the full amount or a deposit for a product before you ship or build your product.

Pay-per-click advertising—a business model by which advertisers pay a Web site based on the amount of times their ad is clicked by Internet users.

Pitch book—a detailed information packet provided to potential acquirers about the financial performance, business model, and operating plan of a business.

Pitch-offs (or demo days)—events or conferences where you usually pitch for a short amount of time to several investors all at once. These are often held by universities and local entrepreneurial organizations.

Winning a pitch-off results in a certain amount of prize money, which varies anywhere from the low five figures to seven figures.

Pivoting—changing direction or trying something new when some aspect of your business model isn't working (i.e., market, price, sales method, product features). For example, if you are unsuccessfully selling your product to restaurants, you could "pivot" and begin trying to sell it to a different market, such as hotels or grocery stores.

Premature scaling—trying to grow operating expenses and overbuild product features before substantial customer growth has occurred.

Pretailing (or pre-commerce)—preselling products.

Principle of affordable loss—a calculation that founders should make to figure out how much they're willing to lose to start a business. They should figure out the upper limit to what they're willing to lose, calculate a worst-case scenario of losses, and then weigh that against how important it is to them to give the idea their best try.

Product integration paid partnership—a partnership with a company that will license your product, patent, or technology to other firms in exchange for a set license fee. Oftentimes, start-ups might license only parts of their intellectual property. For example, a start-up may embed its product into another company's core product to make a more compelling offer.

Licensing—giving a partner legal permission to sell, promote, publish, or perform other activities with your product, brand, or business.

Ramen profitability—the point when a start-up is earning just enough income to pay its founder the bare minimum to live on—or enough to buy inexpensive ramen noodles.

Return on investment (ROI)—amount of profits or income received on an established amount of capital investment. For example, if your annual profit is $100,000 and your investment capital is $1 million, your ROI is 10 percent for that time period.

Revenue-based funding (RBF)—firms that offer a fixed amount of money but do not charge interest on a fixed schedule; rather, they take a percentage of the start-up's revenue over the term of the deal, which is limited to a "cap" amount negotiated as part of the deal. Once the cap is reached, the deal is completed.

Revenue-sharing sales and marketing partnerships—partnerships with companies that promote your product within their existing sales channels. These partnerships enable you to sell and market to wider audiences than your own capabilities allow.

Scaling—the ability of a company to grow its operating margins (profits) as its revenue increases.

Scarcity model—a business model where the customer must make a purchase before you pay your vendors.

Search engine optimization (SEO)—how companies increase the visibility of their Web sites to customers through such practices as word choice, titles, images, and links to their own Web sites from other Web sites.

Seed capital—pre-revenue money used by a start-up company for operating expenses, research and development, and capital expenditures.

Service-to-product model—a business model where a service is provided to the customer and that service transforms into a product.

Social capital—seeking help from people you know in order to leverage their business skills, connections with other people, and resources they may have.

Software as a Service (SaaS)—a business model in which software is licensed to customers on a subscription basis. Unlike installed software that is purchased and installed on local servers or computers, SaaS software resides on an external, off-site service accessed via the Internet.

Soft product launch—the act of announcing a new product to a limited audience in order to gain feedback before releasing it to a wider audience.

Stakeholder—anyone who is vested in the success of your firm, such as employees, customers, shareholders, partners, and suppliers. A challenge for founders is balancing out all their different needs and wants.

Stock option plan—contract between your company and a person (i.e., employee, partner) that provides him or her the right (but not the obligation) to buy shares of stock at a predetermined price within a fixed period of time. Stock options incentivize those vested in your company to increase the value of your company.

Strategic corporate partner—a larger, more established company, which may be private or public, that has created investing arms.

Strategic merger—when a company purchases another with a plan to combine it with its own business to improve its products, services, and profits.

Subscription model—a business model where the product or service is delivered to a customer on an ongoing basis, and the customer pays an ongoing, periodic fee.

Super-angel investment groups—a hybrid between angel investors and venture capitalists, these groups pool together the investment money of a number of individuals, and the investment decisions are made by a management team. They typically offer funding between $250,000 and

$500,000 and attach fewer strings to their offer than a venture capital firm.

Surging growth—the stage when a business's revenue growth rates are very high—often 30 percent or much greater. During this stage, the complexity of managing the organization also increases.

Term sheet—a negotiable document provided by an investor (i.e., venture capitalist) that describes the terms and conditions by which an investment will be made into your company. A term sheet outlines the investment amount, ownership, and legal terms, such as issuing new shares of stock, raising additional money, selling the company, and appointing directors to the board.

Tinkering—the process during which founders are beginning to explore the viability of their ideas—normally before they quit their day jobs.

Value proposition—how your product will solve your customers' problems and satisfy their needs.

Vaporware—a product that is announced to the public but is not yet manufactured into a finished product. Vaporware is often a demonstration of the product that is planned.

Variable costs—costs that rise and fall with your sales volume. Examples of variable costs include packaging, raw materials, shipping, and supplies.

Venture capital—professionally managed capital invested into high-growth-potential start-ups. The minimum investment into each company is normally $500,000, but the average investment is $3–$5 million.

Vesting schedule—an agreement that makes the award of shares or stock options of a company to an employee or partner contingent on work being completed.

Waterfall approach—a product design methodology wherein projects (i.e., writing requirements, designing, engineering, verifying, implementation) are completed sequentially. Each project phase isn't started until the previous one is completed.

Endnotes

1   Jeff Shore, "These 10 Peter Drucker Quotes May Change Your World," *Entrepreneur*, September 16, 2014, http://www.entrepreneur.com/article/237484.

2   Brad Stone, "Storming the Campuses," *The New York Times*, March 21, 2008, http://www.nytimes.com/2008/03/21/technology/21ivygame.html?n =Top%2FReference%2FTimes%20Topics%2FSubjects%2FC%2FComputer%20 and%20Video%20Games&_r=0.

3   Alyson Shontell, "How One Startup Had Millions In Funding And 100,000 Users—And Still FAILED," *Business Insider*, August 19, 2010, http://www .businessinsider.com/how-gocrosscampus-startup-failed-2010-8?op=1.

4   Alexia Tsotsis, "Monsanto Buys Weather Big Data Company Climate Corporation For Around $1.1B," *TechCrunch*, October 2, 2013, http://techcrunch.com /2013/10/02/monsanto-acquires-weather-big-data-company-climate-corporation -for-930m/.

5   Nick Gonzalez, "Eventvue Grabs Angel Round Over The Weekend," *TechCrunch*, September 24, 2007, http://techcrunch.com/2007/09/24/eventvue-grabs -angel-round-over-the-weekend/.

6   MG Siegler, "Eventvue's Next Event: Deadpool. Co-Founder Shares Mistakes.," *TechCrunch*, February 5, 2010, http://techcrunch.com/2010/02/05/eventvue -deadpool/.

7   "Eventvue Post-Mortem," Josh Fraser and Rob Johnson, Facebook, February 5, 2010, https://www.facebook.com/notes/eventvue/eventvue-post-mortem /470086850385.

8   "Mark Zuckerberg: The Evolution of a remarkable CEO," Matt Marshall, *VentureBeat*, October 2, 2009, http://venturebeat.com/2009/10/02/mark -zuckerberg-the-evolution-of-a-remarkable-ceo/.

9   Sam Gustin, "Groupon Fires CEO Andrew Mason: The Rise and Fall of Tech's Enfant Terrible," *Time Magazine*, March 1, 2013, http://business.time.com/2013 /03/01/groupon-fires-ceo-andrew-mason-the-rise-and-fall-of-techs-enfant -terrible/.

10   Jim Clifton, "Why Entrepreneurs Matter More Than Innovators," *Gallup Business Journal*, November 22, 2011, http://www.gallup.com/businessjournal /150707/Why-Entrepreneurs-Matter-Innovators.aspx.

11   "Santa Ana District Newsletter," U.S. Small Business Administration, June 2009, Volume 2, Number 4, https://www.sba.gov/sites/default/files/Santa%20 Ana%20District%20Newsletter%20-%20June%202009.pdf.

12 Mark Henricks, "Do You Really Need a Business Plan?," *Entrepreneur*, December 2008, http://www.entrepreneur.com/article/198618.

13 Steve Blank, *The Startup Owner's Manual* (Pescadero, CA: K&S Ranch, Inc., 2012), Apple iBooks, chap. 2.

14 J.D. Harrison, "When we were small: Under Armour," *The Washington Post*, November 12, 2014, http://www.washingtonpost.com/business/on-small -business/when-we-were-small-under-armour/2014/11/11/f61e8876-69ce-11e4 -b053-65cea7903f2e_story.html.

15 "About us," Poseidon Web Site, August 28, 2015, http://www.poseidonsaveslives .com/ABOUTUS.aspx.

16 Lance A. Bettencourt and Anthony W. Ulwick, "The Customer-Centered Innovation Map" *HBR's 10 Must Reads on Innovation (with featured article "The Discipline of Innovation" by Peter F. Drucker)* (Boston: Harvard Business School Publishing Corporation, 2011), Apple iBooks.

17 George S. Day, "Is It Real? Can We Win? Is It Worth Doing?: Managing Risk and Reward in an Innovation Portfolio," *HBR's 10 Must Reads on Innovation (with featured article "The Discipline of Innovation" by Peter F. Drucker)* (Boston: Harvard Business School Publishing Corporation, 2011), Apple iBooks.

18 Larry Keeley, *Ten Types of Innovation: The Discipline of Building Breakthroughs* (Hoboken, NJ: Wiley, 2013), introduction.

19 Ibid., p. 13.

20 Rob Adams, *If You Build it Will They Come* (Hoboken, NJ: Wiley, 2010), p.1.

21 Gene Landrum, *Profiles of Genius—Thirteen Creative Men Who Changed the World* (Amherst, NY: Prometheus Books, 1993), p. 162.

22 Ibid., p. 135.

23 Marc Benioff, *Behind the Cloud* (San Francisco: Jossey-Bass, 2009), p. 9.

24 James Warren, "Why Experts Get It Wrong," *The Atlantic*, April 1, 2011, http://www.theatlantic.com/national/archive/2011/04/why-experts-get-it -wrong/73322/.

25 Ibid.

26 "Playboy Interview: Steve Jobs, by David Sheff, Playboy," Longform.org, August 28, 2015, http://longform.org/stories/playboy-interview-steve-jobs.

27 Robert Young and Wendy Goldman Rohm, *Under the Radar: How Red Hat Changed the Software Business—and Took Microsoft by Surprise* (Coriolis, 1999).

28 Malcolm Gladwell, "The Sure Thing," *The New Yorker*, January 18, 2010, http://www.newyorker.com/magazine/2010/01/18/the-sure-thing.

29 Jessica Naziri, "Dollar Shave Club co-founder Michael Dublin had a smooth transition," *Los Angeles Times*, August 16, 2013, http://articles.latimes.com/2013 /aug/16/business/la-fi-himi-dubin-20130818.

30 Jefferson Graham, "Dollar Shave Club's Dubin: From YouTube star to CEO," *USA Today*, June 9, 2014, http://www.usatoday.com/story/money/business/2014 /06/09/ceo-profile-dollar-shave-clubs-michael-dubin/9993045/.

31 John Seabrook, "Revenue Streams—Is Spotify the music industry's friend or its foe?," *The New Yorker*, November 24, 2014, p. 72–73.

32 Max Marmer, "Startup Genome Report Extra on Premature Scaling," *Startup Genome*, March 2012, http://gallery.mailchimp.com/8c534f3b5ad611c0ff8aeccd5 /files/Startup_Genome_Report_Extra_Premature_Scaling_version_2.1.pdf.

33   John Mullins, *The Customer-Funded Business* (Hoboken, New Jersey: John Wiley & Sons, Inc. 2014), Apple iBooks, chap. 1.

34   Noam Wasserman, *The Founder's Dilemmas* (Princeton, NJ: Princeton University Press, 2012), p. 88.

35   Ibid., p. 113.

36   "Annual Venture Capital Investment Tops $48 Billion in 2014, Reaching Highest Level in Over a Decade, According to the MoneyTree Report," National Venture Capital Association, Jaunary 16, 2015, http://nvca.org/pressreleases/annual -venture-capital-investment-tops-48-billion-2014-reaching-highest-level-decade -according-moneytree-report/.

37   Richard L. Brandt, *Jeff Bezos and The Rise of Amazon.com* (New York: Portfolio/ Penguin 2011), Google eBook Chap. 7.

38   Noam Wasserman, *The Founder's Dilemmas* (Princeton, NJ: Princeton University Press, 2012), Apple iBook, chap. 6.

39   Ibid.

40   Ryan Allis, *Zero to One Million* (New York: McGraw-Hill, 2008), p. 27.

41   Sramana Mitra, "How Startups Overcome the Capital Gap," *Harvard Business Review*, July 10, 2013, https://hbr.org/2013/07/how-startups-overcome-the-capi.

42   Noam Wasserman, *The Founder's Dilemmas* (Princeton, NJ: Princeton University Press, 2012), Apple iBook, chap. 9.

43   William R. Kerr, Josh Lerner & Antoinette Schoar, "The Consequences of Entrepreneurial Finance: A Regression Discontinuity Analysis," Harvard Business School Working Knowledge, April 15 2011, http://hbswk.hbs.edu/item /6347.html?wknews=041910.

44   "How to Raise $1M as a First-Time Entrepreneur," Gagan Biyani, Udemy Blog, September 8, 2010, https://blog.udemy.com/udemy-fundraising/?siteID =TnL5HPStwNw-.

45   "Love Money," Investopedia, August 26, 2015, http://www.investopedia.com /terms/l/lovemoney.asp.

46   McGuinness, "Amazing $40m Gift; A Lancaster Woman Gives Stock Gains to Hamilton Foundation," 2000, *The Hamilton Spectator*.

47   Adam Janofsky and Angus Loten, "Repeat Crowdfunding Reaps Rewards for Entrepreneurs," *Wall Street Journal*, April 15, 2015, http://www.wsj.com/articles /repeat-crowdfunding-reaps-rewards-for-entrepreneurs-1429143285?tesla=y.

48   Chris Atchison, "The Pitfalls of Crowdfunding," Profitguide.com, December 23 2013, Richter.ca.

49   Paul Graham, "Do Things That Don't Scale," PaulGraham.com, July 2013, http:// paulgraham.com/ds.html.

50   Charles Spinosa, Fernando Flores, and Hubert Dreyfus, *Disclosing New Worlds: Entrepreneurship, Democratic Action, and the Cultivation of Solidarity* (Cambridge, MA: The MIT Press, 1999), 46.

51   Nicole Robinson, "Five Things You Should Know Before Starting a Business," *Forbes*, June 11, 2013, http://www.forbes.com/sites/yec/2013/06/11/five-things -you-should-know-before-starting-a-business/.

52   Roy F. Baumeister and John Tierney, *Willpower: Rediscovering the Greatest Human Strength* (New York: Penguin Press, 2011), chap. 4.

53   Arthur L. Stinchcombe, "Social Structure and Organizations," *Handbook of Organizations*, ed. James G. March (Chicago:Rand McNally, 1965), p 142–193.

54   Rob Walker, *Buying In: What We Buy and Who We Are* (New York: Random House, 2009), p. 66.

55   "Ecommerce Conversion Rates," Dave Chaffey, SmartInsights.com, April 7, 2015, http://www.smartinsights.com/ecommerce/ecommerce-analytics/ecommerce-conversion-rates/.

56   "Bubble Wrap Was Originally Designed to be Used as Wallpaper," Daven Hiskey, TodayIFoundOut.com, November 23, 2011, http://www.todayifoundout.com/index.php/2011/11/bubble-wrap-was-originally-designed-to-be-used-as-wallpaper/.

57   Peter Cohen, "Jurassic Park: How P&G Brought Fabreze Back to Life," *Forbes*, February 19, 2012, http://www.forbes.com/sites/petercohan/2012/02/19/jurassic-park-how-pg-brought-febreze-back-to-life/2/.

58   "Founders School Video Transcript | Entrepreneurial Selling | Entrepreneurial Sales Model," Kauffman Founders School, August 27, 2015, http://www.entrepreneurship.org/Founders-School/Transcripts/Entrepreneurial-Selling/Transcript-Entrepreneurial-Sales-Model.aspx.

59   "2012 SaaS Conversions Benchmark," Totango.com, August 27, 2015, http://www.totango.com/wp-content/uploads/2012/11/2012-SaaS-Conversions-Benchmark2.pdf.

60   Nick Lowe, "Cruel to be Kind," Comp. Ian Gomm and Nick Lowe, 1979.

61   "2012 SaaS Conversions Benchmark," Totango.com, August 27, 2015, http://www.totango.com/wp-content/uploads/2012/11/2012-SaaS-Conversions-Benchmark2.pdf.

62   "The Ultimate List of Marketing Statistics," Hubspot.com, August 27, 2015, http://www.hubspot.com/marketing-statistics.

63   Alex Strachan, "Nova Episodes Appeal to Greater Minds," *The Gazette*, February 9, 2011, C6.

64   Manta.com, Manta Media Inc. 2012, http://www.manta.com/mb_35_A62D102T_000/certified_public_accountant (accessed October 4, 2012).

65   "Do Things That Don't Scale," Paul Graham, PaulGraham.com, July 2013, http://paulgraham.com/ds.html.

66   Jenna Wortham, "In Tech, Starting Up by Failing," *NY Times*, January 17, 2012, http://www.nytimes.com/2012/01/18/business/for-some-internet-start-ups-a-failure-is-just-the-beginning.html?_r=0.

67   Ralph Waldo Emerson, *Letters and Social Aims*. Biblio life, 2008, p. 223.

68   Steve Blank, "Why the Lean Startup Changes Everything," *Harvard Business Review*, May 2013, http://www.nytimes.com/2012/01/18/business/for-some-internet-start-ups-a-failure-is-just-the-beginning.html?_r=0.

69   "Entrepreneurship and the US Economy," Bureau of Labor Statistics, May 7, 2014, http://www.bls.gov/bdm/entrepreneurship/bdm_chart3.htm.

70   Deborah Gage, "The Venture Capital Secret: 3 out of 4 Start-Ups Fail," The Wall Street Journal, September 20, 2012, http://online.wsj.com/news/articles/SB10000872396390443720204578004980476429190?mg=reno64-wsj.

71   "Techstars Delivers the Best Results," Techstars.com, November 2, 2015, http://www.techstars.com/companies/.

72   "On the Lifecycle Dynamics of Venture-Capital- and Non-Venture-Capital-Financed Firms," Manju Puri and Rebecca Zarutskie, National Bureau of Economic Research, August 2008, http://www.nber.org/papers/w14250.

73   "Ramen Profitable," Paul Graham, PaulGraham.com, July 2009, http://www
     .paulgraham.com/ramenprofitable.html.
74   David Sarno, "Apple's iPhone Takes Big Bites Out of Wireless Carrier's Profits,"
     Los Angeles Times, February 10, 2012, http://articles.latimes.com/2012/feb/10
     /business/la-fi-iphone-blues-20120211.
75   "What is the Average Conversion Rate: A 2013 Update," Kevin Gold, Search
     Marketing Standards, August 22, 2013, http://www.searchmarketingstandard
     .com/what-is-the-average-conversion-rate.
76   Alyson Shontell, "The Tech Titanic: How Red-Hot Startup Fab Raised $330
     Million and Then Went Bust," *Business Insider*, February 6, 2015, http://www
     .businessinsider.com/how-billion-dollar-startup-fab-died-2015-2.
77   Benjamin Franklin, *The Autobiography of Benjamin Franklin*, (Mineola, NY:
     Dover), 1996, p. 51.
78   "Startup Genome Report Extra on Premature Scaling," Max Marmer, Bjoern
     Lasse Herrmann, Ron Berman, Ertan Dogrultan, Startup Genome, March 2012,
     http://gallery.mailchimp.com/8c534f3b5ad611c0ff8aeccd5/files/Startup
     _Genome_Report_Extra_Premature_Scaling_version_2.1.pdf.
79   "Amp'd Raises $107M More," Katie Fehrenbacher, Gigaom.com, March 21, 2007,
     https://gigaom.com/2007/03/21/ampd-raises-107m-more/."What Were They
     Thinking: Amp'd Mobile's Mad Credit Strategy," Matt Marshall, VentureBeat
     .com, July 20, 2007, http://venturebeat.com/2007/07/20/what were they
     -thinking-ampd-mobiles-mad-credit-strategy/.Olga Kharif, "Amp'd Mobile
     Runs Out of Juice," *Bloomberg Business*, June 5, 2007, http://www.bloomberg
     .com/bw/stories/2007-06-05/ampd-mobile-runs-out-of-juicebusinessweek
     -business-news-stock-market-and-financial-advice.
80   Issie Lapowsky, "Jason Goldberg: What Went Wrong at Fab," *Inc*, January 7,
     2014, http://www.inc.com/issie-lapowsky/jason-goldberg-what-went-wrong
     .html.
81   Mike Isaac, "Where Profit Margins Are Hefty, Online Upstarts Muscle In,"
     New York Times, September 23, 2014, http://www.nytimes.com/2014/09/24
     /technology/24shave.html?_r=0.
82   "Marketo Announces Fourth Quarter and Full Year 2014 Results," Marketo
     .com, February 10, 2015, http://investors.marketo.com/releasedetail.cfm
     ?ReleaseID=895745.
83   "Marketo Investor Update," Marketo.com, February 2015, http://files
     .shareholder.com/downloads/AMDA-1S4SOT/42727918x0x812716/40DD98D8
     -0EF3-449A-92F0-A58EE7F3A1CF/MKTO_Presentation_Feb_2015_wide_-_final
     .pdf.
84   Fernando Suarez and Gianvito Lanzolla, "The Half-Truth of First-Mover
     Advantage," *Harvard Business Review*, April 2005, https://hbr.org/2005/04/the
     -half-truth-of-first-mover-advantage.
85   Jim Edwards, "WHERE ARE THEY NOW? The Kings Of The '90s Dot-Com
     Bubble," *Business Insider*, October 18 2013, http://www.businessinsider.com
     /where-are-they-now-the-kings-of-the-90s-dot-com-bubble-2013-10#ixzz3jx
     Kluxfo.
86   "Summary of Startup Genome Report Extra: Premature Scaling," Compass,
     August 25 2015, http://blog.startupcompass.co/pages/summary-of-startup
     -genome-report-extra-premat.

87 Ibid.
88 "Scalability," Investopedia.com, August 25, 2015, http://www.investopedia.com/terms/s/scalability.asp#ixzz3XPwM79vH.
89 "Scalability," Divestopedia.com, August 25, 2015, http://www.divestopedia.com/definition/970/scalability.
90 André B. Bondi, "Characteristics of Scalability and Their Impact on Performance," AT&T Labs: Network Design and Performance Analysis Department, January 2000, http://www.researchgate.net/publication/221556521_Characteristics_of_scalability_and_their_impact_on_performance.
91 Jean-Claude Larréché, *The Momentum Effect* (Upper Saddle River, New Jersey: Prentice Hall, 2008), Apple iBook, chap 3.
92 Youngme Moon, *Different: Escaping the Competitive Herd* (New York: Crown Business, 2010) Apple iBooks, introduction.
93 Maggie Zhang, "9 Of The Craziest Things Founders Have Done To Make Their Startups Successful," Business Insider, July 9, 2014, http://www.businessinsider.com/crazy-things-founders-have-done-to-make-their-startups-successful-2014-7#the-founder-of-pinterest-personally-wrote-to-thousands-of-users-7.
94 Seth Godin, *The Purple Cow* (New York: Penguin Group, 2002), p. 3.
95 Ryan Allis, *Zero to One Million: : How I Built A Company to $1 Million in Sales . . . and How You Can, Too* (New York: McGraw-Hill 2003), p. 27.
96 "iContact," CrunchBase, August 27 2015, https://www.crunchbase.com/organization/icontact.
97 "ArsDigita: From Start-Up to Bust-Up," Philip Greenspun, Waxy.org, 2001, http://waxy.org/random/arsdigita/.
98 "Uber," CrunchBase, August 27 2015, https://www.crunchbase.com/organization/uber.
99 Yael V. Hochberg, Michael J. Mazzeo, and Ryan C. McDevitt, "Specialization and Competition in the Venture Capital Industry" *SSRN ELECTRONIC JOURNAL*, October 2011, http://www.researchgate.net/publication/228200501_Specialization_and_Competition_in_the_Venture_Capital_Industry)?.
100 Russ Garland, "Venture Capital Returns Rebound, But Beating Public Markets Remains a Challenge," *Wall Street Journal*, October 31, 2013, http://blogs.wsj.com/venturecapital/2013/10/31/venture-capital-returns-rebound-but-beating-public-markets-remains-a-challenge/.
101 Diane Mulcahy, "Six Myths About Venture Capitalists," *Harvard Business Review*, May 2013, https://hbr.org/2013/05/six-myths-about-venture-capitalists.
102 Deborah Gage, "The Venture Capital Secret: 3 Out of 4 Start-Ups Fail," *The Wall Street Journal*, September 20, 2012, http://www.wsj.com/articles/SB10000872396390443720204578004980476429190.
103 "135 Startup Failure Post-Mortems," CB Insights, August 17, 2015, https://www.cbinsights.com/blog/startup-failure-post-mortem/.
104 "MoneyTree Report Q4 2014/ Full-year 2014," PriceWaterhouseCoopers, National Venture Capital Association, Data Provided by Thomson Reuters, August 27 2015,https://www.pwcmoneytree.com/Reports/FullArchive/National_2014-4.pdf.
105 Richard T. Curtin and Paul D. Reynolds "Business Creation in the United States: Panel Study of Entrepreneurial Dynamics II Initial Assessment," *Foundations and Trends in Entrepreneurship*, Vol. 4, No. 3 (2008) p. 158.

106 "MoneyTree Report Full-year 2013," PriceWaterhouseCoopers, National
     Venture Capital Association, Data Provided by Thomson Reuters, http://www
     .pwc.com/en_US/us/technology/assets/pwc-moneytree-q4-and-full-year-2013
     -summary-report.pdf.
107 Arnobio Morelix, "Kauffman @ SXSW: 4 Insights from the Fastest Growing
     Companies in America," Kauffman Foundation, March 17 2015, http://www
     .kauffman.org/blogs/growthology/2015/03/kauffman-sxsw-insights-from-the
     -fastest-growing-companies-in-america.
108 Daniel Isenberg and Daniel Lawton, "How to Finance the Scale-Up of Your
     Company," *Harvard Business Review*, August 18, 2014, https://hbr.org/2014/08
     /how-to-finance-the-scale-up-of-your-company/.
109 Martin Zwilling, "Super Angels Answer the Prayers of Startups Starved for
     Funding," *Entrepreneur*, December 19 2014, http://www.entrepreneur.com
     /article/240972.
110 Chris Russell, "Clayton Christensen's Outlook on RBF's Disruptive Capabilities,"
     Rock & Hammer Ventures, August 27, 2015, http://www.rockandhammerventures
     .com/clayton-christensens-outlook-on-rbfs-disruptive-capabilities/.
111 "Revenue Based Funding," Startup Owl, August 27, 2015, http://startupowl.com
     /resources/startup-boosters/revenue-based-funding/.
112 Scott Edward Walker, "Demystifying the VC term sheet: Board control,"
     VentureBeat, March 14, 2011, http://venturebeat.com/2011/03/14/demystifying
     -the-vc-term-sheet-board-control/#.
113 Nicole Leinbach-Reyhle, "Shedding Hierarchy: Could Zappos Be Setting An
     Innovative Trend?," *Forbes*, July 14, 2014, http://www.forbes.com/sites
     /nicoleleinbachreyhle/2014/07/15/shedding-hierarchy-could-zappos-be-setting
     -an-innvoative-trend/.
114 Tony Hsieh, "A Memo from Tony Hsieh," Zappos Insights, April 8 2015,
     http://www.zapposinsights.com/blog/item/a-memo-from-tony-hsieh.
115 Gary Hamel, "First, Let's Fire All the Managers," *Harvard Business Review*,
     December 2011, https://hbr.org/2011/12/first-lets-fire-all-the-managers.
116 Jason Fried, "Why I Run a Flat Company," *Inc.*, April 2011, http://www.inc.com
     /magazine/20110401/jason-fried-why-i-run-a-flat-company.html.
117 Rebecca Greenfield, "Zappos CEO Tony Hsieh: Adopt Holacracy or Leave,"
     FastCompany, March 30 2015, http://www.fastcompany.com/3044417/zappos
     -ceo-tony-hsieh-adopt-holacracy-or-leave.
118 Peter F. Drucker, *Innovation and Entrepreneurship: Practice and Principles*
     (New York: Harper & Row, Publishers, Inc., 1993), p. 197.
119 Jerry Kaplan, "Video: Five Biggest Mistakes That Entrepreneurs Make,"
     Stanford University's Entrepreneurship Corner, October 1 2003, http://ecorner
     .stanford.edu/authorMaterialInfo.html?mid=364.
120 "William Seward Biography," Biography.com, August 27, 2015, http://www
     .biography.com/people/william-seward-21010687#later-life-legacy-and-lesser
     -known-facts.
121 "Salmon P. Chase Biography," Biography.com, August 27, 2015, http://www
     .biography.com/people/salmon-p-chase-38185#senate-seat-and-presidential
     -runs.
122 Adrienne Sanders, "How to Preserve a Startup Culture as a Company Grows,"
     Insights by Stanford Business, March 11, 2015, https://www.gsb.stanford.edu
     /insights/how-preserve-startup-culture-company-grows.

123 Joel Peterson, "Top 10 Hiring Mistakes, #1: Hiring Yourself," LinkedIn, May 29 2013, https://www.linkedin.com/pulse/20130529070259-11846967-top-10-hiring -mistakes-1-hiring-yourself?trk=mp-reader-card.

124 "Irving L. Janis, Psychology: Berkeley," Calisphere: University of California, 2011, http://content.cdlib.org/view?docId=hb4t1nb2bd;NAAN=13030&doc.view =frames&chunk.id=div00032&toc.depth=1&toc.id=&brand=calisphere.

125 Gino Wickman, *Traction* (Dallas: BenBella Books, Inc., 2012), Apple iBook, chap. 4.

126 "The 18 Mistakes That Kill Startups," Paul Graham, October 2006, http://www .paulgraham.com/startupmistakes.html.

127 "Expecting the Unexpected From Jeff Bezos," David Streitfeld and Christine Haughney, York Times Online, August 17, 2013, http://www.nytimes.com/ 2013/08/18/business/expecting-the-unexpected-from-jeff-bezos.html?_r=0.

128 "Jessica Herrin: 'I Feel Like I'm in the Happiness Business'," Erika Brown Ekiel, Stanford Graduate School of Business, September 24, 2012, https://www.gsb .stanford.edu/insights/jessica-herrin-"i-feel-im-happiness-business".

129 Quote, Nelson Mandela, ThinkExist.com, accessed August 28 2015, http:// thinkexist.com/quotation/as_a_leader-i_have_always_endeavored_to_listen _to/148828.html.

130 "Leading From Behind," Linda Hill, Harvard Business Review Online, May 5, 2010, https://hbr.org/2010/05/leading-from-behind/.

131 Max De Pree, *Leadership Is an Art* (Phoenix: Crown Press, 2004), p. 28.

132 James Surowiecki, "A Fair Day's Wage," *The New Yorker*, February 9, 2015, http://www.newyorker.com/magazine/2015/02/09/fair-days-wage.

133 "Turnover Rates Inching Up," Compdata Surveys, Dolan Technologies Corp., September 12, 2012, http://www.compdatasurveys.com/2012/09/12/turnover -rates-inching-up/.

134 "Parkinson's Law," Royal Commission on the Civil Service, The Economist Online Archives, November 19, 1955, http://www.economist.com/node /14116121#footnote1.

135 Schlender, Brent, "How A Virtuoso Plays The Web Eclectic, Inquisitive, and Academic: Yahoo's Jerry Yang Reinvents the Role of the Entrepreneur," *Fortune Magazine*, March 6, 2000.

136 Fleming, David. "To Each His Own," *ESPN Magazine*, March 10, 2010.

137 Ibid.

138 "Thinking of Selling Your Company? 8 Things to Consider First," Scott Gerber, Mashable, July 18, 2014, http://mashable.com/2014/07/18/startup-selling-considerations/.

139 "A Unicorn? In Israel?," Noam Bardin, LinkedIn, April 3, 2014, https://www .linkedin.com/pulse/20140403204459-174756-a-unicorn-in-israel.

140 "me + alex quit google. (dodgeball forever!!!!)," Dennis Crowley, Flickr, April 12, 2007, https://www.flickr.com/photos/dpstyles/460987802/.

141 "Dennis Crowley: Google acquisition of Dodgeball a failure," Hamish McKen- zie, Pando, October 11, 2012, http://pando.com/2012/10/11/foursquares-dennis -crowley-google-acquisition-of-dodgeball-a-failure/.

142 "eBay," CrunchBase, accessed August 28, 2015, https://www.crunchbase.com /organization/ebay.

143 "Start-Up Leaders Recall Choice to Cash In or Stay Independent," New York

Times Online, November 17, 2013, http://www.nytimes.com/interactive/2013/11/18/technology/startup-leaders-weigh-decision-to-sell.html?_r=0.

144 "How eBay's purchase of PayPal changed Silicon Valley," Eric M. Jackson, VentureBeat, October 27, 2012, http://venturebeat.com/2012/10/27/how-ebays-purchase-of-paypal-changed-silicon-valley/.

145 "Start-Up Leaders Recall Choice to Cash In or Stay Independent," New York Times Online, November 17, 2013, http://www.nytimes.com/interactive/2013/11/18/technology/startup-leaders-weigh-decision-to-sell.html?_r=0.

146 "In a Sale, Skype Wins a Chance to Prosper," Brad Stone, New York Times Online, September 1, 2009, http://www.nytimes.com/2009/09/02/technology/companies/02ebay.html?_r=0.

147 Ibid.

148 "When Google Wanted To Sell To Excite For Under $1 Million—And They Passed," MG Siegler, TechCrunch, September 29, 2010, http://techcrunch.com/2010/09/29/google-excite/.

149 "Clif Bar & Company," Privco, accessed April 12 2015, http://www.privco.com/private-company/clif-bar-and-company.

150 "Clif Bar sells 20% stake to workers," Steven E.F. Brown, San Francisco Business Times Online, June 29, 2010, http://www.bizjournals.com/sanfrancisco/stories/2010/06/28/daily28.html.

151 "Start-Up Leaders Recall Choice to Cash In or Stay Independent," New York Times Online, November 17, 2013, http://www.nytimes.com/interactive/2013/11/18/technology/startup-leaders-weigh-decision-to-sell.html?_r=0.

152 Richard T. Curtin and Paul D. Reynolds, "Business Creation in the United States: Panel Study of Entrepreneurial Dynamics II Initial Assessment," *Foundations and Trends in Entrepreneurship*, Vol. 4, No. 3 (2008) p. 158.

153 "The Venture Capital Secret: 3 Out of 4 Start-Ups Fail," Deborah Gage, The Wall Street Journal Online, September 20, 2012, http://www.wsj.com/articles/SB10000872396390443720204578004980476429190.

154 Y combinator list, http://yclist.com, December 7, 2015.

155 "Boogie Wipes entrepreneur moves company to Cincinnati," Dan Monk, Cincinnati Business Courier Online, June 15, 2012, http://www.bizjournals.com/cincinnati/print-edition/2012/06/15/boogie-wipes-entrepreneur-moves.html?page=all.

156 Alan J. Smith, "What Entrepreneurs Need to Know When Selling a Private Company," Entrepreneurship.org (Kauffman), December 7, 2015, http://www.entrepreneurship.org/resource-center/what-entrepreneurs-need-to-know-when-selling-a-private-company.aspx.

157 "Pacinian—Pre-Revenue $30 Million Exit," Strategic Exits, accessed August 28, 2015, http://www.exits.com/blog/pacinian-pre-revenue-30-million-exit/.

158 "Unconventional Insights for Managing Stakeholder Trust," Michael Pirson and Deepak Malhotra, Harvard Business School, 2008, http://www.hbs.edu/faculty/Publication%20Files/08-057_17f69d71-6bc0-46b6-ab0a-c42b87c9d546.pdf.

159 "5 Biggest Mistakes Entrepreneurs Make In Selling Their Company," Scott Edward Walker, Walker Corporate Law Group, PLLC, October 6, 2010, http://walkercorporatelaw.com/ma-issues/5-biggest-mistakes-entrepreneurs-make-in-selling-their-company/.

160 "EY Global IPO Trends, 2014 Q4," EY, 2014, http://www.ey.com/Publication
     /vwLUAssets/ey-q4-14-global-ipo-trends-report/$FILE/ey-q4-14-global-ipo
     -trends-report.pdf.
161 "Red Hat Reports Fourth Quarter Results, Revenue of $13.1 Million, Adjusted
     Net Loss of $0.04 Per Share: Robust Revenue Growth Fueled by Open Source
     Solutions for Internet Infrastructure," Red Hat, Inc., March 27, 2000, http://
     investors.redhat.com/releasedetail.cfm?ReleaseID=356511.
162 "GoPro's Nick Woodman On Life As Head Of A Public Company And Micro-
     soft's 'Mistake'," Ryan Mac, Forbes Online, August 1, 2014, http://www.forbes
     .com/sites/ryanmac/2014/08/01/gopros-nick-woodman-on-life-as-head-of-a
     -public-company-and-microsofts-mistake/.
163 James M. Barrie, *Peter Pan.* (New York: Penguin), 1987.
164 "Founder CEOs Are the Best Leaders of Small-Cap Companies," Jim Fink,
     Investing Daily, April 23, 2013, http://www.investingdaily.com/17246/founder
     -ceos-are-the-best-leaders-of-small-cap-companies/.

Index